Fig. I   Class J83 No. 9817 leaving Portobello Yard on trip working to Leith Walk, about 1930.

LOCOMOTIVES OF THE L.N.E.R.

Part 8B

TANK ENGINES — CLASSES J71 TO J94

First Impression February 1971

Published by

THE RAILWAY CORRESPONDENCE AND TRAVEL SOCIETY

1983

Second Impression

ISBN 0 901115 06 1

625. 2'61'0941

C. 60841626

CONTENTS

INTRODUCTION

In this companion volume to Part 8A the story of the L.N.E.R. 0-6-0T engines is continued with classes J71 to J94, comprising the stock from the North Eastern, Hull & Barnsley, North British, Great North of Scotland, East & West Yorkshire Union and Midland & Great Northern Joint, together with the War Department saddle tanks purchased towards the end of the L.N.E.R's existence.

The N.E.R. had some characteristic 0-6-0T designs, including large numbers of the neat little 4ft. 7¼in. and 4ft. 1⅛in. engines (some of the latter actually being built after nationalisation) designed by the Worsdells, and the much bigger rebuilds of Fletcher's BTP 0-4-4T's. There were also the eight side tanks built from material left over after the cancellation of a batch of the ill-fated McDonnell 4-4-0 tender engines folllowing the forced resignation of that engineer from the N.E.R. The H. & B. R. favoured side tanks with typical Stirling cabs and domeless boilers and these were of two classes with different wheel diameters.

On the N.B.R. there were three distinct groups of 0-6-0T. The oldest were the various types of Wheatley saddle tanks, followed by the small Drummond and larger Holmes classes in characteristic Stroudley tradition, and then came the last N.B.R. 0-6-0T type (some built as late as 1919)—the very small Reid dock shunting engines, notable for their outside cylinders, tall chimneys and dumb buffers. The nine 0-6-0T's provided by the G.N.S.R. were the only six-coupled engines owned by that company.

In this work the complete history of each engine owned by the L.N.E.R., or built to its design, is given. Dimensions are quoted as well as full lists of detail alterations and dates of building, rebuilding, renumbering and withdrawal. Illustrations are generally confined to the post-Grouping period as this is primarily an L.N.E.R. history.

Most of the information has been obtained from official sources and it will be noted that in several instances it is at variance with previously published accounts, including such classical historical works as those by E. L. Ahrons and G. F. Bird. In every such case the greatest possible care has been taken to have the details verified and the authors are confident that the version now presented is authentic. Records kept at the various L.N.E.R. locomotive works and elsewhere were not on a uniform basis, particularly of course in the pre-Grouping

period, and this has prevented full documentation of some of the detail variations in certain classes.

Acknowledgements will be found in Part 1, *The Preliminary Survey*, to individuals, firms, organisations and, not least, British Railways, for their assistance in providing material for this Part. In addition, readers are referred to Part 1 for full details of the L.N.E.R.'s history and its policy regarding locomotive construction, classification of engines and boilers, diagrams, numberings, naming, liveries, brakes, tenders, route restrictions and load and power classifications. A full list of locomotive classes and their sub-division into class parts is also included therein.

The individual class articles in this series have been arranged on a uniform basis, each class being divided under sub-headings. This method was preferred by the authors to a chronological history as it facilitates reference, but some unavoidable repetition does occur. The following notes on these sub-headings are offered to assist the reader:—

ENGINES AT GROUPING (or at subsequent date of absorption).—For convenience the locomotive numbers quoted are wherever possible on an L.N.E.R. basis. In some instances, however, locomotives were withdrawn without actually receiving new L.N.E.R. numbers.

STANDARD L.N.E.R. DIMENSIONS.—These are on a uniform basis for each class and have generally been taken from the first engine diagram issued by the L.N.E.R. for the class concerned, unless otherwise stated. The pitch of the boiler is its centre line height above rail level. Boiler diagram numbers refer to those brought into use from 1928 onwards by the L.N.E.R. These numbers have also been used for locomotive classes which became extinct before that date where the particular boiler type survived in use on some other class at 1928 and thus received a diagram number.

REBUILDING.—Generally this section is confined to major rebuilding, or reboilering with a different type of boiler. All other variations appear under other headings, e.g. "Details" and "Brakes".

ENGINE DIAGRAMS.—The diagrams issued by the L.N.E.R. are listed under this heading. Generally the diagrams were prepared at the end of the year quoted and issued early in the following year. In certain classes an indication is given of major variations not recognised by the issue of a diagram.

SUMMARY.—(i) Engine Numbers: An L.N.E.R. number shown in brackets indicates that it was never actually borne. Dates of renumbering are given, except in the case of many of the 1924 L.N.E.R. numbers where the relevant information is not uniformly available. (ii) Rebuilding and other alterations: As this work is primarily a history from Grouping to the present day, the summary normally lists only alterations that occurred after 1923. Alterations made in pre-Grouping days are therefore generally confined to the body of the article on each class, except that, where a particular alteration to a class was initiated before Grouping and continued by the L.N.E.R., complete details will be given in the Summary.

Dates of building, rebuilding and detail alterations are on the basis customarily employed by the various companies before Grouping. For the L.N.E.R. and B.R. periods they are "to traffic," i.e. when the locomotive took up revenue earning work. Differences may thus occur between these and previously published information where, for instance, "ex-works" or "official" rebuilding dates may have been quoted. "Ex-works" frequently meant the date an engine emerged from the erecting shop; a further period then elapsed during which time it ran one or more trial trips and was painted and varnished. Rebuilding dates were often recorded when a new boiler was allotted to or installed on an engine then under repair and could precede the date the engine returned to traffic by several months. From about 1929, ex-works dates ceased to be quoted in L.N.E.R. records, dates to traffic being solely used thereafter.

0-6-0T CLASSES
SUMMARY OF CLASS TOTALS

31st December

Class	Rly.	1-1-23	1923	1924	1925	1926	1927	1928	1929	1930	1931	1932	1933	1934	1935	1936	1937	1938	1939	1940	1941	1942
J50	G.N.	10	10	20	20	47	52	52	61	74	78	85	85	87	88	88	88	93	102	102	102	102
J51	G.N.	30	30	30	30	30	30	30	21	14	10	3	3	1								
J52	G.N.	88	97	112	115	118	120	122	124	129	132	136	136	136	136	134	134	134	132	132	132	132
J53	G.N.	49	40	25	22	19	17	15	13	8	5	1	1	1								
J54	G.N.	56	52	45	40	38	32	19	16	9	5	1										
J55	G.N.	28	32	39	39	37	42	39	32	19	16	15	10	5	5	3	2	2	2	2	2	2
J56	G.N.	5	5	5	4	4	3	1	1	1	1											
J57	G.N.	8	8	8	8	8	8	8	7	5	4	2	1	1	1	1	1					
" 7 "	G.C.	2																				
J58	G.C.	14	12	12	11	8	8	4	1													
J59	G.C.	26	19	13	9	9	6	2														
J60	G.C.	4	4	4	4	4	4	4	4	4	4	4	4	4	4	4	4	4	4	4	4	4
J61	G.C.	2	2	2	2	2	2	2	1	1												
J62	G.C.	12	12	12	12	12	12	12	12	12	12	12	12	12	11	11	4	4	4	4	4	4
J63	G.C.	7	7	7	7	7	7	7	7	7	7	7	7	7	7	7	7	7	7	7	7	7
J64	M.S.L.	—		2§	2	2	2	1														
J65	G.E.	20	20	20	20	20	20	20	20	19	16	14	14	14	12	11	5	5	5	5	5	5
J66	G.E.	49	49	49	49	49	49	49	49	49	49	49	49	49	49	43	31	28	19	18	18	18
J67	G.E.	51	51	51	51	51	51	51	51	51	51	51	51	51	51	51	40	47	54	56	56	56
J68	G.E.	20	30	30	30	30	30	30	30	30	30	30	30	30	30	30	30	30	29	28	28	28
J69	G.E.	109	109	109	109	109	109	109	109	109	108	108	108	108	108	108	108	101	94	79	79	79
J70	G.E.	12	12	12	12	12	12	12	12	12	12	12	12	12	12	12	12	12	12	12	12	11
" 44 "	N.E.	5	5	4	2																	
J71	N.E.	119	119	119	119	120	120	120	120	120	120	120	110	110	108	103	90	90	87	87	87	87
J72	N.E.	75	75	75	85	85	85	85	85	85	85	85	85	85	85	85	85	85	85	85	85	85
J73	N.E.	10	10	10	10	10	10	10	10	10	10	10	10	10	10	10	10	10	10	10	10	10
J74	N.E.	8	8	8	8	8	8	8	8	7												
J75	H.B.	16	16	16	16	16	16	16	16	16	16	16	16	16	16	16	3	2	1	1	1	1
J76	N.E.	10	10	10	10	7	4	1														
J77	N.E.	60	60	60	60	60	60	60	60	60	60	60	55	54	53	53	53	53	52	52	52	52
J78	N.E.	—				2	2	2	2	2	2	2	1	1	1	1						
J79	N.E.	2	2	2	3	3	3	3	3	3	3	3	3	3	3	2						
J80	H.B.	3	3	3	3	3	3	3	2													
J81	N.B.	1	1																			
J82	N.B.	24	23	16	4																	
J83	N.B.	40	40	40	40	40	40	40	40	40	40	40	40	40	40	40	40	40	40	40	40	40
J84	N.B.	3	2																			
J85	N.B.	1	1																			
J84	E.W.Y.	—	2†	2	2	2	2	1	1													
J85	E.W.Y.	—	1	1	1	1	1	1	1	1	1	1										
J86	N.B.	1	1																			
J88	N.B.	35	35	35	35	35	35	35	35	35	35	35	35	35	35	35	35	35	35	35	35	**35**
J90	G.N.S.	6	6	6	6	6	6	6	6	6	6	5	5	3	1							
J91	G.N.S.	3	3	3	3	3	3	3	3	2	2	1										
J93	M.G.N.	—														9	9	9	9	9	9	9
Total		1024	1024*	1017	1003	1017	1014	983	964	943	920	909	884	875	866	848	791	791	783	768	768	767

3

31st December

Class	1943	1944	1945	1946	1947	1948	1949	1950	1951	1952	1953	1954	1955	1956	1957	1958	1959	1960	1961	1962	1963	1964	1965	1966	1967
J50	102	102	102	102	102	102	102	102	102	102	102	102	102	102	102	99	87	67	29	12					
J52	132	132	132	132	132	132	132	127	126	122	113	97	65	45	27	7	3	2							
J55	2	2	2	2	1																				
J60	4	4	4	4	2																				
J62	4	4	4	4	3	3	1	1																	
J63	7	7	7	7	7	7	7	7	7	7	6	6	4	1											
J65	5	5	5	5	4	3	2	2	2	2	1	1	1												
J66	18	18	18	18	18	18	18	14	9	3	3	1													
J67	56	57	50	46	45	44	44	39	36	34	34	30	20	11	7										
J68	28	28	29	29	29	29	29	29	29	29	29	29	29	29	29	22	10	3							
J69	79	78	84	88	89	90	90	95	98	100	96	96	96	95	92	87	62	43	29	11					
J70	11	11	11	11	11	11	10	10	9	8	4	4													
J71	87	87	87	86	81	80	80	76	71	67	64	58	49	39	30	23	14	4							
J72	85	85	85	85	85	85	100	105	113	113	113	113	113	113	113	108	100	78	34	18	4				
J73	10	10	10	10	10	10	10	10	10	10	10	10	9	9	8	5	3								
J75	1	1	1	1	1	1																			
J77	52	48	47	46	46	43	42	40	38	38	37	32	28	21	16	7	5	1							
J83	40	40	40	40	39	39	39	39	39	39	39	39	39	34	32	21	18	16	11						
J88	35	35	35	35	35	35	35	35	35	35	35	34	33	32	31	20	16	10	7						
J93	8	7	5	5	3	1																			
J94			74	75	75	75	75	75	75	75	75	75	75	75	75	75	75	69	66	45	24	13	3	2	
Total	766	761	758	830	818	808	816	806	799	784	761	727	662	603	557	449	374	279	158	75	28	13	3	2	Nil

* The official stock total at 31/12/23 for the 0-6-0T classes was 1026, this being due to the erroneous inclusion of two ex-N.B.R. engines (class J82 No. 1289 and J84 No. 1270) in the 1924 year withdrawals whereas they had actually been withdrawn during 1923.

§ Three J64 class engines were added to stock during 1924, but one was withdrawn later that year.

† Three J84 class engines from the E.W.Y.U.R. were taken into stock during 1923, but one was withdrawn almost immediately.

CLASSES J71 to J94

Because of its considerable mineral traffic, the N.E.R. contributed the largest number of 0-6-0T's, 289 engines, to L.N.E.R. running stock, despite the fact that 102 0-6-2T's were also available for similar duties, neither figure including the H. & B.R. contribution of nineteen 0-6-0T's, and twenty-four 0-6-2T's.

The oldest of the N.E.R. 0-6-0T's were the sixty Fletcher "290" class engines dating from 1874. They had started life as class BTP 0-4-4T's (see class G6, Part 7, pp. 99-103), but between 1899 and 1921 were rebuilt at York and Darlington as six-coupled shunting engines with 4ft. 1¼in. wheels. They were classified J77 by the L.N.E.R. and were sturdy, long-lived engines, bigger than the majority of N.E.R. 0-6-0T's. Withdrawal took place between 1933 and 1961.

In 1881 Fletcher produced a goods version of his BTP class and twelve were built. The wheel diameter was 4ft. 6in., but some engines later received 4ft. 9in. wheels. Ten engines survived to become class J76 on the L.N.E.R. and all had by then been altered from well tanks to side tanks. They were withdrawn during 1926-29.

The N.E.R. "44" class consisted of seven engines built in 1881-83 which were the final version of Fletcher's saddle tanks. T. W. Worsdell followed the design closely with his E class of 1886 (see below), which however had side tanks, and between 1898 and 1902 the "44" class were rebuilt with side tanks so that they became similar to the E class. Five "44" class engines entered L.N.E.R. stock, but never received any L.N.E.R.

4

classification although withdrawal was not completed until 1926.

When McDonnell resigned from his position as Locomotive Superintendent of the N.E.R. in September 1884, material was on order for eight more of his ill-fated " 38 " class 4-4-0's. These engines were not proceeded with and the materials were used to construct a like number of 4ft. 7¼in. 0-6-0T's during 1885. They became class J74 at Grouping and were withdrawn in 1930-31.

T. W. Worsdell introduced his standard class E shunting tank in 1886 and 120 were built during the next ten years. The wheels were 4ft. 7¼in. in diameter and the cylinders 16in. × 22in., except on the last twenty to be built which had 16¾in. cylinders. The L.N.E.R. classified these engines J71. One was in Service Stock until 1926. Withdrawal commenced in 1933 but was not completed until 1961.

In 1898 Wilson Worsdell built the first of the E1 class, a more powerful version of his brother's E class, with 6in. smaller wheels and 17in. × 24in. cylinders, although the boiler was identical. By 1922 seventy-five were in service and became class J72 at Grouping. During 1925 ten additional engines were built at Doncaster and then, after an interval of twenty-four years, twenty-eight more were constructed by British Railways in 1949-51. The class was withdrawn between 1958 and 1964, but remained represented in Departmental Stock until 1967.

The largest N.E.R. 0-6-0T's were Wilson Worsdell's ten 4ft. 7¼in. L class built in 1891-92. These had 19in. × 24in. cylinders and boilers standard with the P class 0-6-0 mineral engines (L.N.E.R. class J24). Classified J73, they were withdrawn during the years 1955-60.

Two small crane tanks with 3ft. 6¼in. wheels were built by T. W. Worsdell in 1888. At Grouping they were classified J78 and were included in service stock, but were transferred to running stock in 1926. Two similar engines, but without cranes, were built in 1897 and became J79. A third engine of this latter type was completed in 1907 and was used as a service locomotive before being transferred to running stock in 1925. Classes J78 and J79 were both eliminated in 1937.

Matthew Stirling designed two classes of 0-6-0T for the H. & B.R. Three engines with 5ft. 0in. wheels for branch passenger work were built in 1892 and were classified J80 by the L.N.E.R. During 1901-8 sixteen more were constructed, but with wheels 6in. less in diameter. These engines became class J75. All nineteen engines had domeless boilers when built, but the majority received new

boilers with domes under the L.N.E.R. Class J80 was withdrawn in 1930-31, whilst the J75's were scrapped in 1937-39, except for one engine which lingered on until 1949.

The N.B.R. had 105 0-6-0T's at Grouping as well as 75 0-6-2T's, although post-Grouping additions to the latter raised their total also to 105. The oldest N.B.R. 0-6-0T's taken over at Grouping were the six survivors of Wheatley's saddle tanks, made up from four different classes. Class J86 was allotted to the one remaining engine of Wheatley's first 5ft. 0in. design, of which two had been constructed in 1870. Fifteen similar engines turned out in 1871-73 and one of these still existed at Grouping to form class J81. A 4ft. 3in. version appeared in 1870 and nine were built. Again one engine survived in 1923 and became class J85. The other Wheatley 4ft. 3in. saddle tanks which came into the L.N.E.R. started life as 0-6-0 tender engines (built in 1873-74) but had been rebuilt as tank engines during 1889-95. Three, out of an original total of 20 rebuilds, were handed over to the L.N.E.R. and formed class J84. The above four classes all became extinct in 1924.

It will be noted that class J86 was not in the correct sequence according to wheel diameter, due to the fact that the L.N.E.R. Engine Diagram showed the wrong figure of 4ft. 3in.

Between 1875 and 1878 Drummond built twenty-five 4ft. 6in. 0-6-0T engines for passenger work on the N.B.R. They had side tanks and were an enlarged version of Stroudley's well-known " Terrier " type on the L.B. & S.C.R. One of the Drummond engines was withdrawn before Grouping and the L.N.E.R., who classified them J82, scrapped the remainder by the end of 1926.

No further 0-6-0T's were built for the N.B.R. until 1900 when Holmes introduced his large and powerful 4ft. 6in. side tanks which became J83 on the L.N.E.R. The forty engines in the class were turned out within a period of two years. Withdrawal took place between 1947 and 1962.

The latest N.B.R. 0-6-0T's were Reid's 3ft. 9in. dock shunters with outside cylinders and dumb buffers. They were introduced in 1904 and thirty-five were constructed down to 1919. All survived to become class J88 on the L.N.E.R. and were withdrawn in 1954-62.

For the G.N.S.R., Manson had six 4ft. 6in. 0-6-0T's built by Kitsons in 1884. Three further engines came from the same builders during the following year, differing slightly in that the boiler was set further forward and there was an increase in overall length and width. The two series were classified J90 and J91 respectively by the L.N.E.R., the former becoming extinct in 1936 and the latter in 1934. These were the only six-coupled engines owned by the G.N.S.R.

The L.N.E.R. classification system had been prepared in September 1923 and as far as the 0-6-0T's were concerned, the whole of the series J50 to J91 was used, except for J64, J87 and J89 which were left blank. J64 may have been intended for the G.C.R. class "7" engines, but the last of these was withdrawn in July 1923. It may also have been the intention to use J87 for the earliest of the N.B.R. Reid dock tanks, which differed in some respects from the later engines of this type. In the event they were all classified J88. There were no known candidates for the classification J89, however. There were a number of later acquisitions to the ranks of the L.N.E.R. 0-6-0T's and these were included in the classification system as shown below.

When the East & West Yorkshire Union Railways Company was absorbed on 1st July 1923, two classes of 0-6-0ST were added to L.N.E.R. stock, comprising three engines with 4ft. 0in. wheels and one having 3ft. 9in. wheels. Either some delay took place in classifying these engines, or there was duplication, because they became classes J84 and J85 respectively, these classifications having already been adopted for some of Wheatley's saddle tanks off the N.B.R. The Wheatley engines disappeared by the end of 1924, however, and the duplication ceased. The E. & W.Y.U. J84 class became extinct in 1930 and J85 followed in 1933.

In July 1924 the blank classification J64 was taken by the three Mid-Suffolk Light Railway 0-6-0T's absorbed at that time (see Part 8A).

The original classification system had allocated Z4 to the three G.E.R. 0-6-0 crane tanks, but in April 1927 they became J92 at the end of the 0-6-0T series. These three engines remained as service locomotives for the rest of their existence and, as such, are not described in this book, but will be dealt with in Part 10. Similarly, No. 3470A, one of Patrick Stirling's small 4ft. 2in. saddle tanks with 16in. cylinders, will be described in Part 10. This engine was the only one of its type at Grouping and was employed as a service locomotive at Boston Sleeper Depot until scrapped in 1927. It never received any L.N.E.R. classification.

From 1st October 1936 the M. & G.N. locomotive stock became the responsibility of the L.N.E.R., although not included in L.N.E.R. stock returns until 1937. The nine

3ft. 7in. outside-cylinder side tanks became class J93, although not in fact so classified until 1942. They had been built at Melton Constable between 1897 and 1905, and some incorporated parts taken from Cornwall Mineral Railways engines built in 1874. Withdrawal took place in 1943-49. An outside cylinder 0-6-0ST was also taken over from the M. & G.N. This was No. 16A, built by Fox, Walker & Co. in 1877 for the Great Yarmouth & Stalham Light Railway. It became works shunter at Melton Constable and, as such, became an L.N.E.R. service locomotive, receiving no classification. It too will be dealt with in Part 10.

The large number of 0-6-0T's used on suburban passenger work by the G.E.R. had a considerable influence on the construction programme for this type of engine by the L.N.E.R. Apart from the fulfilment in 1923 of an order for ten of the G.E.R. J68 class engines, the only additions up to 1940 were ten of the N.E.R. light J72 type and sixty-two of the heavy G.N.R. J50 class. The old shunting engines on the G.N., G.C. and N.B. Sections when scrapped were replaced by G.E.R. 0-6-0T's released from suburban passenger duties upon the construction in the years 1925-28 of 112 N7 class 0-6-2T's. On the G.N.S. Section however the replacements for their 0-6-0T's were J72 class engines from North Eastern sheds.

By the end of 1939, just after the outbreak of the Second World War, the number of classes of 0-6-0T had been halved and the running stock total of such engines had dropped from 1,024 at Grouping to 783. A definite shortage of shunting engines existed during and after the War and this was to some extent rectified when, in 1946-47, the L.N.E.R. purchased seventy-five 0-6-0 saddle tanks from the Ministry of Supply. This was the only entirely new class of 0-6-0T introduced by the L.N.E.R. and received the classification J94. The design, based on a standard Hunslet Engine Co. type, had been adopted for Government use during the 1939-45 War. The J94's were withdrawn between 1960 and 1967.

No further additions were made to this wheel arrangement by the L.N.E.R., but, as already mentioned, twenty-eight J72's were built by B.R. during the period 1949-51. This class, introduced in 1898, thus achieved the extraordinary record of being built over a period of fifty-four years by the N.E.R., L.N.E.R. and B.R. The class only remained intact for seven years and withdrawal was completed within the next six years.

CLASS 44

N.E.R. CLASS 44—FLETCHER
4ft. 7¼in. ENGINES

ENGINES AT GROUPING (Built 1881-83):
44/9, 94/8, 106. TOTAL 5.

The North Eastern Railway had always used a number of small shunting engines, but in the late 1860's Edward Fletcher built a few new engines at Gateshead of a more substantial design (class " 5 "). They were short-coupled long-boilered saddle tanks and between 1872 and 1875 a further fifty generally similar engines came from outside contractors (see table below). In 1875/6 twenty more saddle tanks were delivered by outside builders for the Central Division (the old Stockton & Darlington, with additions) and in these the design was changed to one having the rear coupled wheels behind the firebox. The " 44 " class, which was built five years later at Gateshead, was a development of these engines. Over the same period, from the late 1860's until the early 1880's, both short and long boilered shunting engines were also turned out as " rebuilds " from Gateshead Works. The history of these engines is complex, but in the main they used the newer parts of small old passenger and goods engines which had themselves been rebuilt or renewed in the 1860's, only to be displaced about ten years later by the new engines of such classes as " 398 " and " 901 " then being built. To utilise the relatively new boilers and other parts of some of these old small engines, a considerable number of saddle tanks were built along the lines of one or other of the designs of new engines mentioned above.

The " 44 " class was thus the final version of a long development of saddle tank engines and the only one to survive to Grouping, though by then rebuilt with side tanks as described below.

The " 44 " class consisted of only seven engines. In this design Fletcher used the longer 24in. stroke as in the case of the old goods engines rebuilt as saddle tanks and at least two of the new " 44 " class engines, Nos. 106 and 140, were built with second-hand crank axles. The wheels were 4ft. 6in. in diameter, larger than normal for shunting engines, except for No. 98 which had 4ft. 0in. wheels when built until they were replaced with 4ft. 6in. wheels between 1894 and 1902, probably in 1898 when the engine was rebuilt.

Neither T. W. Worsdell nor his brother Wilson Worsdell favoured saddle tanks and a large programme of building new side tank shunting engines was started. The first of these new standard classes was class E (L.N.E.R. J71) introduced in 1886, followed in 1898 by class E1 (J72). The E class retained the 4ft. 6in. nominal wheel size of the " 44 " class but the cylinders reverted to the 22in. stroke, whereas E1 class reversed the position, reverting to the 4ft. 0in. wheels of Fletcher's earlier engines but having the 24in. stroke of the " 44 " class. When, after fifteen to twenty years' service, the boilers of the " 44 " class needed replacement, it was decided to rebuild the engines with side tanks as well.

The rebuilding of Fletcher's saddle tank shunting engines to conform with the ideas of the brothers Worsdell had been started earlier, in 1892/3. At this date the Gateshead engines of 1867-69 had been withdrawn, as had some of the rebuilds of 1871-81, while others had been reboilered and/or had received 16in. diameter cylinders, but had not been otherwise rebuilt. In 1890 a start was made to reboiler the " 1350 " class and again no other rebuilding took place except that 16in. cylinders were fitted if new cylinders were required. The case of the " 964 " class was

Date	Class	Makers	Cylinders	Wheels	Boiler
1867-9	" 5 "	Gateshead	14½″ × 22″	4′ 2″	long
1872-3	" 964 "	Black, Hawthorn	14¾″ × 22″	4′ 2″	,,
1873-5	,,	Stephenson	,,	4′ 0″	,,
1875-6	" 1350 "	Hawthorn	15″ × 22″	4′ 0″	short
1871-81 (about)	" 30 " " 48 " and " 287 "	Gateshead (rebuilds)	15″ × 22″ and 15″ × 24″	4′ 0″	long and short
1881-3	" 44 "	Gateshead	15″ × 24″	4′ 6″	short

7

different. Fifteen were withdrawn unrebuilt between 1887 and 1893, ten being scrapped and five sold. During 1891 and 1892 twenty were reboilered but not rebuilt and then in 1892 and 1893 the remaining fifteen were reboilered and extensively rebuilt as side tanks with 16in. cylinders if these had not already been fitted. Even more significant, however, was the alteration from short to long coupled design, with a new cab and a rear bunker. Apart from having only 4ft. 0in. wheels, they were now very similar to class E and were at first included in that class, although later they came to be known as class "964A". In reviewing this extensive rebuilding, Wilson Worsdell came to the conclusion that a rebuild cost nearly three-quarters of the cost of a new engine and this assessment would seem to imply that in future he would be likely to favour building new engines rather than such substantial rebuilding. The reboilering in 1895-97 of the last five of the "1350" class engines without conversion to side tanks was in line with this view.

The position was, however, different in the case of class "44" when these engines needed rebuilding. The basic similarity of the "chassis" to class E meant that by replacing the superstructure and boiler they became almost uniform with that class. This rebuilding was duly carried out on the whole of class "44" between the years 1898 and 1902. The rebuilds had the running plate set high so that the splashers and sandboxes were like those on class E1 (4ft. 0in. wheels) then in production, rather than E which had the same size wheels as class "44". This was again a reflection of the contemporary new engines, whereas the "964A" rebuilds of 1892-93 had small wheels but the large splashers of the current E design.

Two "44" class engines were withdrawn before Grouping, namely No. 46 (built 4/1882, withdrawn 4/1919) and No. 140 (built 4/1883, withdrawn 7/1914). No L.N.E.R. classification was given to the five survivors (which was also the case with several other N.E.R. classes, such as the "398" 0-6-0's and "901" and "1440" 2-4-0 types) as they were evidently ear-marked for early withdrawal, this usually taking place when they next became due for general repairs. No. 106, which had received a new boiler in April 1918, was however given a general overhaul by the L.N.E.R. in August 1923 and by January 1926 it was the only survivor (fig. 2). In September the same year a shortage of spare boilers for class J71 caused it to be recalled to Darlington and withdrawn, its boiler going to No. 399 of that class.

Standard Dimensions at Grouping

No L.N.E.R. engine diagram was issued and these dimensions are from N.E.R. records.

Cylinders (2 inside)	16″ × 24″
Motion	Stephenson with slide valves
Boiler:	
Max. diam. outside	3′ 8″
Barrel length ...	10′ 0″
Firebox length outside ...	4′ 4″
Pitch	6′ 10″
Diagram No. ...	73
Heating surface:	
Firebox	73 sq. ft.
Tubes (139 × 1¾″)	658 sq. ft.
Total	731 sq. ft.
Grate area ...	11.3 sq. ft.
Boiler pressure ...	140 lb./sq. in.
Coupled wheels ...	4′ 7¼″
Tractive effort (85%)	13,233 lb.
Length over buffers	28′ 4¾″
Wheelbase ...	6′ 6″ + 7′ 1″ = 13′ 7″
Weight (full) ...	36T 0c
Max. axle load ...	13T 15c
Water capacity ...	690 gallons
Coal capacity ...	1T 5c

Rebuilding

The individual rebuilding dates for the "44" class were as follows:

No.	Date
44	3/1901
46	2/1902
49	10/1899
94	4/1900
98	12/1898
106	12/1899
140	10/1900

When the boilers provided on rebuilding the "44" class engines themselves became due for replacement Nos. 98 and 49 were given further new boilers in September 1908 and October 1910 respectively, whilst Nos. 44 and 94 received second-hand boilers from "964A" class engines in March 1915 and October 1916. Finally, No. 106 was given a new boiler in April 1918. Of the two engines which were withdrawn before Grouping, No. 46 had had a new boiler in August 1912, but No. 140 was withdrawn without receiving a fresh boiler.

Details

After the substantial rebuilding in 1898-1902 their appearance was altered very little. Three coal rails had been added to the top of the bunker and although originally open, plates had been put behind these rails long before Grouping. Ramsbottom safety valves in the usual polished brass casing were used throughout, but these engines carried only a single whistle (of the bell-shaped type) mounted on the firebox between the safety valves and the spectacle plate. Sandwich type bufferbeams were used at both ends and the buffers were of the tapered-shank variety. Quite substantial single-step foot-steps were mounted just behind the leading axle in addition to the steps to the cab. For the valves and cylinders, screw-down displacement type lubricators were fitted on the sides of the smokebox, but on No. 106 at its L.N.E.R. repair, these were changed to tallow cups. For the axleboxes, there were oil-boxes mounted on the front ends of the tanks. Before Grouping No. 106 was trans-ferred to Shildon and was fitted on both sides at the leading end with shunting poles for moving wagons on adjoining lines in Shildon Wagon Works (see class J71, p. 13). No. 106 was the only one of the class fitted with these poles, retaining them until withdrawn.

Brakes

The " 44 " class engines were fitted throughout their life with steam brake only.

Allocation and Work

When first built the whole class worked in the Northern Division of the N.E.R. By Grouping the five survivors were spread amongst four sheds, No. 44 being at East Hartlepool, Nos. 49 and 98 at Sunderland, No. 94 at Heaton, and No. 106 at Shildon, and it was from these sheds that they were with-drawn. Their end was hastened by the allocation of new E1 class engines to each of these sheds during 1922. In their last years, the " 44 " class engines were confined mainly to the shunting of wagons close to their sheds.

Engine Diagram

None issued.

Summary of 44 Class

1923 No.	Maker	Built	Withdrawn
44	Gateshead	12/1881	6/24
106	,,	6/1882	9/26
94	,,	8/1882	1/26
98	,,	9/1882	6/25
49	,,	1/1883	2/25

CLASS J71

N.E.R. CLASS E—T. W. WORSDELL
4ft. 7¼in. (and 4ft. 1¼in.) ENGINES

ENGINES AT GROUPING (Built 1886-95): 27, 50/4, 70/7, 84, 103/37/44/61/5/8/76/7/9/81, 221/4/5/37/9-42/4/8/52/4/60/1/8/72/5/8/80/ 5/6/96/9, 301/4/17/26/38/47/99, 400-3/47-53/ 78/82/92-6/9, 501/33/41/72/7/84, 802/11, 969/ 72/7/8/80, 1083/4/5/95, 1103/23/34/40/2/3/4/ 51/3/5/7/63/7/96-9, 1314, 1666/88/9/90, 1735/ 58/89/96/7, 1831-6/61-4. TOTAL 119.
In addition, No. 263 was in Service Stock until August 1926.

When T. W. Worsdell came to the N.E.R. towards the end of 1885 there was a consider-able backlog of repair work, particularly the fitting of new boilers. This had arisen partly from the large number of engines built in the years 1870-76 when the locomotive stock was expanding rapidly, the boilers of which were now due for renewal. Another major cause was that Alexander McDonnell had started to reorganise the boiler shops at Gateshead, but this had resulted in an unfortunate

reduction in the number of new boilers being built and fitted at a time when the need was particularly urgent.

As outlined under class " 44 " a large number of shunting engines dated, or had boilers dating, from the late 1860's or early 1870's. These engines were saddle tanks, and many were also short-coupled, which did not fit into the scheme of things as seen by Thomas W. Worsdell.

In 1886 the first of the new standard shunting engines emerged from Darlington Works. They differed from Worsdell's other standard classes of engine in that they were neither compounds nor were they fitted with Joy's motion. In view of the duties for which they were designed neither of these variations is surprising, but the result was that the shunting tank was much more a develop-ment of the " 44 " class than any other of the new designs were of preceding engines of their own wheel arrangement. The similarity

9

to class "44" became very noticeable after this class was rebuilt by Wilson Worsdell with the side tanks and new cabs and bunkers. The new class was designated E and it should be noted that when some of the "964" class were rebuilt (see p. 8) they were at first included under class E.

Darlington Works continued building these engines for ten years until 1895, when 120 had been constructed, Wilson Worsdell being responsible for the later engines. Since they had neither compounding nor Joy's motion he made little change to the design in evolving his own standard class, smaller wheels and larger cylinders being the principal changes made in the E1 class which followed (see J72). The boiler was unchanged in its principal features and was used on classes E and E1 and also on the rebuilt classes "44", "1350" and "964A".

The class E engines were originally all built for goods shunting and were fitted with steam brake only, though a number latterly had continuous brakes. The last twenty, as built, had cylinders enlarged from 16in. to 16¾in. diameter. Nine of the ten engines

built in 1892-93 were given second-hand wheels 6in. less in diameter than standard for the class.

No. 263 had been allocated to Service Stock before Grouping and was used as one of the shunters at North Road Works, Darlington. In August 1926 it was transferred to Running Stock although still used on the same duties.

The class remained intact until the slump in trade of the early 1930's, which resulted in the first ten J71's being withdrawn between August and November 1933. Further inroads were made each year up to the outbreak of war, with a particularly heavy reduction of thirteen engines in May 1937, most of which had been in store as surplus to requirements. A few more were withdrawn just after hostilities began, leaving 81 still in stock at the end of the L.N.E.R. After nationalisation only five more disappeared in the first three years, but the advent of the diesel shunter hastened their demise, and the last to survive was No. 68233 (ex-No. 326), withdrawn in February 1961 at the ripe old age of exactly seventy-four years.

Engine Nos.	No. built	Date
144/65, 299, 317, 261, 304/99, 27, 326, 533	10	1886-87
70, 168, 263/72/8, 347, 493/4/9, 811	10	1887
242/68/75/85/6, 403, 541/84, 1123/63	10	1888
1167, 84, 221/4/5, 453/92/5/6, 501	10	1889
1083, 239, 50, 241/4/54/60/96, 338, 400, 54, 103/76/7/9/81, 248, 478/82, 802	20	1890
77, 161, 252/80, 447/8, 301, 401/49-52, 572/7, 1085, 1103/40/2/53/7	20	1891-92
237/40, 402, 1084/95, 1143/4/51/5, 1314	10	1892
1196-9, 969/72, 137, 977/8/80	10	1892-93
1666, 1735/96/7, 1831-6	10	1894
1134, 1758/89, 1688/9/90, 1861-4	10	1895

Standard L.N.E.R. Dimensions at Grouping

Cylinders (2 inside)	16″ × 22″ or 16¾″ × 22″
Motion	Stephenson with slide valves
Boiler:	
Max. diam. out-side	3′ 8″
Barrel length ...	10′ 0″
Firebox length outside ...	4′ 4″
Pitch	6′ 6″
Diagram No. ...	73
Heating surface:	
Firebox	73 sq. ft.
Tubes (139 × 1¾″)	658 sq. ft.
Total	731 sq. ft.
Grate area ...	11.3 sq. ft.
Boiler pressure ...	140 lb./sq. in.

Coupled wheels ...	4′ 7¼″
Tractive effort (85%)	12,130 lb. or 13,300 lb.
Length over buffers	28′ 8¾″
Wheelbase ...	6′ 6″ + 7′ 2″ = 13′ 8″
Weight (full) ...	37T 12c
Max. axle load ...	13T 14c
Water capacity ...	690 gallons
Coal capacity ...	1T 5c

Compared with the dimensions at Grouping, the coal capacity as first built without coal rails, was one ton. The length over buffers was originally 27ft. 9½in. but the addition of wooden sandwich buffing plates and the later pattern of N.E.R. buffers increased this to 28ft. 8¾in. The last twenty engines with 16¾in. cylinders on average weighed 12 cwt. less than the standard engines, the L.N.E.R. diagram giving the latter.

L.N.E.R. Renumbering

The eighty-seven engines existing when the 1943 scheme was prepared were allotted Nos. 8230 to 8316 and all survived to receive them, although No. 1861 only ran as No. 8315 from 17th March to 20th April 1946, when it was withdrawn.

Details

When the ten engines forming the batch of 1892-93 were built, some second-hand material was used and all these engines received previously used wheels. Except for No. 978, which had the normal 4ft. 6in. nominal size for the class, all received 4ft. wheels (fig. 11). Only four of these engines, Nos. 969/77/8/80, had new tyres when built. Of the nine, Nos. 137, 969/72/7/80, 1196-9, which had 4ft. wheels when built, Nos. 137 and 1196 received new wheels of standard size by 1912, but the exact date is not certain. The index to the L.N.E.R. Engine Diagram Book of 1924 did not recognise the existence of the seven which still had small wheels, though later they were recorded and No. 1197 is shown as having its wheels changed in August 1935 and No. 972 received standard wheels in March 1936. It is known that No. 969 still had its smaller wheels when withdrawn in September 1933. On the other hand, when the Engine History Sheets were begun in 1934, No. 1199 was shown as then having 4ft. 6in. wheels and this is supported by photographic evidence, whereas Nos. 977/80 and 1198 were still shown as 4ft. wheels and no subsequent change was entered.

Another variation within the class as built is to be noted in the shape of the frames at the ends. The first eighteen engines had them cut square, thus coming well below the bufferbeams. Angle brackets were fitted to take vertical oak planks which were used as buffers when moving chaldron wagons. Commencing with No. 499 the bottom corners at each end of the frames were cut away in an arc which finished where the guard irons were attached (fig. 3). However, some of the engines built in 1892 and 1893 also received the square-ended frames (fig. 6). From these and the original batch several survived unaltered into B.R. days. No. 68291 still had them at withdrawal in April 1956 and others noted with them were Nos. 68300 (in 1952), 68238 (in 1953), 68233/98 (in 1954) and 68235/9 (in 1955).

The frames on the altered engines generally conformed to the shape introduced on No. 499, but No. 68230 (ex-165) differed in having its frames at the rear end cut away in a straight line which sloped downwards from the buffer beam, the front end of the frames being in the customary arc form.

When first built the last twenty engines had 16¾in. cylinders, whereas the preceding one hundred had 16in. cylinders. The stroke in all cases was 22in. Engines in both series received new cylinders of different sizes and in some cases more than one change was made. The changes made before Grouping were:—

Rebuilt to 16in.

1690	7/02 (b)	1861	4/18 (b)	402	8/18 (d)	1735	12/21 (b)

Rebuilt to 16½in.

286	6/03 (c)	1084	3/04	1314	8/06	1199	10/06 (c)
326	5/07	978	10/09	478	3/10	1153	2/12
137	4/14						

Rebuilt to 16¾in.

237	12/02	811	4/03	1167	11/03 (a)	1197	7/05
338	10/05	1095	9/06	980	6/07	240	9/07
402	9/07 (c)	495	10/07	1085	9/08	1140	10/08
533	11/08	260	3/09	1196	5/09	452	8/09
492	9/09	449	1/10	1083	8/10	493	10/10
1163	11/10	239	8/11	165	11/11	496	12/11
27	3/12	225	3/12	977	3/12	286	2/15 (d)
448	2/16	248	3/17	299	11/18	1198	5/19
177	8/19	400	7/20	399	6/21	244	12/21

Rebuilt to 17in.

1155	8/10	1199	3/21 (d)

Rebuilt to 18in.

1688	10/03 (b)

Notes
(a) Second-hand from No. 1688.
(b) Originally had 16¾in. cylinders.
(c) Altered again before 1923.
(d) Second alteration.

Further changes noted in the N.E.R. registers in 1923 and 1924 were two engines altered from 16¾in. to 16in., Nos. 1862 (3/23) and 1833 (1/24), and three 16in. engines altered to 16¾in., Nos. 577 (3/23), 447 (5/23) and 296 (10/24).

As already mentioned, when the index to the L.N.E.R. Diagram Book was prepared in 1924, no cognisance was taken of the engines still having 4ft. wheels. However, lists of engines with 16 and 16¾in. cylinders were given, but not for those of 16½, 17 or 18in. The position was further complicated because cylinder changes made after 1912, and some made before that date, were ignored in preparing these lists. Starting from this discrepancy between the N.E.R. and L.N.E.R. records, it has proved impossible to verify any subsequent changes. A North Eastern Area register of 1928 gave all the engines, but was based on the 1924 list, adding in those missing from that list, though not necessarily taking account of all changes. Finally, a revised index of about 1942 showed those engines listed as 16¾in. in 1924 as still the same, showed No. 1688 as 18in. and the remainder, whether 16, 16½ or 17 in., were all treated as being 16in. Once thus recognised, the special position of No. 1688 was entered on the engine history sheet and although new cylinders had been fitted in September 1930 and again in February 1952, it was still recorded as having 18in. cylinders up to its withdrawal in 1959. Even here there is an element of doubt since one of the works copies of the 1920 engine list had been annotated to show No. 1688 as altered back to 16¾in. in September 1930. This engine was fitted with 18in. cylinders for work at Dunston Staiths on the Tyne and, in a Freight Train Circular dated April 1925, was still separately shown as being allowed to work heavier loads from Norwood Junction Sidings to the staiths than the other engines of the class, as also was class J72 No. 1741 which had cylinders larger than normal for these same duties.

Although there were no major dimensional alterations to the boilers, there was a change from the three ⅜in. butt-jointed plates of the barrel to 7/16in. thick plates by Grouping. On boilers built from November 1936 a single ½in. plate was used for the barrel.

Boilers used on this class were fully interchangeable with class J72 and after Grouping were used indiscriminately between these two classes. Taking one example, the boiler put new into J72 No. 2311 in December 1920 was subsequently put into J71 No. 237 (in June 1935), into J72 No. 2173 (in October 1939) and finally into J71 No. 286 where it served from October 1943 until cut up in

November 1946. These boilers were also used by N.E.R. class "44" and when No. 49 of that class was scrapped in February 1925, its boiler was then used from July 1925 to March 1929 in J71 class No. 1157, but none used on class "44" was ever put into the J72 class. Another 0-6-0T class which disappeared before Grouping, N.E.R. "964A", also used this type of boiler and although many of that class were sold out of service, some were scrapped and the boilers from Nos. 873 and 967 withdrawn in 1916 each served more than twelve years in J72 class No. 1722 and 1747 respectively. Boilers of this type were also found suitable for stationary use and indeed three went straight into that type of service and were never in a locomotive, although originally intended for that purpose. For example, out of a batch of ten spare boilers built in 1912, seven were put into class J71, one each into classes J72 and "964A", and the other was used throughout its life as a heating boiler at Wakefield Street stables in Hull. A case surely of facilitating horse power rather than of developing it.

By Grouping 380 of these boilers had been built, 25 by Armstrong, Whitworth & Co. (for the batch of J72's turned out by them in 1922), but all the others by Darlington. Prior to Grouping, the interchange of boilers was not customary.

In L.N.E.R. days another 159 of these boilers were built, 90 by Darlington, 59 by an outside contractor (Hawthorn, Leslie & Co.) and the other ten by Doncaster, for the new J72's built there in 1925. Including these ten, 62 boilers began their service on the J72 class, the others all going to J71 engines.

British Railways built another 103 Diagram 73 boilers, of which 28 went into new engines Nos. 69001-28, and another 53 were first used by J72 class, the remainder going to J71 class. All these B.R. boilers were built by Darlington, the last one as late as June 1957 and, inevitably, the life of many was only a few years. The full total of Diagram 73 boilers thus ran to 642, built over the years 1886-1957.

The older boilers were fed through clack boxes mounted on the side of the barrel ahead of the tanks, but latterly the feed was via the faceplate. All 120 engines originally had the Ramsbottom type of safety valve enclosed in the customary polished brass casing, but from about 1914, replacement boilers had Ross pop valves (cf. figs. 3 and 5). On such small-boilered engines, escaping steam from the pop valves tended on occasion to obscure visibility when shunting. The reaction of the crews to this was to fit makeshift covers around the safety valves. This difficulty was ultimately recognised and from about 1938 covers of similar type to those used with the Ramsbottom valves were put on to enclose the pop valves (fig. 9). Across the top of these covers, the Ramsbottom valves had a relieving lever, not of course fitted, or required, with pop valves and the presence (or absence) of this lever (or 'tail' as it was known) gives the clue to the type of safety valve used.

Two types of buffer were in use on the class, the majority of engines having the type with a tapered shank and solid spindle, but in L.N.E.R. days a few (such as Nos. 103/77, 225/37/85, and 1163) had parallel shank buffers with a large diameter hollow spindle. (figs. 5 and 6). From about 1932 onwards L.N.E.R. Group Standard buffers were fitted to quite a number of J71's, generally in conjunction with L.N.E.R. draw-hooks and couplings in place of the N.E.R. pattern in which the top link was shackled to the drawhook (fig. 8). Originally, steel plate bufferbeams were standard on the class, but most engines ultimately had the front buffer-beam augmented to a sandwich type by the addition of a wooden plank faced by a further steel plate (figs. 3 and 5). Known exceptions were No. 8292 which still had a single steel plate at the front in May 1947 and Nos. 68260/4 noted in similar condition in the early 1950's. Of the engines built with squared frame ends to support wooden dumb buffers between the normal spring buffers for moving chaldron wagons, Nos. 1197/9 seem to have been the last ones running so fitted, being noted in 1932 and 1933 respectively (fig. 6).

Five of this class, Nos. 50, 241/99, 802 and 977, were allocated to Shildon at Grouping and, whilst No. 299 was transferred to Dairy-coates in October 1934, the other four remained at Shildon until closure took place in July 1935, when they were transferred to nearby West Auckland shed. As was customary on shunting engines at Shildon, they had shunting poles fitted to hinged brackets on the footplate angle iron at the front end for moving vehicles on adjacent lines when working in the Wagon Works there (fig. 7). No. 977 additionally had shunting poles at the back end. In use, the poles extended at an angle horizontally from the engine and connected to any convenient point on the wagon to be pushed along the adjoining track. The method was finally condemned due to men being hurt when the poles splintered. In July 1939 Nos. 50 and 802 were noted without shunting poles (but with the brackets still in position) whilst Nos. 977 and 241 still had them. The last-mentioned engine (as B.R. No. 68255) was still running with the poles as late as May 1949. In addition to these J71's, class "44" No. 106, J72 No. 2192 and J77 No. 956 carried shunting poles for use at Shildon.

Nos. 278 and 977 did not have the usual stay to the front footsteps and the latter engine also differed in having sliding shutters to the cab cut-outs.

All 120 engines originally had a bell-shaped high-pitched whistle mounted on the firebox between safety valves and cab front. In December 1909 an instruction was issued by the N.E.R. that all shunting engines were to be changed to low-toned whistle i.e. the organ-pipe type (fig. 5). A modification dated October 1910 made an exception to this instruction for all shunters at the Hartlepools where the low-toned whistle had proved unsuitable. So whilst the majority changed to the organ-pipe type, a few retained the original bell shape.

Whilst the normal smokebox door fastening was a pair of handles, a number of J71's carried a wheel and handle in L.N.E.R. days (figs. 3 and 5). No. 1861 at Blaydon in August 1939 was the last so noted and wheels seem to have disappeared in the war years.

Originally the bunker tops were devoid of coal rails, but around the turn of the century these were added and plated on the inside from 1910 onwards. Three rails were standard but in 1923, Nos. 978 and 1789 only had two, whilst No. 286 only had two as late as 1929. Subsequently all three were brought into line and noted with three rails.

Two of this class, Nos. 285 and 453, each spent more than ten years in the Scottish Area working from Eastfield shed, but neither was ever fitted with the extra long footboard for shunters to ride on as was the general custom on shunting engines in that area.

A special fitting confined to shunting engines working pilot duties in the Newcastle and Gateshead areas was a red spectacle glass which could be turned in front of a lamp mounted on a special bracket on the right-hand side of the smokebox. By operating a rod passing through the boiler handrail, the driver could alter the lamp indication to red without leaving the footplate (fig 8). In use at Grouping, this fitting remained on the engines concerned into B.R. days, although two out of the six so fitted left the Newcastle area in 1934 and 1938. Those so equipped were Nos. 70, 103, 403/82, 501 and 1834, which were all engines fitted for shunting of coaching stock. In addition, J72 No. 8687 was similarly equipped in January 1948.

In June 1934, Nos. 225 and 299 were fitted with spark arresters in connection with their work on the docks at Hull. Another Alexandra Dock engine, No. 286, carried around that time a clumsy wire basket and hinged lid on top of its chimney. Later, others were provided with spark arresters inside the smokebox, mostly for working in the extensive timber yards at the Hartlepools.

One detail for which the reason has not been discovered concerns two engines only, Nos. 263 and 449, which had small subsidiary splashers outside the normal ones to their leading coupled wheels (fig. 5). Both were Darlington based engines before and after Grouping, No. 263 as one of the Works Pilots, and they may possibly have figured in a trial requiring some gear driven off the leading crankpin, such as the recording of mileage during shunting operations.

A local fitting by York shed to some of their pilot engines was a small rain shield to the eaves of the cab. Nos. 1085, 1140, 8286 (237) and 8310 (1134) were all noted with these shields.

Liveries

As an aid to visibility during the wartime blackout, No. 980 had luminous paint applied to its front bufferbeam in December 1943, but this experiment was not extended. Then as a contrast to the wartime austerity and drabness, No. 8286 of York appeared on 31st May 1947 painted in apple green with black and white lining. It also displayed "LNER" above 8286 in cream painted Gill Sans characters, but without any shading (fig. 9). This special treatment was not extended to any further J71 class engines, although others besides No. 8286 were still engaged full time as passenger pilots at main line stations. Following its next general repair, this time at Gateshead, this engine emerged in January 1950 as No. 68286 and with the B.R. lion and wheel crest. The apple green paint was changed to the darker B.R. green and the lining was omitted from the ends of the sandwich type front bufferbeam (fig. 10). Unfortunately its next visit to works, in June 1952, proved to be its last because it was then withdrawn.

Brakes

Originally the whole class was fitted with steam brake only. In December 1899 No. 296 was additionally fitted with Westinghouse apparatus for train brakes, the only one ever equipped with this combination of steam brake on engine and Westinghouse for train, and then in December 1902 No. 1197 had its steam brake changed to Westinghouse and also received train connections. The next changes heralded the start of passenger pilot duties for this class, and took place in

November/December 1909 when four York engines (Nos. 237, 399, 1134/67) and four Newcastle engines (Nos. 179, 501, 811 and 1834, working from Borough Gardens shed) were equipped with vacuum apparatus for train brakes. It will be noted that these station pilots at York and Newcastle were not equipped with Westinghouse brake and when shunting Westinghouse stock the release chains had to be pulled; for this reason there were two shunters per engine. About the same time, another York engine (No. 1140) was altered to Westinghouse brake with vacuum ejector for duties as York Carriage Works pilot. Then as late as June 1922 two more York engines, Nos. 1163 and 1831, received Westinghouse brake for both engine and train (fig. 4). Thus at Grouping the brake position was that eight engines were equipped with steam and vacuum, one with Westinghouse and vacuum, one with steam and Westinghouse, three with Westinghouse for engine and train, the remaining 107 being as built, with steam brake on engine only. Of the odd engines, No. 296 still had steam on engine and Westinghouse for train when withdrawn in August 1933, and No. 1140 changed in September 1929 from Westinghouse and vacuum to steam and vacuum, whilst the three Westinghouse engines reverted to steam brake on engine only, No. 1163 in July 1929, 1197 in March 1930 and 1831 in November 1937.

During 1928-33 ten more steam braked engines were fitted with vacuum apparatus for train working, these being Nos. 254/75, 403/82/95/9, 972/8, 1085, 1157, for which individual dates are given in the Summary (fig. 8). Also, in 1928 the vacuum brake (and steam heating equipment) were taken from No. 811, one of the engines fitted before Grouping, and put on No. 1690. Thus from November 1937 there were eighteen fitted with steam and vacuum, all the other survivors having steam brake only and there were no subsequent changes.

By Grouping all thirteen engines then running with continuous brakes were also equipped with steam heating connections at both ends. In addition, Nos. 254/75, 403/82 had this equipment, although they were steam braked only, likewise Nos. 70 and 103, but with connections only at the back end. Nos. 254/75, 403/82 subsequently received vacuum ejectors, as recorded above, whilst the other J71's which were fitted with vacuum ejector during the same period were also given steam heating fittings (at both ends), Nos. 495/9, 1085, 1157, 1690 concurrently and Nos. 972 and 978 later on (in June 1929 and September, 1930 respectively). No. 811 lost its steam heating fitment in January 1928

Fig. 2   Class "44" No. 106 at Shildon shed, 1923.

With shunting pole.   Tallow cup on side of smokebox.

Fig. 3   Class J71 No. 453 at Eastfield shed, 1928.

Ramsbottom safety valves, wheel and handle fastening on smokebox door, steel plate front bufferbeam, curved frame ends, pre-1928 livery of black with red lining.

Fig. 4   Class J71 No. 1163 at Darlington, 1925.

Westinghouse brake

Fig. 5   Class J71 No. 263 at Darlington, about 1936.

Ross pop safety valves, organ pipe whistle, subsidiary splashers at
front end, sandwich type front bufferbeam, buffers with tapered
shanks and solid spindles, twin handles on smokebox door.

Fig. 6   Class J71 No. 1199 at Hull in 1932.

Square-ended frames with dumb buffers for moving chaldron wagons.
Conventional buffers have parallel shanks and hollow spindles.

Fig. 7   Class J71 No. 50 at West Auckland.

Shunting pole.

Fig. 8   Class J71 No. 403 at Darlington, June 1935.

Steam brake and vacuum ejector, Group Standard buffers, extra lamp
bracket and red spectacle glass on side of smokebox.

Fig. 9   Class J71 No. 8286 at York, June 1947.

L.N.E.R. green livery, Ross pop safety valves with trumpet-shaped cover.

Fig. 10   Class J71 No. 68286 at York, May 1950.

B.R. green livery.

Fig. 11   Class J71 No. 972, also D22 No. 673 and D17/1 No. 1637 inside Selby
shed, August 1932.

The J71 has wheels 6in. smaller in diameter than normal—note relative buffer heights.

Fig. 12   Class J71 No. 1758 leaving Easingwold for Alne whilst on loan to the
Easingwold Railway, June 1932.

Fig. 13   Class J72 No. 1734, about 1923.
Worsdell series (short bunker, steel plate bufferbeams, Ramsbottom
safety valves), stay to front step added.

Fig. 14   Class J72 No. 2181 at Bank Top shed, Darlington, 1923.
Raven series (longer bunker, sandwich bufferbeams, Ross pop safety valves,
breather pipe on side tank).

Fig. 15   Class J72 No. 2190 at South Dock shed, Sunderland,
May 1946.
Ross pop safety valves inside trumpet-shaped cover (note how steam is
being carried clear of windows, compare fig. 6), steel plate rear
bufferbeam, N.E.R. drawhook and tapered buffers.

Fig. 16   Class J72 No. 500.
                 Doncaster-built engine.

Fig. 17   Class J72 No. 69016 at Scarborough shed, August 1952.
        B.R. series (Group Standard buffers, Downs' sanding at front, rear
                        sandbox below bunker).

Fig. 18   Class J72 No. 2331 in North Road Works yard,
                        Darlington, 1939.
                 With mechanical stoking apparatus.

(to No. 1690), whilst No. 1197 had its apparatus removed in April 1930, followed by No. 1831 in November 1937. No. 103 also lost its heating equipment, probably some time after 1934.

A point of interest is that none of the J71's with passenger fittings ever had screw couplings and even when No. 68246 was hired to the Easingwold Railway to run that company's passenger service, still retained three-link couplings. Likewise when No. 1758 (with steam brake only) worked the Easingwold passenger trains in June 1932, it too kept three-link couplings.

British Railways

Eighty-one of the original 120 survived to be taken over by B.R., all of them well over fifty years old, and only nine of these did not have 60,000 added to their numbers. Five of these nine (Nos. 8247/9/77, 8310/1) did get BRITISH RAILWAYS on their tanks and the E prefix to their numbers, so only Nos. 8231/43/85/8 of the nationalised engines failed to receive some form of B.R. livery.

Allocation and Work

The majority of J71's were despatched to the North-East coast ports where they were engaged in shunting, especially within the dock areas where curvature and weight restrictions precluded the use of larger engines. Many were also employed on local trip work, moving loads between the many freight depots, wharves and warehouses, sometimes involving runs of up to ten miles. Several were used as carriage shunters in the yards at Heaton and elsewhere having certain specified tasks at sheds far removed from the docks and mineral yards. Selby made use of a couple for passenger and freight traffic on the lightly-laid branch to Cawood and another acted as the N.E.R. representative at the Midland shed at Normanton, a tradition which was upheld into the B.R. period.

To the traveller on the East Coast route they were a familiar sight as station pilots, particularly at York where Nos. 237 and 1167 were specially selected and well maintained, each serving as passenger pilot there for sixty years. Quietly simmering in some bay platform or in the centre road, they would suddenly come to life and with great alacrity descend on the rear of a main line express to attach or detach coaches, vans or horse-boxes and whisk them away to a nearby siding or cattle dock. Their facility for quick acceleration and precision braking was renowned.

Two of the class, Nos. 263 and 1142, were allocated to the curious engine shed within the confines of Darlington Works where they were employed in the towing of dead engines from the " crossing " storage sidings into the Works yard, as well as shunting in the Works yard. Others were employed in the sidings and foundries flanking the Works.

A handful of J71's dominated the Shildon reception yards where, apart from the heavy concentration of minerals, their duties included the movement of crippled wagons into, and new and repaired wagons out of, the Shildon wagon shops. Consequent upon the closure of Shildon shed in 1935 these tanks were transferred for stabling purposes to neighbouring West Auckland shed.

Just after Grouping the 120 engines were spread over twenty-two sheds. No less than twenty-one of the class were at East and West Hartlepool where they were employed amidst the complicated network of lines serving the docks, timber ponds, coal staiths and fish quays. Some effort was needed in hauling the many curious patterns of internal user timber wagons and bogies laden with pit props and sawn timber from the congested wharves to the storage yards, particularly those along the Cliff House branch.

Twelve of the class were located at Borough Gardens for trip work and shunting among the many Tyneside yards, depots and private traders' sidings radiating eastwards from Gateshead along the south bank of the Tyne. The number based at Borough Gardens gradually declined, though to some extent they were replaced by J72's. However, with the concentration of Tyneside freight depots in the late 1950's, their usefulness declined sharply and their home shed eventually demolished to make way for a new diesel-operated freight terminal. In 1923 Blaydon housed eight which worked in the network of yards and connecting spurs around Team Valley and Dunston on the southwest bank of the Tyne, whilst Heaton had ten to cover a multitude of duties on the north bank of the river, including much carriage shunting. The eight engines at Tyne Dock led energetic lives, chiefly in helping to assemble mineral wagons for the coal export staiths and acting as bankers for trains leaving the dock area up the difficult 1 in 40 grades. The five which had their home amid the long decaying pile of brickwork at Middlesbrough shed were employed in the nearby docks. Further engines were at Hull including a batch of seven based at the Alexandra Dock shed of the former H. & B.R. as a result of the prompt withdrawal of a number of old tank engines owned by that company when it was absorbed into the N.E.R. in 1922. From 1930 onwards these seven were gradually replaced by J72's, and both classes could often be found at weekends at the large parent depot of Springhead.

The remaining J71's were scattered in ones and twos, at Selby, Carlisle, Neville Hill, Normanton and Botanic Gardens. Those at Botanic Gardens were stationed at this passenger depot as a matter of convenience, being fairly close to the freight yards at Sculcoates.

Oddly enough, with one exception, and then not until B.R. days, the class was never represented north of the Tyne on the N.E.R. system, other than at Heaton. The exception was No. 8284 which was shedded at Tweedmouth from June 1948 to September 1953. Similarly, apart from those at Shildon, they were completely absent from the many lines and small depots in West Durham. Sunderland had only a single J71, and this had been transferred by 1935, and in general they were never to be found at the smaller sheds. Unlike the J72's which eventually found homes in the four corners of the L.N.E.R. system, the J71's seldom ventured away from their native heath, although two of them, Nos. 285 and 453, went from Carlisle to Eastfield in 1926 where they remained until withdrawn in 1936 and 1939 respectively, and No. 77 moved to Wrexham in 1940 for a four-year spell. At Eastfield the duties of Nos. 285 and 453 consisted of little more than moving dead engines between that running shed and Cowlairs Works.

At the end of 1935 the distribution pattern was very similar to that at Grouping, though twelve of them had been withdrawn in the meantime. The allocations at Hull and York had each increased by five and remained static well into B.R. days. The odd South roundhouses at York acted as sanctuaries to these engines following a hard day's work in the Severus and Clifton yards, where they operated alongside the J72's and J77's. The war brought very few changes in allocation and there were no withdrawals during the war years. At the close of 1948, with the total

down to eighty, the overall pattern remained much the same as before and although West Hartlepool still boasted a dozen engines, those at Alexandra Dock had disappeared for ever and only one remained at Tyne Dock.

The mid-1950's saw the arrival of the diesel shunter and as these grew in number they displaced the J71's, and steady withdrawals left only thirty-nine by the end of 1956. Over the next two or three years many of the survivors were frequently transferred to replace withdrawn engines. Of the last four, all withdrawn in February 1961, No. 68233 (old 326, one of the first ten built) was at West Hartlepool, where it had been since October 1934, whilst No. 68275 had lingered on at Normanton, though earlier in its career it had been at Darlington, Hull and York. The other two, Nos. 68272/8, had found a brief home at the new ultra modern depot at Thornaby.

Sales

When No. 304 was withdrawn in February 1936 it was sold to Cowpen Coal Co., where it became Cambois No. 12 and acquired a hideous straight-sided chimney. In June 1938 No. 1144 (withdrawn in May 1937) was also sold and became Ryhope Coal Co. No. 3. They were scrapped in 1954 and in January 1960 respectively.

Engine Diagram

Section D, 1924. Details given both for engines with 16in. and with 16¾in. diameter cylinders. No mention was ever made that some engines had 6in. smaller wheels, but at December 1942 a note was added that one engine had 18in. diameter cylinders.

Classification: Route availability 1; B.R. power class 0F until May 1953, then unclassified.

Summary of J7I Class

B.R. No.		1946 No.		1923 No.	Maker	Built	Brake at Grouping	Subsequent Alterations	Withdrawn
—		—		144	Darlington	11/1886	S	—	5/37
68230	10/51	8230	11/46	165	,,	11/1886	,,	—	1/60
(68231)		8231	10/46	299	,,	12/1886	,,	—	7/51
—		—		317	,,	12/1886	,,	—	5/36
68232	5/49	8232	11/46	261	,,	1/1887	,,	—	2/57
—		—		304	,,	1/1887	,,	—	2/36
—		—		399	,,	1/1887	S & VE	—	11/33
—		—		27	,,	2/1887	S	—	9/33
68233	9/48	8233	10/46	326	,,	2/1887	,,	—	2/61
68234	10/50	8234	6/46	533	,,	2/1887	,,	—	8/54

B.R. No.		1946 No.		1923 No.	Maker	Built	Brake at Grouping	Subsequent Alterations	Withdrawn
68235	4/48	8235	5/46	70	Darlington	4/1887	S	—	11/60
68236	3/50	8236	12/46	168	,,	4/1887	,,	—	11/55
—		—		263*	,,	4/1887	,,	—	5/37
—		8237	11/46	272	,,	5/1887	,,	—	7/47
—		—		278	,,	5/1887	,,	—	11/35
68238	6/50	8238	12/46	347	,,	5/1887	,,	—	9/55
—		—		493	,,	6/1887	,,	—	7/39
68239	3/52	8239	11/46	494	,,	6/1887	,,	—	11/56
68240	6/48	8240	12/46	499	,,	6/1887	,,	+ VE 9/31	9/56
—		—		811	,,	6/1887	S & VE	S 1/28	5/37
—		—		242	,,	4/1888	S	—	10/36
—		—		268	,,	4/1888	,,	—	8/39
—		8241	1/47	275	,,	4/1888	,,	+ VE 7/30	7/47
—		—		285	,,	5/1888	,,	—	12/36
68242	11/49	8242	11/46	286	,,	5/1888	,,	—	8/58
(68243)		8243	12/46	403	,,	5/1888	,,	+ VE 6/30	3/50
68244	1/51	8244	6/46	541	,,	6/1888	,,	—	4/58
—		—		584	,,	6/1888	,,	—	2/35
68245	11/48	8245	3/46	1123	,,	6/1888	,,	—	4/59
—		—		1163	,,	6/1888	W	S 7/29	10/33
68246	4/49	8246	2/46	1167	,,	7/1889	S & VE	—	11/58
—		—		84	,,	7/1889	S	—	8/33
(68247)		8247	5/46	221	,,	7/1889	,,	—	8/51
68248	4/48	8248	5/46	224	,,	8/1889	,,	—	7/51
—		—		225	,,	8/1889	,,	—	5/37
—		—		453	,,	8/1889	,,	—	2/39
(68249)		8249	11/46	492	,,	8/1889	,,	—	1/53
68250	4/48	8250	12/46	495	,,	9/1889	,,	+ VE 3/29	4/59
—		—		496	,,	9/1889	,,	—	5/37
68251	11/51	8251	6/46	501	,,	9/1889	S & VE	—	1/59
68252	12/50	8252	4/46	1083	,,	5/1890	S	—	4/57
68253	8/50	8253	5/46	239	,,	5/1890	,,	—	9/57
68254	10/51	8254	6/46	50	,,	6/1890	,,	—	11/60
68255	1/49	8255	4/46	241	,,	6/1890	,,	—	8/52
68256	6/48	8256	8/46	244	,,	6/1890	,,	—	7/54
—		8257	8/46	254	,,	6/1890	,,	+ VE 9/30	5/47
68258	5/51	8258	8/46	260	,,	7/1890	,,	—	11/54
—		—		296	,,	7/1890	S & W	—	8/33
68259	12/49	8259	4/46	338	,,	7/1890	S	—	9/55
68260	2/49	8260	12/46	400	,,	7/1890	,,	—	3/60
—		8261	9/46	54	,,	9/1890	,,	—	3/47
68262	7/48	8262	4/46	103	,,	9/1890	,,	—	1/60
68263	5/49	8263	1/47	176	,,	9/1890	,,	—	6/59
68264	12/48	8264	11/46	177	,,	9/1890	,,	—	1/60
68265	3/49	8265	11/46	179	,,	9/1890	S & VE	—	8/59
68266	11/49	8266	12/46	181	,,	9/1890	S	—	2/57
68267	9/50	8267	12/46	248	,,	9/1890	,,	—	11/57
—		—		478	,,	10/1890	,,	—	9/33
68268	8/49	8268	11/46	482	,,	10/1890	,,	+ VE 9/30	5/52
68269	9/50	8269	11/46	802	,,	10/1890	,,	—	10/60

B.R. No.		1946 No.		1923 No.	Maker	Built	Brake at Grouping	Subsequent Alterations	Withdrawn
68270	3/50	8270	6/46	77	Darlington	11/1891	S	—	11/55
68271	10/48	8271	12/46	161	,,	11/1891	,,	—	5/54
68272	12/51	8272	12/46	252	,,	11/1891	,,	—	2/61
68273	9/50	8273	12/46	280	,,	11/1891	,,	—	11/57
—		—		447	,,	11/1891	,,	—	5/37
—		—		448	,,	11/1891	,,	—	5/37
—		8274	12/46	301	,,	1/1892	,,	—	6/47
—		—		401	,,	1/1892	,,	—	9/36
68275	12/48	8275	12/46	449	,,	1/1892	,,	—	2/61
68276	9/48	8276	12/46	450	,,	1/1892	,,	—	11/56
—		—		451	,,	1/1892	,,	—	5/37
(68277)		8277	1/47	452	,,	1/1892	,,	—	11/50
68278	4/48	8278	1/47	572	,,	2/1892	,,	—	2/61
68279	3/51	8279	12/46	577	,,	2/1892	,,	—	6/57
68280	2/50	8280	2/46	1085	,,	2/1892	,,	+ VE 12/33	5/57
68281	7/50	8281	2/46	1103	,,	2/1892	,,	—	11/53
68282	11/50	8282	2/46	1140	,,	3/1892	W & VE	S & VE 9/29	10/53
68283	9/48	8283	2/46	1142	,,	3/1892	S	—	7/59
68284	8/50	8284	2/46	1153	,,	3/1892	,,	—	10/55
(68285)		8285	2/46	1157	,,	3/1892	,,	+ VE 3/29	10/48
68286	1/50	8286	5/46	237	,,	7/1892	S & VE	—	6/52
68287	1/50	8287	5/46	240	,,	7/1892	S	—	11/56
—		—		402	,,	7/1892	,,	—	9/33
(68288)		8288	2/46	1084	,,	7/1892	,,	—	11/50
68289	10/50	8289	2/46	1095	,,	7/1892	,,	—	6/55
68290	4/48	8290	3/46	1143	,,	7/1892	,,	—	1/59
—		—		1144	,,	7/1892	,,	—	5/37
68291	7/48	8291	2/46	1151	,,	8/1892	,,	—	4/56
68292	1/49	8292	2/46	1155	,,	8/1892	,,	—	10/54
—		—		1314	,,	8/1892	,,	—	5/37
68293	6/49	8293	5/46	1196	,,	11/1892	,,	—	9/56
68294	7/49	8294	5/46	1197	,,	11/1892	W	S 3/30	11/56
68295	11/48	8295	3/46	1198	,,	11/1892	S	—	2/59
68296	8/49	8296	3/46	1199	,,	11/1892	,,	—	6/58
—		—		969	,,	1/1893	,,	—	9/33
68297	9/50	8297	6/46	972	,,	1/1893	,,	+ VE 6/29	5/56
68298	8/51	8298	10/46	137	,,	1/1893	,,	—	3/57
68299	10/49	8299	8/46	977	,,	1/1893	,,	—	12/52
68300	9/49	8300	8/46	978	,,	1/1893	,,	+ VE 9/30	3/55
68301	3/49	8301	12/46	980	,,	1/1893	,,	—	11/56
—		—		1666	,,	11/1894	,,	—	8/33
68302	10/48	8302	2/46	1735	,,	11/1894	,,	—	8/51
68303	11/49	8303	11/46	1796	,,	11/1894	,,	—	6/55
68304	10/51	8304	11/46	1797	,,	12/1894	,,	—	11/54
68305	8/48	8305	3/46	1831	,,	12/1894	W	S 11/37	11/58
68306	12/50	8306	5/46	1832	,,	12/1894	S	—	7/58
68307	6/48	8307	5/46	1833	,,	12/1894	,,	—	6/55
68308	9/50	8308	5/46	1834	,,	12/1894	S & VE	—	5/58
—		—		1835	,,	12/1894	S	—	5/37
68309	9/48	8309	5/46	1836	,,	12/1894	,,	—	5/60

B.R. No.		1946 No.	1923 No.	Maker	Built	Brake at Grouping	Subsequent Alterations	Withdrawn
(68310)		8310	3/46	1134	Darlington	8/1895	S & VE	—	12/50
—		—		1758	,,	9/1895	S	—	9/33
(68311)		8311	3/46	1789	,,	9/1895	,,	—	8/51
68312	6/51	8312	5/46	1688	,,	10/1895	,,	—	2/59
68313	11/48	8313	3/46	1689	,,	10/1895	,,	—	9/56
68314	9/50	8314	3/46	1690	,,	10/1895	,,	+ VE 1/28	5/60
—		8315	3/46	1861	,,	10/1895	,,	—	4/46
—		—		1862	,,	10/1895	,,	—	5/37
—		—		1863	,,	11/1895	,,	—	5/37
68316	2/51	8316	3/46	1864	,,	11/1895	,,	—	10/60

* No. 263 was a Service Locomotive at Darlington until August 1926.

CLASS J72

N.E.R. CLASS E1—WILSON WORSDELL
4ft. 1¼in. ENGINES

ENGINES AT GROUPING (Built 1898-1922): 462, 1715/8/20/1/2/8/32/3/4/6/41/2/4/6/7/9/61/3/70, 2173-92, 2303-37. TOTAL 75.

ENGINES BUILT AFTER GROUPING (1925): 500/12/6/24/42/66/71/4/6/81. TOTAL 10.

ENGINES BUILT AFTER NATIONALISATION (1949-51): 69001-28. TOTAL 28.

T. W. Worsdell had introduced his class E 0-6-0T design (L.N.E.R. J71) in 1886 and Wilson Worsdell continued to build them down to 1895, by which time they totalled 120. This was the only large class designed by T. W. Worsdell to have Stephenson's rather than Joy's valve gear and none were compounds, so that Wilson Worsdell's chief causes of dislike for his brother's work were missing.

However, Wilson Worsdell generally preferred smaller wheels for goods and shunting and in due course developed class E1, similar to class E but having larger cylinders 17in. × 24in. instead of 16in. × 22in. and wheels 6in. less in diameter. It may be noted that similar changes were made between the B1 and U 0-6-2T classes (L.N.E.R. N8 and N10) and between the C1 and P1 0-6-0's (J21 and J25), as well as the dropping of Joy's valve gear.

Both the change to 24in. stroke and to 4ft. nominal wheels were reversions to earlier practice on the N.E.R., Fletcher having used wheels of this size for most of his shunting engines and 24in. stroke in many, including his final design (see "44" class). The reversion to smaller wheels had been antici-

pated in that ten of the E class were built with second-hand wheel centres and, of these, nine had 4ft. wheels. In addition to these nine engines, fifteen of Fletcher's "964" class saddle tanks were rebuilt as side tanks very similar to class E retaining their 4ft. or 4ft. 2in. wheels.

Twenty E1 class engines were built in 1898-99, but no additions were made to the class until after Raven had succeeded Worsdell as C.M.E. Then some modification was made to the design for future construction, such as heavier frames, longer bunkers and other features in line with contemporary N.E.R. practice. Twenty engines were turned out in 1914 and a further ten in 1920. Regarding the latter, difficulty was being experienced at that time, not long after the end of the First World War, in obtaining materials for the construction of new big engines of the S3 4-6-0 and D 4-4-2T classes then on order. However, sufficient material could be obtained to build ten E1 class shunting engines and in April 1920 it was decided to do this in order to keep new construction going at Darlington during the remainder of that year. At the same time an order was placed with Armstrong, Whitworth & Co. for another twenty-five for delivery by February 1921. Considerable delay occurred in the execution of this latter order, the boilers not being built until September to December 1921 and the completed engines were not delivered until April to October 1922.

After Grouping, the L.N.E.R. had ten more built in 1925, surprisingly at Doncaster Works. They were turned out concurrently with N2 class 0-6-2T's Nos. 892-7, hence the lack of continuity in the works numbers. The 1930 building programme included twenty J72's and the 1931 programme a further eighteen, but these orders were cancelled, this being due in part to the successful development of the Sentinel 0-4-0T's and also to the decline in trade at that time.

In the Thompson standardisation scheme of 1943 for locomotives, class J50 was selected for heavy goods shunting with an unspecified light shunting engine to be added later and the J72 class was amongst those listed to be withdrawn when needing boiler renewals. This had not been implemented by 1946 when Peppercorn took over as C.M.E. and in his modifications to the scheme J50 was dropped, due to the purchase of the M.O.S. 0-6-0ST's (class J94), and J72 included. An order was placed for the latter on the 1946 building programme but they

were deferred until 1949 (after nationalisation) when fifteen were built at Darlington. Five more appeared in 1950 and the final eight in 1951, fifty-three years after the first one was constructed.

Ultimately engines of this class were used from Keith in the far north, Glasgow in the north-west, Wrexham in the west, to Ipswich in the east and Neasden in the south. Sheds which had belonged to all seven major constituent companies of the L.N.E.R. housed them at some time or another, a unique record for any class of L.N.E.R. engine.

The class remained intact until the end of June 1958, No. 68718 being the first to be withdrawn, and there was particularly heavy slaughter in both 1960 and 1961. Normal service by the class ceased in October 1964, but two were then transferred to Service Stock, No. 58 (ex-69005) being the final one to be withdrawn in October 1967.

Engine Nos.	Maker	Works Nos.	No. built	Date
462, 1715/8/21/2/32/44/6/ 61/70	Darlington	—	10	1898
1720/8/33/4/6/41/2/7/9/63	,,	—	10	1899
2173-92	,,	—	20	1914
2303-12	,,	—	10	1920
2313-37	Armstrong, Whitworth & Co.	391-415	25	1922
500/12/6/24/42/66/71/4/6/81	Doncaster	1621/4/6/7/30/1/ 3/4/5/6	10	1925
69001-15	Darlington	2082-96	15	1949
69016-20	,,	2097-2101	5	1950
69021-8	,,	2149-56	8	1951

Standard L.N.E.R. Dimensions at Grouping

Cylinders (2 inside)		17″ × 24″
Motion		Stephenson with slide valves
Boiler:		
Max. diam. outside		3′ 8″
Barrel length ...		10′ 0″
Firebox length outside ...		4′ 4″
Pitch		6′ 6″
Diagram No. ...		73
Heating surface:		
Firebox		73 sq. ft.
Tubes (139 × 1¾″)		658 sq. ft.
Total		731 sq. ft.
Grate area		11.3 sq. ft.
Boiler pressure ...		140 lb./sq. in.
Coupled wheels ...		4′ 1¼″
Tractive effort (85%)		16,760 lb.

Length over buffers		28′ 9¾″ (a)
Wheelbase ...		6′ 8″ + 7′ 0″ = 13′ 8″
Weight (full) ...		38T 12C (a)
Max. axle load ...		14T 7C (a)
Water capacity ...		690 gallons
Coal capacity ...		1T 0C (b)

(a) The weight and overall length relate to engines built in 1914-25. The length over buffers and total weight of the engines built in 1898-99 were 27ft. 10¼in. and 36 tons 14 cwt., whilst the figures for the B.R. built engines were 29ft. 2¾in. and 39 tons 12 cwt.

(b) This figure was incorrect. For the first twenty engines it was 1 ton 5 cwt. and for the remainder 2 tons.

L.N.E.R. Renumbering

The eighty-five engines existing when the general renumbering scheme was prepared in 1943 were renumbered from 8670 to 8754 inclusive between January and July 1946, in sequence of building date.

Development

N.E.R.

The E1 class utilised the same type of boiler as class E and on the same pitch, despite the difference in wheel size. Tanks, cab and bunker were all similar, but a visible difference was the smaller front splasher and combined sandbox to suit the smaller wheels. The wheel spacings were altered from 6ft. 6in. + 7ft. 2in. on class E to 6ft. 8in. + 7ft. 0in. The cylinder stroke was 2in. longer and there was an addition of 1in. to the frame length at the front end, which brought the length over buffers to 27ft. 10½in. The bunker had coal rails fitted and the capacity was quoted as 1 ton, the same as on class E which at that time did not have any coal rails. When that class was eventually fitted with coal rails the bunker capacity was raised to 1 ton 5 cwt. and this is the figure which should have been shown on the E1 class engine diagram. The weight in working order of these first twenty engines was 36 tons 14 cwt.

Raven changed the design when further engines were built in 1914 and a 6in. longer bunker stated as holding 1 ton 10 cwt. of coal, was provided (but see below). The coal rails were plated on the inside and a horizontal handrail was fixed to the rear of the bunker. The latter feature never appeared on the first twenty engines. The main frames were made much deeper between the coupled wheels and wooden sandwich bufferbeams were fitted at front and rear in place of the steel plate variety on the earlier engines (cf. figs. 13 and 14). The buffer cases were of plainer appearance, but again had thin spindles. The overall length of this series was 28ft. 9¾in. There were other detail differences, such as the replacement of the Ramsbottom safety valves by the Ross pop variety (these being provided with a small cover around the base), a conspicuous breather pipe was fitted to each side tank, the front footsteps had external strengthening stays, and the smokebox door was fastened by means of a wheel and handle instead of twin handles. These differences added nearly two tons to the overall weight, the official figure being 38 tons 12 cwt.

The earlier engines were brought into line in respect of some of these alterations, such as plates behind the coal rails, Ross pop valves on replacement boilers, front footstep stays, and wheel and handle smokebox fastenings. From about 1932, the earlier engines began to get the wooden sandwich type of bufferbeam at the front end only, and it is probable that all twenty were so treated. Conversely, some of the Raven series (e.g.

Nos. 2182/8/90) lost the rear wooden sandwich bufferbeams and were given steel plate bufferbeams in their place. The bunkers of the engines thus altered then projected beyond the bufferbeams (fig. 15).

The Armstrong Whitworth engines, Nos. 2313-37, originally carried small rectangular makers' plates on their front sandboxes, but most, if not all, of these plates were removed at their first shopping and at which they received their L.N.E.R. livery.

L.N.E.R.

The ten J72's built at Doncaster in 1925 (to Engine Order 304) followed the Raven style in nearly all respects, even to the N.E.R. buffers, sandwich bufferbeams and the Darlington type of smokebox door, with forked ends to the straps at the hinge end and wheel and handle fastening (fig. 16). It appears that these engines were entirely constructed at Doncaster to Darlington patterns, despite the distinct difference from their own standards.

Some time after the delivery of these ten engines, a query concerning the capacity of the bunkers appears to have arisen at Doncaster. The matter was taken up with Darlington and a trial was arranged whereby coal was carefully weighed into the bunker of one of the later series of J72's which was found to hold just 2 tons, which was half a ton more than the figure shown on the engine diagram. The diagram was altered to show 2 tons in December 1927, but when it was re-issued in 1946 the figure of 1½ tons was again shown.

B.R.

The twenty-eight new J72's, Nos. 69001-28, turned out from Darlington in 1949-51 were similar in most respects to their predecessors, but were brought up to date in several matters of detail, such as the fitting of twin handles on the smokebox door and Group Standard buffers and drawgear (albeit still with the wooden sandwich bufferbeams) and this increased the overall length to 29ft. 2¾in. (fig. 17).

These engines were provided with Downs' sanding equipment in the leading sandboxes following successful trial of this on Nos. 68675, 68732/44 (all of Heaton shed) from September, 1948. Hitherto ordinary gravity sanding had been standard on the class. The new equipment was the subject of a patent by locomotive foreman Downs for a sanding gear in which the heat from a small steam pipe within the sandbox kept the sand fluid and avoided clogging from condensation. The rear sandboxes were situated below the running plate instead of in the cab. The B.R.-built engines were one ton heavier, at 39 tons 12 cwt. On their leading sandboxes they carried elliptical polished brass works number plates, a feature shared with the ten built at Doncaster. The final eight were turned out new with vacuum ejectors.

Details

In September 1904, No. 1741 was fitted with cylinders 18in. × 24in. giving it a tractive effort of 18,788 lb. In January 1937 it was again fitted with new cylinders, presumably of the same dimensions because in the 1942 Diagram Book Alterations, the L.N.E.R. for the first time took cognisance of this difference. No. 1741 was the only one so altered and was used at Dunston Staiths on the Tyne (see class J71, p. 12).

The boilers used on class J72 were identical and completely interchangeable with class J71 (which see at p. 12). However, prior to Grouping the exchanging of boilers was not practised to any degree. The first twenty J72's had Ramsbottom safety valves, but commencing with the next series, built in 1914, a change was made to Ross pop valves. The boilers on this latter group remained with the original engines and were never used elsewhere. By Grouping all the original boilers built in 1898-99 had been replaced, seventeen by new ones and the other three after short service on other classes. Of the pre-Grouping boilers, that put into No. 2303 new in October 1920 achieved a noteworthy length of life. With intervals as spare of only nine months, six months and two months, it was in constant use on J72 class Nos. 2303, 2183, 68733 and 68733 until July 1962, an actual service life of more than forty years. The reason could be found in that for almost thirty of those years it worked in the north of Scotland where the feed water was kinder to boilers than elsewhere.

As mentioned under class J71, when that class eventually received boilers fitted with Ross pop safety valves, the proximity of the valves to the cab windows was a nuisance to the enginemen. Various unofficial forms of diverting the steam upwards were put into practice, from pieces of piping on one, or both, valves, to paint cans on which top and bottom had been removed. Ultimately, "Authority" recognised the real need and usually solved it by fitting a similar trumpet shape of cover as had been used with Rams-bottom valves, which completely hid the pop valves (fig. 15). Scotland produced its own variety, however (fig. 20).

A single whistle was mounted on the firebox between the safety valves and cab front. Originally of the bell-shaped high-pitch type, from December 1909 this was changed to the organ-pipe low-toned type on all except those engines then based at the Hartlepools sheds. There was apparently no further need for high-pitched whistles at the Hartlepools by Grouping and only No. 2334 was noted in the original numbering with a bell-shaped whistle, but it was not a Hartle-pools engine. Two of the Scottish-based engines as Nos. 8749/50 had the bell shape by 1947 and in B.R. livery Nos. 68710/1/41/2 were the only others observed.

In May/June 1948, the four J72's allocated to Bidston shed were fitted with a shorter chimney to give a maximum height from rail of 11ft. 0½in. (see Part 1, fig. 130). This was a reduction of ten inches and brought the top of the chimney to the same height as that of the dome. These shorter chimneys were cast-iron, in the same style as the original and in no way detracted from the neat and tidy appearance associated with the class. No. 68671 was altered at Darlington Works and Nos. 8701/14 and E8727 at Wrexham, under which shed Bidston came for maintenance. At that time all four engines normally worked in Birkenhead docks, but the purpose of the alteration was to permit them to act as substitutes should either of the little J62 class saddle tanks allocated to Wrexham not be available to work the Connahs Quay-Buckley branch which had a low bridge. When the last J62 was withdrawn in November 1951, a J72 took over the working of the branch. The shorter chimneys were retained until these J72 engines were withdrawn. Two of the class working in Scotland fared much worse. By May 1945 Inverurie Works had fitted No. 566 (which became No. 8750) with a chimney of plainer shape from a class Y9 0-4-0T (fig. 20), but from Cowlairs in June 1949, No. 68709 appeared with a stovepipe chimney on which a deep collar at the top only made appearances worse (fig. 21). These odd chimneys were retained until withdrawal. Several others in Scotland lost the inner rim at the chimney top, those noted being Nos. 2312, 8709, 68686/9.

During L.N.E.R. days there was a definite change towards two handles in place of a wheel and handle for fastening the doors and by 1939, few if any J72's maintained by Darlington still had a wheel. On the eight which went to Scotland in 1932-9, Nos. 542/66 and 2192 had already been changed, but the other five still had a wheel and at least Nos. 68710/17/9 remained so fitted when they first acquired B.R. livery. By May 1954, No. 68717 had changed to two handles, but No. 68719 probably retained its wheel to withdrawal in January 1961 as a photograph taken in May 1959 shows one still fitted, almost certainly the last one in use.

Group Standard buffers replaced the earlier types on quite a number of the class, No. 2184 receiving them as early as July 1931. With G.S. buffers, the overall length of the engine was increased by 5in., to 29ft. 2¾in. Beginning in December 1947 vacuum ejectors were fitted to a number of J72's to enable them to operate as passenger pilots (see Brakes) and, where not already fitted, it was intended that they should have G.S. buffers, but not all were altered. The fitting of G.S. buffers, which were longer than the N.E.R. buffers, necessitated the replacement of the N.E.R.-pattern drawhooks (which had their coupling links attached by means of a shackle—fig. 15) by the standard variety, which projected further. Some engines which retained N.E.R. buffers also had standard drawhooks and these had pads inserted between the base of the buffers and the buffer-beam.

The only J72 allocated to Shildon, No. 2192 (fig. 19), was fitted with shunting poles (see class J71, p. 13).

When No. 2192 left Shildon in 1935, the poles were removed, but the anchoring brackets remained in place and, indeed, were not removed until after 1950. Another curiosity, this time amongst the Scottish based engines, was No. 2183 which, as late as August 1937, was still carrying CLASS E1 on its front bufferbeam, although not in Darlington style.

In January 1948 No. 8687 had the additional lamp bracket fitted to the right-hand side of the smokebox and operating rod with red glass, as described under class J71 (see page 13), and was the only J72 to have this fitment.

In Scotland it was normal practice to fit goods shunting engines with shunters' steps, which extended from the normal lower step giving access to the cab, to a supporting bracket hung from the inside of the rear bufferbeam. These extra steps were placed on both sides of the engine and were accompanied by a horizontal handrail on each bunker side. The six J72 class which went to the Northern Scottish Area in 1932/4 were all so equipped soon after their arrival, but the two which went to Eastfield in 1939 did not then receive similar treatment. Indeed No. 2326 (and as 68733) never got the steps, but No. 68709 had them fitted in May 1948 (fig. 21). Of the four B.R. engines, Nos. 69012-5, which worked in Scotland from early 1952, at least one, No. 69014, was so fitted.

In the early 1930's, when Nos. 2184, 2307/20 were working in Birkenhead Docks from Bidston shed, they were fitted with hinged spark arresters on the tops of their chimneys. These were later removed at dates not recorded, but in July 1952 an authorisation was issued for three Bidston engines, Nos. 68671, 68701/27, to be fitted with spark arresters, this time of the internal type within the smokebox. In February 1936, during general repairs at Darlington, Nos. 462 and 2308 of Hull Alexandra Dock shed had been fitted with internal spark arresters for their work in the timber pit prop yards which had recently been the scene of a very extensive fire. Some fifteen years later, two more Alexandra Dock engines Nos. 69003/10, were fitted with cage type spark arresters, most probably this time for hauling trains of petrol tank wagons from the large oil depot at Saltend on the Humber.

To meet wartime blackout conditions, in December 1943 No. 1749 of Darlington shed had its bufferbeam treated with luminous paint and, in the following month, three Middlesbrough engines Nos. 2173, 2306/33 received similar treatment. Probably the war also stifled the proper development of an interesting experiment on No. 2331 (fig. 18). In May 1939, this engine was sent to Messrs. Robert Stephenson & Hawthorns' to be fitted with Nu-Way mechanical stoking gear. In the Nu-Way system, coal was carried from the bottom of the bunker to the firebox by two revolving spirals driven by a small steam turbine mounted below the bunker. The turbine also drove two fans which provided currents of air to blow the coal from the ends of the spirals into the firebox. The exhaust from the turbine was discharged from a pipe just behind the rear left corner of the cab, and this pipe, and the air pipes were easily visible. A maximum coal feed of 300 lb. per hour was possible. The engine re-entered service in July 1939. In September it was additionally equipped with a thermo pump for controlling automatically the supply of boiler feed water. The object of these alterations was to make the engine capable of being single manned, but this was objected to by the men's representatives. The engine appears to have been in regular use until the complete mechanical stoking gear and pump were removed at Darlington Works in April 1947.

Soon after nationalisation, a trial was made of Jay-Gee smoke eliminators and three J72 class participated in this experiment, No. 68677 being fitted in April 1948 and Nos. 68743/7 in the following month (see under class J50 p. 50, Part 8A for description). The apparatus was taken off Nos. 68743/7 in January 1951 and from No. 68677 in September 1951. The only external evidence was an extra pipe from cab to smokebox just above and similar in appearance to the blower connection.

23

Liveries

Down to 1928 normal L.N.E.R. practice was to fully line out black painted engines, goods as well as passenger, and the ten new engines from Doncaster appeared with single thin red lining round the tanks, cab and bunker, along the footplating, around the wheel rims and centres, and edging the front sandboxes and boiler cleading bands. This treatment failed to survive their first shoppings in 1928-30 and from then until the autumn of 1937, the whole class was in unrelieved black. In 1937 two Gateshead J72's were fitted with vacuum ejectors and carriage warming apparatus, with hose connections front and rear, so that they could be used on empty carriage shunting at Newcastle Central station. As they would be more in the public eye, they were accorded the full red lining treatment on their black livery. No. 2313 appeared thus in August 1937, followed by No. 1720 in September, and so they remained until wartime austerity drove them into unlined black again from August and May 1940 respectively. In 1947 both were still at Gateshead shed and equipped for carriage shunting, but this time only one was selected for special painting. No. 8680 (ex-1720) appeared in May 1947 in L.N.E.R. green with full black and white lining, but with hand painted and unshaded letters and numbers in Gill Sans characters (fig. 22). At its next shopping in October 1949 it appeared again in L.N.E.R. green paint, fully lined, but with the B.R. emblem in place of L.N.E.R. and numbered 68680. There was a further change in March 1952 when the green gave way to black, but with the B.R. red, cream and grey lining. Then from August 1957 the emblem was changed to the lion-holding-the-wheel variety, but at the next shopping in December 1959 the lining was omitted and this engine rejoined the rank and file for its last days.

Special treatment for class J72 was, however, revived the following year when Nos. 68723/36, which were then used for carriage shunting duties at Newcastle and York stations respectively, were painted in the original N.E.R. green lined livery during the course of general repairs in May 1960 at Darlington, but with their B.R. numbers in the customary place on the tank sides. Ahead of the number was the latest B.R. emblem, balanced on the other side of the number by the N.E.R. coat of arms (fig. 23). In 1961 No. 68736 joined No. 68723 at Newcastle Central and they continued to run in their green livery until they were withdrawn in September and October respectively.

Throughout L.N.E.R. days, the standard position for displaying the number was on the tank sides, and this was continued after nationalisation on all engines which Darlington maintained, and on the twenty-eight new engines built subsequently. After nationalisation the predominating influence in the Scottish Region was mainly L.M.S., whose practice latterly had been to show tank engine numbers on the bunker sides. As and when the eight Scottish-based J72's received B.R. livery from early 1948, their numbers were moved from the tanks to the bunkers (fig. 20). Similar treatment was meted out to Nos. 69012-5 when they were shopped in Scotland after going there in 1952.

Brakes

When built, the first eighty-five engines had steam brake only, and it was not until 1937 that any change was made. Then Nos. 1720 and 2313 were given vacuum ejectors and carriage warming apparatus. A further ten years elapsed before any more were altered, due to the J72 class taking over further carriage shunting which had hitherto been undertaken by the J71 class. Between December 1947 and October 1948, thirteen J72's were fitted with vacuum ejectors, and three more were equipped in May/August 1950 (fig. 23). As the first five to be dealt with, Nos. 8687/9/93, 8702/23, did not simultaneously receive steam heating equipment and hose connections, they were called back to Darlington early in 1948 for these to be fitted. The remainder were given heating gear when the vacuum ejectors were fitted. When B.R. Nos. 69001-20 were built in 1949-50, they had steam brake only, but Nos. 69021-8 built in 1951 were turned out with vacuum ejectors in addition to the steam brake and with carriage heating connections at both ends.

From September 1953, as withdrawal of vacuum-fitted J71 and J77 class engines was accelerated, their brake equipment was transferred to the J72 class, a process which continued until February 1960. By that date considerable inroads were also being made into the J72's. Ultimately a total of forty-one J72's which had originally been steam braked only received vacuum equipment in addition to the eight built with it in 1951. In all cases, only the three-link couplings were fitted as their passenger shunting duties were confined to empty stock workings. On the occasion when No. 68736 worked an R.C.T.S.-S.L.S. North Eastern Tour on 29th September 1963, it was fitted temporarily with screw couplings at each end. Dates for the fitting of vacuum ejectors are given in the Summary.

British Railways

The eighty-five L.N.E.R. J72's were all taken over by British Railways, and between March 1948 and September 1951 they were renumbered 68670-68754, and to them were added Nos. 69001-28 as new engines. Withdrawal of the class commenced in June 1958 and proceeded rapidly. The final two engines, Nos. 69005/23, were transferred to Service Stock in October 1964, and were renumbered as Departmental 58 and 59. At first they were stationed at North Blyth for use in de-freezing coal wagons on Blyth shipping staiths. They served only one winter on this job and were then moved to Gateshead where No. 58 was tried (unsuccessfully) on supplying steam for cleaning the bogies of diesel locomotives and for de-icing points in Tyne Yard. After a long period in store, first at Heaton and then at Tyne Dock, No. 59 was sold in September 1966 (see below) and No. 58 was withdrawn in October 1967 and disposed of for scrap in January 1968.

Allocation and Work

Although this class ultimately spread to the four corners of the L.N.E.R., transfers were infrequent some and individual engines established some impressive long-service records. For example, No. 1746 was always at York. The first allocation of the 1898-99 engines immediately set the pattern for where these engines were likely to be found: Hull received 6, West Hartlepool 4, Borough Gardens 3, York and Heaton 2 each with single engines at Darlington, Tyne Dock and Stockton. When reinforced by a further twenty in 1914, the new engines all went to sheds in Co. Durham, 8 to West Hartlepool, 4 each to Sunderland and Borough Gardens, 2 to Tyne Dock and one each to Darlington and Shildon. Of the next ten, Middlesbrough was the chief beneficiary, getting five and the availability of another twenty-five enabled some to be sent to Blaydon and Ferryhill, the remainder strengthening existing allocations and replacing some which had moved to Gateshead and a single one, No. 1718, which moved to Starbeck from Hull in 1919. The distribution in early L.N.E.R. days was as shown in the first column of the attached table.

This pattern had not been disturbed at the time the ten new engines came from Doncaster at the end of 1925 and once again a new shed received J72 class, Neville Hill getting three, although one of them stayed only six weeks before going to Dairycoates, where it joined two other new ones. One of the Doncaster-built engines went to Alexandra Dock and the other four found homes at Sunderland (2), York and Ferryhill (one each).

	1923	1939	1948	1951
Gateshead	5	6	6	9
Borough Gardens	5	7	7	7
Heaton	6	9	8	7
Blaydon	4	–	–	4
Hexham	–	–	–	1
Tyne Dock	3	2	3	4
Sunderland	5	5	5	5
West Hartlepool	7	15	10	10
East Hartlepool	5	–	–	–
Darlington	7	–	2	6
Ferryhill	1	–	–	–
Middlesbrough	5	6	7	10
Stockton	2	–	–	–
Shildon	1	–	–	–
West Auckland	–	–	2	3
York	10	10	10	11
Scarborough	–	–	–	1
Starbeck	1	–	–	–
Neville Hill	–	2	3	2
Dairycoates	8	–	2	3
Alexandra Dock	–	12	8	14
Kittybrewster	–	5	6	6
Eastfield	–	2	2	2
Thornton	–	1	–	–
Bidston	–	2	4	3
Wrexham	–	–	–	1
Neasden	–	1	–	–
Doncaster	–	–	–	2
Ipswich	–	–	–	2
Total	75	85	85	113

Changes were still quite rare down to 1937, despite the departure of three to the Southern Area in 1929-30 and six to the Northern Scottish Area in 1932-34. The first to leave were Nos. 2184 and 2320 from Heaton to Doncaster in October 1929 and about six months later both moved to Bidston for working on Birkenhead Docks, a duty in which they were joined by No. 2307 in December 1930. Apart from No. 2320 going to Neasden from November 1935 to March 1940 (mainly for shunting at Harrow-on-the-Hill), these three spent the rest of their careers on the L.N.E.R. either at Bidston or Wrexham and at the beginning of 1942 they were joined by No. 1715. These were the four to get the shorter chimneys (see page 22). After nationalisation they continued on their customary duties for a time, but in 1952 No. 68714 moved to Birkenhead shed where it remained until 1957, returning then to Wrexham. During the following year this latter shed passed from London Midland to Western Region ownership and Nos. 68714/27 were noteworthy as being on W.R. book stock for a short time. Both were soon sent to Bidston and 16XX class pannier tanks took over their duties at Wrexham. For a few

25

months in 1939 Nos. 516 and 2178 were also at Bidston, but returned to the N.E. Area.

Two J72's had been tried in Scotland soon after Grouping, the first being in July 1924 when No. 1733 was shedded at St. Margaret's for a brief period, during which it shunted at Portobello on trial against J66 No. 278 from Great Eastern. (This was part of a series of coal consumption trials for shunting engines held at that time and necessitated six other J72's temporarily leaving the N.E.R. system, Nos. 1720/46, 2307 to New England and Nos. 2309/13/33 to Colwick.) Then from March 1925 to January 1926 No. 2190 was stationed at Eastfield for shunting duties around Cowlairs. The first permanent transfers of J72's to the Scottish Area were Nos. 2183, 2303/10/2 in March 1932, followed by Doncaster-built Nos. 542/66 in December 1934. They were mainly intended to replace the G.N.S.R. 0-6-0T's of classes J90 and J91, two being allocated to Keith and the other four to Kittybrewster, for shunting and trip work there and at the Waterloo goods station in Aberdeen. No. 2310 however went to Thornton, where it was employed on various pilot duties in Fife, including Kirkcaldy and Methil, before joining the other five at Kittybrewster in 1943. The class reappeared at Eastfield with the arrival of Nos. 2192 and 2326 there early in 1939 to replace a pair of J71's which Eastfield had used since 1926 for shunting at Cowlairs.

In 1937-39 the allocation was affected both by the closure of Ferryhill and East Hartlepool sheds and also the determined efforts which were then being made in the N.E. Area to reduce the number of classes at individual sheds, so that at the end of 1939, before any moves due to war conditions took place, the allocation was as shown in column two of the table.

Changed traffic conditions during the War affected this class to a surprisingly small degree, the only significant moves arising from the substantial reduction in timber imports at Hull and the Hartlepools. Both Alexandra Dock and West Hartlepool sheds each lost one third of their 1939 allocation, the sheds which gained being Dairycoates and Darlington (where the J72 class had been quite common up to 1938), also West Auckland where they had not previously been allocated. At the end of the L.N.E.R.'s existence in 1947, the sheds housing them were as shown in the third column of the table.

When the new engines were built in 1949-51, twenty-four of them went to former North Eastern sheds, initial allocation being as follows:— Alexandra Dock (4), Darlington (4), Gateshead (1), Middlesbrough (2), West Auckland (1), Tyne Dock (1), Dairycoates (2), York (2), Sunderland (1), Blaydon (4) and Heaton (2). After only a week, York passed on No. 69016 to Scarborough, whilst Blaydon also immediately sent No. 69026 to Hexham where it spent eighteen months before returning to its parent shed. The other four new engines, Nos. 69012-5, had a somewhat chequered career. In the last week of December 1949 they went new to Doncaster but only No. 69014/5 spent any appreciable time there for in May 1950, Nos. 69012/3 were sent to Ipswich, where they were never popular. In February 1952, these four were all transferred to Scotland, again to sheds with little previous experience of the class. Nos. 69012/3 went to Thornton, No. 69014 to St. Margaret's and No. 69015 to Parkhead. The St. Margaret's engine was generally utilised at South Leith and was joined there in 1957 by No. 69013. From 1958 onwards several moves were made by the Scottish-based J72's (including some of the Kittybrewster engines and the Eastfield pair referred to earlier), these being to Kipps and to former L.M.S. depots at Polmadie, Motherwell, Hamilton and Dumfries.

Until August 1937, the engines of class J72 concentrated entirely on goods shunting and short local trip workings, but then they began to replace class J71 as carriage shunters at main stations. The change-over began very slowly, and was deferred by the onset of the war, but as described when dealing with brakes, the pace quickened appreciably from the end of 1947. So they were equally capable of, and just as likely to be seen on transferring a heavy load of minerals or timber between docks and yards as attaching a horsebox or a few fish vans to a passenger train. Their slender appearance was very deceptive compared with power output.

From 1953 the N.E. Region made increasing use of 350 and 204 h.p. diesel shunters and this, coupled with the steady withdrawal of the older J71 and J77 classes, led to numerous changes in allocation of class J72. Sheds which had not had them on their books previously were Tweedmouth, Haverton Hill, Selby, Normanton, Springhead, and the new depot at Thornaby, opened on 1st June 1958. The former G.N.R. shed at Ardsley and the L. & Y. shed at Goole, both by then in the N.E. Region, also received representatives of the class. Withdrawal of the class took place between 1958 and 1964, some of the B.R.-built engines having a working life of as little as eleven years. As mentioned earlier, two of the class survived for a few years in Departmental Stock and one of these, No. 69023, has been privately preserved.

Sales

Departmental No. 59 was purchased in September 1966 by Mr. R. Ainsworth, who had it repainted in North Eastern Railway green livery with black and white lining. The original number 69023 was restored and the smokebox numberplate put back. Nameplates *Joem* (a contraction of the names of Mr. Ainsworth's parents, Joseph and Emma) have been affixed to the side tanks. *Joem* is on loan to the Keighley & Worth Valley Railway Preservation Society where it is maintained in working order and can frequently be seen in steam.

Engine Diagrams

Section D, 1924. Drawing shows Raven variety with deeper frames, sandwich type buffer-beams, and longer bunkers. Coal capacity shown incorrectly as 1 ton, amended to 2 tons in December 1927.

1946. Revised diagram to smaller scale. Coal capacity shown as 1½ tons. Length over buffers increased from 28ft. 9¾in. to 29ft. 2¾in.

Classification: Route availability 2; B.R. power class 2F.

Summary of J72 Class

B.R. No.		1946 No.		1923 No.	Maker	Works No.	Built	Vacuum Ejector Fitted	Withdrawn
68670	2/50	8670	6/46	462	Darlington	—	12/1898	—	1/60
68671	5/48	8671	5/46	1715	,,	—	12/1898	—	2/60
68672	9/51	8672	6/46	1718	,,	—	12/1898	—	10/61
68673	3/48	8673	1/46	1721	,,	—	12/1898	—	5/61
68674	4/48	8674	1/46	1722	,,	—	12/1898	—	10/61
68675	9/48	8675	6/46	1732	,,	—	12/1898	—	9/61
68676	12/48	8676	5/46	1744	,,	—	12/1898	—	9/60
68677	4/48	8677	5/46	1746	,,	—	12/1898	4/48	10/61
68678	10/48	8678	5/46	1761	,,	—	12/1898	10/48	2/61
68679	5/50	8679	4/46	1770	,,	—	12/1898	5/50	6/60
68680	10/49	8680	4/46	1720	,,	—	3/1899	9/37	10/61
68681	9/51	8681	1/46	1728	,,	—	3/1899	—	11/60
68682	8/50	8682	6/46	1733	,,	—	3/1899	—	12/59
68683	7/48	8683	5/46	1734	,,	—	3/1899	7/48	3/61
68684	8/50	8684	1/46	1736	,,	—	3/1899	—	3/61
68685	11/50	8685	3/46	1741	,,	—	3/1899	—	10/60
68686	10/48	8686	3/46	1742	,,	—	4/1899	10/54	8/61
68687	10/48	8687	6/46	1747	,,	—	4/1899	1/48	9/61
68688	6/48	8688	6/46	1749	,,	—	4/1899	—	10/61
68689	4/48	8689	3/46	1763	,,	—	4/1899	1/48	10/61
68690	1/50	8690	7/46	2173	,,	—	8/1914	12/56	2/61
68691	4/48	8691	5/46	2174	,,	—	9/1914	—	12/60
68692	3/48	8692	6/46	2175	,,	—	9/1914	—	10/61
68693	10/48	8693	6/46	2176	,,	—	9/1914	12/47	8/61
68694	12/49	8694	6/46	2177	,,	—	9/1914	—	11/59
68695	5/49	8695	5/46	2178	,,	—	9/1914	—	4/62
68696	12/48	8696	5/46	2179	,,	—	9/1914	5/55	1/61
68697	6/50	8697	3/46	2180	,,	—	9/1914	—	2/60
68698	11/48	8698	5/46	2181	,,	—	9/1914	—	10/61
68699	11/48	8699	5/46	2182	,,	—	10/1914	—	12/58
68700	6/48	8700	4/46	2183	,,	—	10/1914	—	12/58
68701	6/49	8701	5/46	2184	,,	—	10/1914	—	10/60
68702	3/48	8702	6/46	2185	,,	—	10/1914	12/47	8/61
68703	9/50	8703	6/46	2186	,,	—	10/1914	—	10/61
68704	10/48	8704	6/46	2187	,,	—	10/1914	10/48	10/61
68705	4/49	8705	6/46	2188	,,	—	11/1914	—	11/60
68706	6/48	8706	6/46	2189	,,	—	11/1914	—	10/60
68707	5/51	8707	5/46	2190	,,	—	11/1914	10/55	4/62
68708	3/49	8708	6/46	2191	,,	—	11/1914	2/54	8/61
68709	5/48	8709	5/46	2192	,,	—	11/1914	—	2/62
68710	4/48	8710	4/46	2303	,,	—	10/1920	—	3/59
68711	5/48	8711	6/46	2304	,,	—	10/1920	5/48	8/61
68712	8/48	8712	6/46	2305	,,	—	10/1920	—	1/59
68713	3/49	8713	6/46	2306	,,	—	10/1920	4/55	10/61
68714	6/49	8714	5/46	2307	,,	—	11/1920	—	3/60
68715	2/50	8715	6/46	2308	,,	—	11/1920	—	7/61
68716	6/48	8716	6/46	2309	,,	—	11/1920	—	2/61
68717	12/48	8717	4/46	2310	,,	—	11/1920	—	11/61
68718	11/50	8718	5/46	2311	,,	—	12/1920	—	6/58
68719	2/49	8719	4/46	2312	,,	—	12/1920	—	1/61

Summary of J72 Class (continued)

B.R. No.		1946 No.		1923 No.	Maker	Works No.	Built	Vacuum Ejector Fitted	Withdrawn
68720	2/50	8720	6/46	2313	Armstrong, Whitworth & Co.	391	4/1922	8/37	9/61
68721	10/49	8721	6/46	2314	,,	392	4/1922	—	8/61
68722	9/48	8722	5/46	2315	,,	393	4/1922	9/53	2/60
68723	10/48	8723	6/46	2316	,,	394	4/1922	1/48	9/63
68724	5/48	8724	6/46	2317	,,	395	4/1922	9/53	12/60
68725	4/48	8725	6/46	2318	,,	396	4/1922	—	4/60
68726	10/49	8726	6/46	2319	,,	397	4/1922	10/59	6/61
68727	6/49	8727	5/46	2320	,,	398	4/1922	—	2/60
68728	8/48	8728	6/46	2321	,,	399	4/1922	8/48	10/61
68729	1/51	8729	6/46	2322	,,	400	4/1922	—	10/61
68730	12/50	8730	5/46	2323	,,	401	5/1922	—	11/60
68731	6/50	8731	6/46	2324	,,	402	5/1922	11/56	5/60
68732	9/48	8732	3/46	2325	,,	403	5/1922	11/56	10/61
68733	12/50	8733	4/46	2326	,,	404	5/1922	—	7/62
68734	11/50	8734	6/46	2327	,,	405	5/1922	—	10/61
68735	4/48	8735	6/46	2328	,,	406	5/1922	5/48	10/58
68736	8/50	8736	6/46	2329	,,	407	6/1922	8/50	10/63
68737	5/50	8737	6/46	2330	,,	408	6/1922	6/55	8/61
68738	2/49	8738	1/46	2331	,,	409	6/1922	3/57	11/60
68739	8/49	8739	6/46	2332	,,	410	6/1922	—	8/59
68740	10/50	8740	1/46	2333	,,	411	6/1922	—	7/61
68741	6/50	8741	6/46	2334	,,	412	8/1922	—	6/59
68742	5/50	8742	6/46	2335	,,	413	8/1922	5/50	10/61
68743	5/48	8743	6/46	2336	,,	414	9/1922	11/57	10/61
68744	9/48	8744	6/46	2337	,,	415	10/1922	4/56	9/61
68745	11/48	8745	5/46	500	Doncaster	1621	11/1925	—	9/61
68746	9/50	8746	5/46	512	,,	1624	11/1925	3/57	12/58
68747	5/48	8747	5/46	516	,,	1626	11/1925	8/57	10/61
68748	7/51	8748	5/46	524	,,	1627	11/1925	1/48	1/59
68749	8/50	8749	3/46	542	,,	1630	12/1925	—	8/60
68750	5/49	8750	4/46	566	,,	1631	12/1925	—	12/62
68751	4/50	8751	6/46	571	,,	1633	12/1925	—	5/59
68752	1/50	8752	6/46	574	,,	1634	12/1925	—	2/60
68753	5/48	8753	6/46	576	,,	1635	12/1925	—	8/60
68754	9/49	8754	6/46	581	,,	1636	12/1925	2/60	4/62
69001	New	—		—	Darlington	2082	10/1949	—	9/63
69002	,,	—		—	,,	2083	11/1949	—	10/62
69003	,,	—		—	,,	2084	11/1949	9/59	12/63
69004	,,	—		—	,,	2085	11/1949	—	9/63
69005	,,	—		—	,,	2086	11/1949	1/57	10/64(a)
69006	,,	—		—	,,	2087	11/1949	—	12/63
69007	,,	—		—	,,	2088	11/1949	—	10/62
69008	,,	—		—	,,	2089	12/1949	1/57	12/63
69009	,,	—		—	,,	2090	12/1949	—	9/63
69010	,,	—		—	,,	2091	12/1949	—	10/62
69011	,,	—		—	,,	2092	12/1949	—	12/63
69012	,,	—		—	,,	2093	12/1949	—	2/61
69013	,,	—		—	,,	2094	12/1949	—	1/62
69014	,,	—		—	,,	2095	12/1949	—	2/62
69015	,,	—		—	,,	2096	12/1949	—	9/61
69016	,,	—		—	,,	2097	1/1950	2/57	10/64
69017	,,	—		—	,,	2098	1/1950	—	4/62
69018	,,	—		—	,,	2099	1/1950	1/57	10/62
69019	,,	—		—	,,	2100	1/1950	—	12/63
69020	,,	—		—	,,	2101	1/1950	—	12/63
69021	,,	—		—	,,	2149	4/1951	When new	9/63
69022	,,	—		—	,,	2150	4/1951	,,	12/62(b)
69023	,,	—		—	,,	2151	4/1951	,,	10/64(a)
69024	,,	—		—	,,	2152	4/1951	,,	9/63
69025	,,	—		—	,,	2153	4/1951	,,	12/63
69026	,,	—		—	,,	2154	5/1951	,,	4/62
69027	,,	—		—	,,	2155	5/1951	,,	10/62
69028	,,	—		—	,,	2156	5/1951	,,	10/64

(a) Nos. 69005/23 were renumbered 58 and 59 in Departmental Stock from October 1964 and were condemned in October 1967 and September 1966 respectively.

(b) No. 69022 was withdrawn on 31/12/62, but included in the B.R. 1963 statistical year withdrawals.

CLASS J73

N.E.R. CLASS L—WILSON WORSDELL
4ft. 7¼in. ENGINES

ENGINES AT GROUPING (Built 1891-92): 544-53. TOTAL 10.

These ten engines were constructed at Gateshead Works between December 1891 and June 1892, and this was the first new N.E.R. design after Wilson Worsdell had succeeded his elder brother T. W. Worsdell as Locomotive Superintendent on 1st October 1890. The latter, who had retired for health reasons, remained as consultant for a further two years.

The L class was ordered for working the Redheugh and Quayside banks on opposite sides of the Tyne and was larger and more powerful than T. W. Worsdell's E class 0-6-0T's (L.N.E.R. class J71).

Compared with class E, which had 16in. × 22in. cylinders, the L class had 19in. × 24in. cylinders and a considerably bigger boiler with a 40% increase in grate area and 50% in heating surface. This boiler was similar to that already in use on T. W. Worsdell's 2-4-2T's (class A) and 2-4-0's (class G). Unlike class E, which had Stephenson motion with valves between the cylinders, class L had Joy's gear with the slide valves above the cylinders. These valves were also somewhat unusual for slide valves in having tail guides, which had cylindrical covers with flat ends, a noticeable feature at the front of the engine and one which they kept throughout their average life of sixty-five years. Indeed, apart from minor details, they were practically unaltered in this long span.

This was a specialised rather than a general-purpose design and in consequence only ten engines were built. The boiler type on class L was used subsequently on Worsdell's next two designs, the class O 0-4-4T's (L.N.E.R. G5) and P 0-6-0's (J24), these totalling 180 engines, and parts were common to all three designs. The first withdrawal of a class L did not take place until 1955, and the class became extinct five years later.

Standard L.N.E.R. Dimensions at Grouping

Cylinders (2 inside)	19″ × 24″
Motion	Joy with slide valves
Boiler:	
Max. diam. outside	4′ 3″
Barrel length ...	10′ 3″
Firebox length outside ...	5′ 6″
Pitch	7′ 1½″
Diagram No. ...	69

Heating surface:

Firebox ...	98 sq. ft.	
Tubes (205 × 1¾″)	995 sq. ft.	
Total	1093 sq. ft.	
Grate area ...	15.6 sq. ft.	
Boiler pressure ...	160 lb./sq. in.	
Coupled wheels ...	4′ 7¼″	
Tractive effort(85%)	21,320 lb.	
Length over buffers	31′ 8″	
Wheelbase ...	7′ 6″ + 8′ 2″ = 15′ 8″	
Weight (full) ...	46T 15c	
Max. axle load ...	18T 6c	
Water capacity ...	1,000 gallons	
Coal capacity ...	2T 10c	

L.N.E.R. Renumbering

During 1946 Nos. 544-53 became 8355-64 in order of building.

Rebuilding

As first built the boilers had 206 tubes, but in later N.E.R. days a different tube arrangement reduced the number to 205. The 206 tubes provided 999 sq. ft. of heating surface making the total 1097 sq. ft. The grate area was given as 15.16 sq. ft.

The original set of boilers on the class remained undisturbed until 1904, when a spare boiler, newly-built at Darlington, was put on No. 548. Apart from three new Gateshead-built boilers put on class L in 1907-8, all subsequent boilers used on the class were built at Darlington. After Grouping, several second-hand replacement boilers were fitted and included some from classes J22 (0-6-0), " 901 " (2-4-0) and F8 (2-4-2T). In 1930 the design of this type of boiler (still designated Diagram 69) was changed to incorporate a barrel constructed from a single rolled plate instead of the three rings hitherto used. In these boilers the number of tubes was reduced to 199 and the total heating surface to 1069 sq. ft., but the overall dimensions remained unaltered. In due course this pattern found its way on to class J73, but only second-hand examples were used.

In 1937 the Diagram 69 boiler underwent a further redesign as type 69A. The single plate barrel was retained, but the number of tubes was increased again to 205. A noticeable feature was the placing of the dome 1ft. 8in. further to the rear (cf. figs. 24 and 27). Although designed to fit classes G5, J24 and J73, the first to be put on to class J73 was on No. 552 in November 1942. The Diagram 69 type continued to be used concurrently and No. 547 kept this pattern of boiler throughout. Engines which carried the 69A pattern are shown in the Summary.

Details

The coal bunkers did not have coal rails originally, but it became standard practice on the N.E.R. to fit them by the turn of the century, and in 1909, an instruction was issued for open coal rails to have plates fitted behind them to reduce spillage. Whilst all the J73 class received rails and the plates behind them, at least in L.N.E.R. days they were not all similar. Nos. 547/9/53 had only two rails, but the other seven engines had three and this position obtained until withdrawal.

Safety valves were of the Ramsbottom type in the usual polished brass casing (fig. 24) and, on J73 class, this type did not disappear until No. 8362 went to Gateshead late in November 1950 for a general repair. The change-over to the Ross pop type (fig. 26) had begun in January 1942 when Nos. 551 and 553 were so equipped. When No. 68362, as it then became, reappeared from works in December 1950 it carried its pop safety valves on a curious mounting. The boiler put into it then had hitherto carried Ramsbottom valves, but these were removed and to their mounting pad was fixed a plate carrying the pop valves. This variation disappeared when No. 68362 received a fresh boiler in January 1954.

The fitting of pop valves to the J73 class does not seem to have caused the difficulties experienced by the footplatemen on the smaller N.E.R. shunting engines, where various devices (official and otherwise) were fitted as shields around the valves and not a single J73 was noted so fitted.

For nearly fifty years this class carried the usual N.E.R. twin whistles, both of the bell type with the larger on the right-hand side, and mounted on pipes protruding through the cab roof (fig. 25). Then from December 1940 (on No. 544) all were fitted with new whistle gear. On Diagram 69A boilers this meant a single whistle, moved to the front of the cab and fixed to a pad on the firebox. On the earlier boilers the change was also to a single whistle, although usually this still protruded through the cab roof. Generally the new whistles were of the bell shape, but in May 1952 No. 68358 was carrying one of the organ type on the cab roof and was the only engine so noted.

The original type of smokebox door fitted to the J73's was only slightly dished and had the customary wheel-and-handle fastening. This latter was still to be seen on Nos. 548/9/50/2 in the mid-1930's when the others had already changed to two handles, but the wheel-and-handle variety had disappeared by the time the engines became Nos. 8355-64 in 1946. In July of that year No. 8357 was fitted with a smokebox front having a pressed joint ring, and the door itself was considerably more dished in appearance. Two others, Nos. 68360/1, were dealt with similarly, but the remaining seven retained the original type.

The original buffers had parallel shanks and hollow spindles and the first engine withdrawn, No. 68358 (ex-547), kept this type throughout and was the only one to do so. These buffers could still be seen on most of the others up to the late 'thirties, although a gradual change was being made to a type with tapered shank and solid spindle, Nos. 546/8/50 being so fitted before the War (fig. 24). The length over buffers of 31ft. 8in. shown on the L.N.E.R. diagram was with this later type of buffer, the figure with the original buffers being 2½in. less overall. By B.R. days eight of the ten were using the newer type but, as already mentioned, No. 547 was never altered. The remaining engine, No. 548, was the only one of the class to be fitted with Group Standard buffers and drawgear (fig. 26). When first constructed, the class was additionally fitted with substantial dumb buffers at both ends, situated between the ordinary buffers and the drawhook. These were for dealing with chaldron wagons, but were removed well before Grouping.

COMPARATIVE BOILER DIMENSIONS

Diagram No. ...				69 (or N.E.R. class L)			69A
			Original N.E.R.	At Grouping	1930		1937
Heating surface (sq. ft.):							
Firebox				98	98	98	98
Tubes				999	995	971	994.4
Total				1097	1093	1069	1092.4
Tubes (1¾in. diameter)				206	205	199	205
Grate area (sq. ft.)				15.16	15.6	15.6	15.54

Fig. 19 Class J72 No. 2192 at Shildon sidings, June 1932.
Shunting pole.

Fig. 20 Class J72 No. 68750 at Kittybrewster shed,
June 1949.
N.B R. Y9 type chimney, Scottish variety of safety valve cover,
B.R. number on bunker.

Fig. 21 Class J72 No. 68709 at Eastfield, May 1948.
Stovepipe chimney, N.B.R. shunters footsteps under bunker with
extra handrail.

Fig. 22   Class J72 No. 8680 at Newcastle Central,
October 1947.

L.N.E.R. green livery, Group Standard buffers, no handrail across rear of bunker.

Fig. 23   Class J72 No. 68723 at Newcastle Central,
September 1962.

N.E.R. green livery with B.R. and N.E.R. crests, vacuum ejector.

Fig. 24   Class J73 No. 550 at Springhead, 1937.

Diagram 69 boiler, Ramsbottom safety valves, buffers with tapered shanks.

Fig. 25   Class J73 No. 545 at Ferryhill shed, August 1936.
Westinghouse brake and vacuum ejector, twin whistles on cab roof.

Fig. 26   Class J73 No. 8359 at West Hartlepool,
August 1947.
Ross pop safety valves, Group Standard buffers and drawgear.

Fig. 27   Class J73 No. 68359 at Northallerton shed, June 1952.
Diagram 69A boiler (with dome further back).

Fig. 28   Class J74 No. 20 at Alexandra Dock shed.
2 coal rails, buffers with parallel shanks.

Fig. 29   Class J74 No. 461.
3 coal rails, buffers with tapered shanks.

Fig. 30   Class J75 H. & B. R. No. 145 (L.N.E.R. 2526) at
Darlington shed, June 1922.
Diagram 71A domeless boiler, H. & B. chimney and buffers, uncased
Ramsbottom safety valves, original pattern of smokebox door with
dog clips, un-plated coal rails, re-railing jack.

Fig. 31   Class J75 No. 2495 at Alexandra Dock shed.

Diagram 71A domeless boiler, H. & B chimney, Ross pop safety valves,
Yorkshire Engine Co. series (shorter front sandboxes with rounded
edges, brass beading on splashers, handrail on tank top curved
downwards at ends), N.E.R. pattern smokebox door with repositioned
handrail above door.

Fig. 32   Class J75 No. 2528, about 1932.

Diagram 71B domed boiler, with boiler handrail repositioned higher,
Kitson series (longer front sandboxes with angular corners,
handrail on tank top secured by stanchions), N.E.R. buffers with
parallel shanks and hollow spindles.

Fig. 33   Class J75 No. 2497 at Springhead shed,
October 1935.

Domed boiler off "901" class 2-4-0 (with clack box on side of barrel
and Ramsbottom safety valves inside brass trumpet cover), N.E.R.
chimney.

Fig. 34   Class J75 No. 8365 at Walton-on-the-Hill shed,
August 1948.

Group Standard buffers, cover plate missing from base of safety valves.

Fig. 35   Class J76 N.E.R. No. 124 at Ferryhill shed.

Front springs above running plate, Westinghouse brake pump mounted on
plate ahead of right-hand tank, small front sandbox, hopper-shaped
rear sandbox.

Fig. 36   Class J76 No. 599 at Bank Top shed, Darlington,
about 1925.

Underslung front springs, Westinghouse pump mounted on left-hand tank,
large front sandboxes.

Brakes

Being intended for goods work, the class was equipped with steam brake. In the winter of 1914, raids by German battle-cruisers on our North-East coast made some sort of defence desirable, and two mobile heavy gun trains were organised with Nos. 544/5 selected for their haulage and servicing. In June 1915 these two engines were fitted with Westinghouse pumps and brake equipment, train heating apparatus with connections at both ends, screw couplings, condensing apparatus for their exhausts, and an extra Westinghouse pump for lifting water from streams when the normal supply was not available. The pumps were mounted on brackets placed at the front corners of the running board, just ahead of the smokebox, one on each side of the engine, that on the left-hand side being for the brakes. When the emergency was over, the right-hand pump and the condensing apparatus were removed, but the Westinghouse brake equipment, heater connections and screw couplings were not disturbed. Later, vacuum apparatus for train working was also added, to No. 544 in July 1930 and to No. 545 in November 1928 (fig. 25). There seems to be no record however of either of these engines being engaged on any normal passenger workings, and in September 1944 all the extra equipment was removed from No. 544. The other one received the same treatment in July 1946. Henceforward both had steam brake only and three-link couplings, but right to the end of their days there was a visible reminder of the part they had taken in the 1914-18 War. The fitting of condensing apparatus necessitated mushroom-shaped breather pipes on the top of each side tank and these were never removed. On its gun duties No. 544 worked around Brotton in North Yorkshire covering the mouth of the Tees and was nominally allocated to Middlesbrough, whilst No. 545 was at Hartley in Northumberland on the coastal lines and was allocated to Blyth.

British Railways

The whole class was taken over by British Railways and between June 1948 and February 1951 their numbers were changed from 8355-64 to 68355-64.

Allocation and Work

The class was put to work on the more arduous banks, especially the Redheugh incline leading from the River Tyne at Dunston up to Gateshead and the Quayside branch (which joined the main line at Manors) on the other side of the river. Later, consequent upon the electrification of the Quayside line, the class was redistributed and the allocation by Grouping, and until the end of 1927, was Ferryhill (Nos. 544/5/7/8/53), Tyne Dock (Nos. 546/51), Pelton Level (Nos. 549/52), with No. 550 at Heaton. The Ferryhill engines spent most of their time pushing eastbound mineral trains up Kelloe Bank from Coxhoe Bridge to Trimdon, where there were numerous collieries and quarries. This was part of the old inland route to East Hartlepool via Castle Eden. In more recent times, to dispense with banking, the laden trains were worked downhill in the opposite direction, continuing to Hartlepool via the former Clarence route through Norton.

The small, out-of-the-way Pelton Level shed was located at the western end of a level stretch of track between a succession of self-acting inclines, all dating back to 1834 and created by the Stanhope & Tyne Railway. Some relief for the volume of mineral traffic over this route from Consett to the coast was provided by the opening in 1894 of the steeply-graded adhesion line from Ouston Junction to Annfield Plain via Beamish. Because numerous collieries were connected to the inclines, they were retained and the duties of Pelton Level engines were to move the wagons (full one way, empty the other) between the foot of Edenhill incline and the head of Waldridge incline, a distance of no more than 1,331 yards. For visits to works, the engines had to go down the Waldridge incline to Stella Gill.

During the period 1927-29 Ferryhill shed parted with Nos. 547/8/53 to East Hartlepool, and the overall allocation then remained undisturbed for another five years. By 1934 one engine sufficed at Pelton Level and No. 552 went to Consett shed before moving on to Borough Gardens.

In May 1937 there was a wholesale withdrawal of N.E. Area 0-6-0T's, thirteen J71 and six J75 being taken out of service, the majority of them from Hull sheds. Some replacements were essential and the first to be gathered together were as varied as J77 class No. 614 from West Hartlepool, A7 class No. 1113 from York, and J73 class No. 552 (the odd man out) from Borough Gardens. This latter was soon joined at Alexandra Dock by No. 550 from Heaton. Soon more of these "stronger engines to work timber traffic on Hull Docks" were desired and No. 549 from Pelton Level (where it was replaced by N9 0-6-2T No. 1652) and Nos. 546/51 from Tyne Dock moved to Alexandra Dock late in 1937, the allocation of the class then being Ferryhill (Nos. 544/5), East Hartlepool (Nos. 547/8/53) and Alexandra Dock (Nos. 546/9-52).

31

In November 1938 traffic requirements caused the transfer of No. 552 to East Hartlepool whilst the closure of Ferryhill shed on the 7th of that month sent Nos. 544/5 to Newport, but there was no work for them and they were transferred to West Hartlepool in March 1939. On 17th April 1939 East Hartlepool shed closed and Nos. 547/8/52/3 also went to West Hartlepool, that shed then losing No. 545 to Alexandra Dock in June, so that when war broke out they were equally divided between West Hartlepool (Nos. 544/7/8/52/3) and Alexandra Dock (Nos. 545/6/9-51). By this time their principal activity was the haulage of heavy trains of timber from the docks to the stacking areas at Hartlepool and Hull.

Altered traffic conditions at Hull during the War resulted in Nos. 545/6/51 being transferred early in 1940 to Selby, where they were used mainly in Gascoigne Wood marshalling yard. They remained at Selby for the rest of their lives. The peripatetic No. 552 spent a short time at Northallerton from late 1940, where it was used on an additional piloting shift at Thirsk, after which it was transferred in succession to Darlington, Heaton and, in 1947 as No. 8363, to Tweed-mouth. At nationalisation the allocation was Alexandra Dock (Nos. 8360/1), Selby (Nos. 8356/7/62), West Hartlepool (Nos. 8355/8/9/64) and Tweedmouth (No. 8363). The Alexandra Dock engines were by then usually employed on the movement of petrol tank wagons from Saltend oil depot on the Humber to the outward marshalling yards. In B.R. days No. 68363 continued its wanderings, going back to Alexandra Dock in 1949, to Botanic Gardens in 1954 and finally, when that shed closed on 14th June 1959, to Dairycoates, where it joined Nos. 68360/1 transferred there earlier from Alexandra Dock. The only other significant move was of No. 68359 from West Hartlepool to Northallerton in 1951 and back again in 1955. Withdrawal of the class began in March of that year with No. 68358 and was completed in November 1960 when No. 68361 of Dairycoates was condemned.

Engine Diagram

Section D, 1924. Drawing shows original style without coal rails.

Classification: Route availability 5; B.R. power class 3F.

Summary of J73 Class

B.R. No.		1946 No.		1923 No.	Maker	Built	Diagram 69A Boiler	With-drawn
68355	2/51	8355	5/46	544	Gateshead	12/1891	9/44-Wdl.	12/58
68356	9/48	8356	3/46	545	,,	12/1891	7/46-Wdl.	8/58
68357	8/48	8357	5/46	546	,,	3/1892	7/51-7/54	1/58
68358	6/48	8358	5/46	547	,,	4/1892	Not fitted	3/55
68359	5/49	8359	5/46	548	,,	4/1892	5/49-Wdl.	12/59
68360	7/48	8360	5/46	549	,,	5/1892	3/51-Wdl.	2/60
68361	12/49	8361	5/46	550	,,	6/1892	6/56-Wdl.	11/60
68362	12/50	8362	5/46	551	,,	6/1892	12/47-12/50, 1/54-Wdl.	9/57
68363	9/50	8363	5/46	552	,,	6/1892	11/42-11/47, 6/53-Wdl.	10/59
68364	10/48	8364	9/46	553	,,	6/1892	6/45-1/52, 11/55-Wdl.	5/60

CLASS J74

N.E.R. CLASS 8—TENNANT
4ft. 7¼in. ENGINES

ENGINES AT GROUPING (Built 1885): 20, 64, 82, 88, 461/7/89, 662. TOTAL 8.

This design of goods shunting engine has sometimes been attributed to McDonnell, but was in fact a legacy of his short reign. He had resigned from the N.E.R. in September 1884 and the first of these class " 8 " engines did not appear until August 1885. By that time the caretaker Locomotive Committee, chaired by Henry Tennant, had designed the " 1463 " class 2-4-0 and sixteen of the twenty were already running. These engines had been designed and built as a matter of urgency because McDonnell's " 38 " class 4-4-0's had proved unsatisfactory. In fact, after his resignation an outstanding order for eight more of the " 38 " class was cancelled although some of the materials for these had already been ordered and were to hand. Once the " 1463 " class had been designed, attention was turned to this surplus material and a minute, dated 5th February 1885, of the Locomotive Committee stated " that with a view to using up material provided for eight additional bogie passenger engines, which are of a kind not required by the Company, it is recommended that eight side tank shunters be constructed to drawings now submitted and tenders be obtained for the wheel centres." Gateshead completed the eight engines between August and December 1885, designating them as class " 8 " from the running number of the first to appear. Obvious McDonnell features were the brass beading round the combined front sandbox and splasher and the left-handed driving position. An unusual feature, not perpetuated on later N.E.R. designs, was the rounded front ends to the side tanks.

In due time class " 8 " received Worsdell boilers and boiler mountings. The class remained intact until February 1930, when No. 64 was withdrawn; No. 662 was sold in January 1931 and the remaining six were withdrawn in August and September of that year.

Standard L.N.E.R. Dimensions at Grouping

Cylinders (2 inside)	17″ × 24″
Motion	Stephenson with slide valves

Boiler:

Max. diam. outside	4′ 3″
Barrel length ...	10′ 3″
Firebox length outside ...	5′ 6″
Pitch	6′ 11⅝″
Diagram No. ...	69

Heating surface:

Firebox ...	98 sq. ft.
Tubes (205 × 1¾″)	995 sq. ft.
Total ...	1093 sq. ft.
Grate area ...	15.6 sq. ft.
Boiler pressure ...	160 lb./sq. in.
Coupled wheels ...	4′ 7¼″
Tractive effort(85%)	17,077 lb.
Length over buffers	27′ 1″
Wheelbase ...	7′ 9″ + 8′ 0″ = 15′ 9″
Weight (full) ...	43T 10c
Max. axle load ...	15T 4c
Water capacity ...	995 gallons
Coal capacity ...	2T 0c

N.E.R. Renumbering

No. 8 was changed to 467 in January 1914 so that the Newport-Shildon electric locomotives could be numbered consecutively.

Rebuilding

The original boilers were amongst the last to be built by the N.E.R. using iron plates and are believed to have been similar in dimensions to those fitted to the McDonnell 0-6-0 and 4-4-0 engines of classes " 59 " (L.N.E.R. J22) and " 38 ". The heating surface figures of the boiler on class " 8 " were probably as follows, although this cannot be confirmed from contemporary evidence.

Firebox ...	...	104 sq. ft.
Tubes ...	...	926 sq. ft.
Total ...	...	1030 sq. ft.

The number of tubes in these boilers was 193, although an earlier version had only 190, and the working pressure was 140 lb. per sq. in. Compared with the standard Worsdell boilers which were fitted as replacements between 1900 and 1905 (see table below), the fireboxes had smaller water spaces and consequently a bigger heating surface and larger grate area (17 sq. ft.). Otherwise the Worsdell boilers had the same overall dimensions and were as shown under " Standard L.N.E.R. Dimensions at Grouping". The main change in appearance was limited to chimneys and safety valves, the latter (originally open Ramsbottom type) all getting the polished brass cover with their Worsdell boilers.

Rather curiously, for as many as eight engines all with a minimum life of forty-five years, their boiler history was consistent. Each engine used three boilers, none of them second-hand, and the first two in every case served their full life in the engine to which first fitted. Of the third set (of similar Worsdell pattern), that on No. 662 was sold with the engine, but the other seven were put in other engines (of G5, J24 and J73 classes) after J74 class had been cut up. Those boilers forming the first change on Nos. 8, 64 and 662 were made at Gateshead, but the remaining five and the subsequent eight were all Darlington built. Dates for these reboilerings were:—

No.	8 (467)	2/05 and	2/22
No.	20	10/00 ,,	10/19
No.	64	5/03 ,,	2/21
No.	82	8/01 ,,	6/20
No.	88	6/00 ,,	8/19
No.	461	11/00 ,,	12/19
No.	489	1/00 ,,	2/18
No.	662	9/02 ,,	11/21

Details

So little regarded was the appearance of this class that no official photograph of them seems to have been taken—at least none has ever been discovered, which is unusual for a North Eastern class. Therefore it is difficult to determine what, if any, were subsequent alterations to portions other than the boilers. Presumably they did not originally have coal rails to their bunkers, nor does No. 662 ever seem to have been so equipped, but by L.N.E.R. days Nos. 20, 64 and 489 had two rails, whilst Nos. 82, 88 and 461 had three, all of them with plates on the inside (figs. 28 and 29). No. 88 had rectangular section rails whereas the others had rails of half-rounded section.

Latterly, smokebox door fastenings also differed, Nos. 20, 82, 88 and 461 being noted with wheel and handle, whereas Nos. 64, 489 and 662 had twin handles. (No. 467 was not observed).

For lubricating the cylinders, tallow cups were provided on each side of the smokebox and for the slide valves there was a single screw-down displacement lubricator on the front of the casing housing these. For axle-box lubrication, oilboxes mounted on the front of the side tanks were fitted.

A single front footstep was provided, but without any stiffening stay as on other classes of N.E.R. 0-6-0T. Two distinct types of buffers were in use latterly, having either tapered shanks (e.g. Nos. 82, 461/89) or parallel shanks (e.g. Nos. 20, 64 and 88) (figs. 28 and 29).

Although officially class J74 on the L.N.E.R., this never appeared on the bufferbeam, which continued to carry CLASS 8, Darlington Works not changing their practice until 1929, too late for these engines to be concerned.

Brakes

This class carried steam brake throughout.

Allocation and Work

Initially the class worked mainly on the Durham side of the Tyne, from Tyne Dock and Borough Gardens sheds in particular. By 1920 No. 20 was at Tyne Dock, No. 88 at Heaton, Nos. 64 and 662 at Gateshead, and the other four at West Hartlepool, but an influx of new class E1 (L.N.E.R. J72) engines in 1920-22 made them largely redundant at these sheds. In May 1922 the eight class " 8 " engines were all sent to Alexandra Dock shed at Hull where, with four class E (L.N.E.R. J71) engines, they replaced H. & B.R. Nos. 1-12, which the N.E.R. authorities condemned practically at first sight as they still carried their 1885-built boilers. Here they spent the rest of their days on dock shunting duties and trip working as far as Springhead marshalling yard.

Sales

In January 1931 No. 662 was sold to the Ashington Coal Co., where it became their No. 5. It was frequently employed on the workmen's trains on that line and was scrapped in August 1938.

Engine Diagram

Section D, 1924. Diameter of smokebox corrected 12/1927 from 4ft. 11in. to 5ft. 0in.

Summary of J74 Class

1923 No.	Maker	Built	Withdrawn
467	Gateshead	8/1885	9/31
20	,,	9/1885	9/31
461	,,	10/1885	9/31
489	,,	11/1885	9/31
662	,,	11/1885	1/31
64	,,	12/1885	2/30
82	,,	12/1885	9/31
88	,,	12/1885	8/31

CLASS J75

H. & B.R. CLASS G3—M. STIRLING
4ft. 6in. ENGINES

ENGINES AT GROUPING (Built 1901-8): 2492-7 (H. & B. 111-6), 2523-32 (H. & B. 142-51). TOTAL 16.

These domeless engines were based on Stirling's earlier 0-6-0T class (see L.N.E.R. class J80) and differed principally in having wheels six inches less in diameter and a lower-pitched boiler. The J75's were essentially built for shunting duties, but an 0-6-2T version (L.N.E.R. N12) was produced at the

same time for transfer work and short-haul mineral trains in the colliery areas.

The J75's were delivered in two batches from contractors as shown below.

The L.N.E.R. rebuilt all but two of the class with domed boilers between 1923 and 1928. Except for one engine, which lasted until 1949, the J75's fell victim to the aftermath of the depression in the 'thirties and were withdrawn between 1937 and 1939.

H. & B. Nos.	Maker	Order No.	Works Nos.	No. built	Date
111-6	Yorkshire Engine Co.	E116	655-60	6	1901-2
142-51	Kitson & Co.	—	4545-54	10	1908

Standard L.N.E.R. Dimensions at Grouping

Cylinders (2 inside)		$18'' \times 26''$
Motion		Stephenson with slide valves
Boiler (domeless):		
Max. diam. outside		$4'\ 3''$
Barrel length ...		$10'\ 0''$
Firebox length outside ...		$5'\ 6''$
Pitch		$6'\ 11''$
Diagram No. ...		71A
Heating surface:		
Firebox		104 sq. ft.
Tubes ($194 \times 1\frac{3}{4}''$)		951 sq. ft.
Total		1055 sq. ft.
Grate area ...		16.25 sq. ft.
Boiler pressure ...		150 lb./sq. in.
Coupled wheels ...		$4'\ 6''$
Tractive effort(85%)		19,890 lb.
Length over buffers		$32'\ 2\frac{1}{2}''$
Wheelbase ...	$7'\ 3'' + 8'\ 3'' = 15'\ 6''$	
Weight (full) ...		47T 7C
Max. axle load ...		17T 16C
Water capacity ...		850 gallons
Coal capacity ...		3T 0C

H. & B.R. and L.N.E.R. Renumbering

Following amalgamation with the N.E.R. on 1st April 1922, the numbers of all H. & B. engines were increased by 3000 during 1922 and 1923. With the possible (though unlikely) exception of No. 146, all the J75 class were actually renumbered. The practice at Springhead Works was to add a 3 to the painted H. & B.R. number, but several J75's visited the N.E.R. works at Darlington and these received cast-brass number plates (see under "Details"). In 1924 the L.N.E.R. allotted numbers 2492-7, 2523-32 to the J75 class in order of construction, the renumbering being completed by the end of that year. One engine, No. 2532, survived long enough to be renumbered under the 1946 scheme and became 8365.

Rebuilding

At the time of amalgamation with the N.E.R., the majority of boilers on H. & B. engines required early replacement. In February 1923, class J75 No. 3116 (2497) was fitted with a domed boiler (fig. 33) from an N.E.R. "901" class 2-4-0 (L.N.E.R. Diagram 69). This boiler was retained by No. 2497 until October 1936, when it was replaced by a further domed boiler to Diagram 71B (see below). The firebox length and barrel diameter of the " 901 " class boiler were the same as the original H. & B. boiler, but the barrel length was 3in. greater. The grate area was less and there were differences in the heating surface and working pressure, as shown in the table below.

In 1924 a redesigned domed version of the original domeless boiler was produced at Darlington for use on classes J75, J80, N12 and N13. These boilers, designated 71B (fig. 32), were fitted between July 1924 and February 1928 to the J75 class with the exception of Nos. 2495 and 2526, which kept domeless 71A boilers (figs. 30 and 31) until withdrawal, and No. 2497, mentioned above. Of the two J75's retaining domeless boilers, No. 2495 was fitted in December 1927 with a new Diagram 71A boiler constructed at Darlington from stocks of parts held at Springhead, whilst in the same month No. 2526 received the second-hand 71A boiler taken from class N13 No. 2405. Nos. 2495 and 2526 still carried these boilers when condemned in May 1937.

The Diagram 71B domed boilers were of similar overall size to the 71A type but there were more tubes and a slightly reduced grate area. The working pressure, however, was increased from 160 to 175 lb. per sq. in.

Details

The six engines built by the Yorkshire Engine Co. had brass beading round the splasher over the leading wheels, whereas the ten Kitson engines were without this beading (cf. figs. 31 and 32). The front sandboxes on the earlier engines had rounded edges and were shorter in length than the Kitson variety, which had their leading edges flush with the front of the smokebox and had angular corners. The latter batch also had a side access hole to the sandbox not found on the first six engines.

The handrails running along the top of the side tanks of the Yorkshire Engine Co. batch were bent downwards at right-angles at each end to a fastening on the tank tops. The similar handrails on the Kitson engines were secured to the tank tops by normal stanchions.

The entire class ultimately lost their H. & B.R. chimneys (fig. 30), but at least Nos. 2494/6 and 2528 retained their original chimney until after the domed boiler was fitted. The replacement chimneys were of N.E.R. cast iron pattern (fig. 33). No. 2527 was unusual in receiving one with a " wind jabber ", or capuchon, with which it was noted in the early 'thirties.

Uncased Ramsbottom safety valves were fitted to the original boilers and No. 2526 retained this type until withdrawal (fig. 30). The other domeless engine, No. 2495, had Ross pop valves on its Diagram 71A boiler (fig. 31) and all the 71B domed boilers had Ross pops. Covers were provided around the base of the pop valves, and these were retained except on the last survivor, No. 8365 (fig. 34). The N.E.R. boiler of Diagram 69 on No. 2497 had Ramsbottom valves enclosed in the usual N.E.R. shapely polished brass cover (fig. 33).

The H. & B.R. whistle was bell-shaped and was fixed to the cab front just behind the safety valves, but all except two of the class ultimately received twin N.E.R. whistles, one bell-shaped and the other of the organ-pipe type, probably when the Diagram 71B domed boilers were fitted. No. 2526 (which remained domeless) retained the single fitting although the whistle itself was changed to the organ-pipe type. No. 2497 was treated similarly, but may have been further altered after the Diagram 69 boiler was replaced by the 71B type seven months before this engine was withdrawn. When shopped at Darlington in December 1924, No. 2529 retained its domeless boiler and single whistle, but this was altered to the organ-pipe type. Twin whistles were fitted when the engine was rebuilt with a domed boiler.

COMPARATIVE BOILER DIMENSIONS

						Domeless	Domed	Domed
Diagram No. ...	...	...	...	...	...	71A	69	71B
Barrel length	...	...	...	...	...	10' 0"	10' 3"	10' 0"
Heating surface (sq. ft.):								
Firebox	...	...	...	...	...	104	98	99
Tubes	...	...	...	...	...	951	995	972
Total	...	...	...	...	...	1055	1093	1071
Tubes (1¾in.)	...	...	...	...	...	194	205	205
Grate area (sq. ft.)	...	...	...	...	...	16.25	15.16	15.5
Boiler pressure (lb./sq. in.) ...	...	...	...	...	150	160	175
Tractive effort (85%) (lb.) ...	...	...	...	...	19,890	21,216	23,197

The original flush-fitting smokebox doors were secured by central handles aided by two dog clips on the lower half (fig. 30). From 1922 onwards these doors were quickly replaced by new ones of Darlington pattern, which had flanges, were more dished, of greater diameter, and had the hinges further apart (fig. 31). Fastening was by twin handles or wheel and handle.

Originally the boiler handrail commenced at the front of the side tanks and ran round the front of the smokebox. When larger doors were fitted, the two domeless engines retained this arrangement except that the portion of rail across the front of the smokebox had to be raised to allow the bigger door to open (cf. figs. 30 and 31). On all the other engines the height of the rail along the sides was also raised, to the same level as the rails along the tank tops (fig. 32), and the opportunity was taken to combine the blower connection with the handrail on the left-hand side.

The bunker coal rails were provided with backing plates when the engines were shopped at Darlington, the last being No. 2531 in May 1927.

After they began to visit Darlington Works for repairs in 1922, N.E.R. black livery was applied. Nos. 3116/42/3/5 (and probably No. 3115) were fitted with large elliptical cast brass N.E.R. style number plates on the sides of the bunkers. Until 1930 Darlington continued to paint " CLASS G3 (HB) " under the number on the bufferbeam, but then changed over to J75.

The L.N.E.R. quickly removed the maker's plates from the sides of the front sandboxes, also the re-railing jacks formerly carried alongside the bunker on the left-hand side (fig. 30). However, No. 2523 was noted still with its jack after it began working from Immingham shed in September 1926.

With two exceptions the whole class retained their original H. & B.R. buffers (fig. 30). No. 2528 latterly had more substantial N.E.R. pattern buffers with hollow shanks having internal springs (fig. 32), whilst No. 8365 (ex-2532) had L.N.E.R. Group Standard buffers (fig. 34).

In February 1936, the shunting engines, mainly J72 class, which worked in the Hull timber yards were fitted with spark arresters inside the smokebox following an extensive fire there. No. 2524 was the only J75 class engine so treated.

Brakes

Steam brake only was fitted.

British Railways

No. 8365 was taken into B.R. stock and was withdrawn by the L.M. Region in January 1949 without being renumbered.

Allocation and Work

The first series, Nos. 111-6, were employed on the Wath and Braithwell branches, whilst for many years others of the class were engaged on shunting work at Cudworth and at Hull.

Under the L.N.E.R. the class was at first largely employed on former H. & B.R. metals in the Hull area, mostly shunting at Alexandra Dock and on short transfer trips. One of the class was normally attached to the wagon shops at Springhead.

In September 1926 No. 2523 was sent to Immingham shed, where it remained until withdrawn in June 1938. Others of the class were also sent to the Southern Area, No. 2529 going first to Immingham before finishing its career at New England. No. 2528 spent several years at Boston with a spell at Peterborough East from June to October 1937. After ten years at Immingham, No. 2532 went to Doncaster in October 1936, where it spent lengthy periods in store. In November 1940 it was moved to Gorton and in the following month to Walton-on-the-Hill. At this latter shed No. 2532 found regular employment at Huskisson Dock and outlived the remainder of the class by ten years, being withdrawn in January 1949.

Engine Diagrams

Not issued.	Engines with Diagram 71A domeless boilers.
Not issued.	Engine 2497 with Diagram 69 domed boiler.
Section D, 1924.	Engines with Diagram 71B domed boilers.

Classification: Route availability 5; B.R. power class 3F.

Summary of J75 Class

B.R. No.	1946 No.	1924 No.	N.E.R. No.	H. & B. No.	Maker	Works No.	Built	Rebuilt Domed Boiler		Withdrawn
								Diag. 69	Diag. 71B	
—	—	2492	3111	111	Yorkshire Engine Co.	655	12/1901	—	12/26	9/37
—	—	2493	3112	112	,,	656	12/1901	—	8/26	6/37
—	—	2494	3113	113	,,	657	12/1901	—	7/24	5/37
—	—	2495	3114	114	,,	658	1/1902	—	—	5/37
—	—	2496	3115	115	,,	659	2/1902	—	6/26	9/37
—	—	2497	3116	116	,,	660	2/1902	2/23	10/36	5/37
—	—	2523	3142	142	Kitson & Co.	4545	1/1908	—	8/27	6/38
—	—	2524	3143	143	,,	4546	1/1908	—	10/27	5/37
—	—	2525	3144	144	,,	4547	1/1908	—	2/28	6/37
—	—	2526	3145	145	,,	4548	2/1908	—	—	5/37
—	—	2527	3146	146	,,	4549	2/1908	—	9/24	9/37
—	—	2528	3147	147	,,	4550	2/1908	—	1/28	3/39
—	—	2529	3148	148	,,	4551	2/1908	—	2/28	7/37
—	—	2530	3149	149	,,	4552	2/1908	—	5/27	5/37
—	—	2531	3150	150	,,	4553	2/1908	—	5/27	6/37
(68365)	8365 5/46	2532	3151	151	,,	4554	3/1908	—	10/27	1/49

CLASS J76

N.E.R. CLASS 124—FLETCHER
4ft. 6in. and 4ft. 9in. ENGINES

ENGINES AT GROUPING (Built 1881-82): 124/71/93/7/8, 211, 598/9, 602, 1059. TOTAL 10.

The North Eastern Railway did not make extensive use of tank engines for either passenger or goods working in its early years, although examples for pilot and other light duties existed. It was not until 1864, ten years after the N.E.R. was formed, that tank engines were built on capital account. When eventually a number of tank classes had been introduced they were regarded as falling into three main groups, passenger, goods and shunting engines. Some notes on the first and last of these groups are given under class G6 (N.E.R. Bogie Tank Passenger) in Part 7 and class " 44 " (N.E.R. class " 44 " 0-6-0T) respectively. The engines of class J76 were the oldest survivors of those classes included under the general heading of goods engines, though in fact the duties of these engines were much more varied than the name suggests and many of the earlier engines included in this category had been built specifically for banking duties.

In 1863 two heavy tank engines were ordered to the designs of Edward Fletcher for banking duties on the Grosmont-Goathland deviation of the Whitby-Pickering line. A few years later four long-boiler 0-6-0 goods engines of 1866 were rebuilt to provide even more powerful banking engines. Then in 1875/82 four more were built at Gateshead for the Redheugh bank. All these banking engines were saddle tanks, and all except the last four were long-boilered.

Meanwhile on the Darlington Section four large long-boilered saddle tanks had been built in 1866 for the " zig-zag " lines at Skinningrove. They were not a success, doing little work in this form, and were rebuilt as tender engines. Later, in 1876 the works at Darlington produced a neat side tank goods engine design, discarding the long-boiler arrangement. Thus when further goods tank engines were to be built at Darlington in 1881 there were several existing designs from which the new class could have evolved.

The new class, however, followed none of these previous designs, but was developed instead from the already very successful 0-4-4 Bogie Tank Passenger (B.T.P. class; L.N.E.R. class G6) engines, even to the extent of having well tanks. With only six

rather than eight wheels, these new engines had a shorter bunker and well tank than was possible on the B.T.P. class, so that coal and water capacity was restricted. This proved to be a weak point in the design and extra tanks were added later which increased the usefulness of these engines.

Although classified as goods engines, some were fitted with Westinghouse brake and were used for passenger trains on short branches when required.

Two engines had been withdrawn by Grouping, No. 609 in July 1911 and No. 610 in May 1917, and the remainder were withdrawn between February 1926 and January 1929. No. 598 was sold and survived at Milford Haven until 1944.

Engine Nos.	Maker	No. built	Date
124/93, 602/9/10, 1059	Darlington	6	1881
171/97/8, 211, 598/9	,,	6	1881-82

Standard L.N.E.R. Dimensions at Grouping

Cylinders (2 inside)	$17'' \times 24''$
Motion	Stephenson with slide valves
Boiler:	
Max. diam. outside	4' 3"
Barrel length ...	10' 7"
Firebox length outside ...	4' 6"
Pitch	7' 4½"
Diagram No. ...	68
Heating surface:	
Firebox ...	84 sq. ft.
Tubes (205 × 1¾")	1025 sq. ft.
Total	1109 sq. ft.
Grate area	12.8 sq. ft.
Boiler pressure ...	160 lb./sq. in.
Coupled wheels ...	4' 9"*
Tractive effort (85%)	16,549 lb.
Length over buffers	30' 11"
Wheelbase ...	7' 8" + 8' 0" = 15' 8"
Weight (full) ...	44т 12c
Max. axle load ...	16т 6c
Water capacity ...	1280 gallons
Coal capacity ...	1т 7c

* Four engines had 4ft 6in. diameter wheels at the time of Grouping.

Rebuilding

The rebuilding of these engines, with saddle tanks in the case of No. 211, or with additional side tanks, did not necessarily involve any other alterations at the time. Indeed the North Eastern Engine Registers did not regard these as sufficiently significant changes for the dates to be recorded. The saddle tank put on No. 211 is said to have been added in 1897 at Darlington and it was also reported in this condition in 1904. All the engines which survived until Grouping had been rebuilt as side tank engines.

The original Fletcher boilers were similar to those fitted to the B.T.P. class being built at about the same time. No contemporary detail drawings have been traced, but the boilers appear to have been 10ft. 6in. long and 4ft. 2in. diameter with 175 tubes of two inches diameter. The tube heating surface was 1074 sq. ft. and firebox 84 sq. ft., the grate area 12.75 sq. ft. and the boiler pressure 140 lb. per sq. in.

Standard Worsdell boilers were fitted to all engines as follows:—

No.	Date	No.	Date
124	12/1896	598	2/1900
171	3/1899	599	4/1900
193	8/1896	602	11/1891
197	10/1897	609	3/1895
198	7/1899	610	7/1896
211	2/1892	1059	2/1893

The two engines which were withdrawn before Grouping, Nos. 609/10 (built July and August 1881 respectively), did not receive further boilers, but all the others were again reboilered between 1911 and 1920. Seven engines received new boilers, but three (Nos. 124, 211 and 602) were given second-hand boilers. That fitted to No. 602 in March 1911 had formerly been fitted to " 1001 " class 0-6-0 No. 1203 in February 1901, while in June 1914 No. 124 received a similar boiler which had first been put on " 1001 " class No. 1205 in March 1901 and transferred to B.T.P. class No. 255 in May 1906. Originally both these boilers had had longer barrels which were shortened for use on the B.T.P. or " 124 " classes. The second-hand boiler used on No. 211 in March 1912 had been put new on to B.T.P. class No. 949 in May 1906. The three engines, Nos. 124, 211 and 602, all received new boilers again in 1919-21.

When first built all the engines had wheels of 4ft. 6in. nominal diameter but between 1906 and 1911 seven, Nos. 124/93/7, 599, 602/9/10, are shown in the registers as altered to 4ft. 9in. wheels and No. 1059 was shown as altered in a new register printed in 1912. The L.N.E.R. diagram book of 1924 showed only the 4ft. 9in. engines on the diagram, but the index listed the engines in two groups without giving any explanation, namely Nos. 171/98, 211 and 598 together and then Nos. 124/93/7, 599, 602 and 1059. Allowing for Nos. 609/10 withdrawn in 1911 and 1917, which had both been altered to 4ft. 9in. wheels, these two groups were the 4ft. 6in. and 4ft. 9in. engines at Grouping.

Details

The frames of these engines were of the deep, slotted variety used by Fletcher down to 1882. They were curved down at the ends and fitted with angle brackets to take the vertical wooden planks used in connection with the chaldron wagons still in use on some of the colliery railways. So far as is known, none of these engines had the cut-away type frames fitted to the later engines of the B.T.P. class, but the change to underhung front springs was made on the later engines of this class (cf. figs. 35 and 36).

All the engines had deep valances to the running plate and substantial wooden sandwich bufferbeams. The buffers were originally of the large-diameter hollow shank type, but later some engines received new buffers with the solid type of spindle. Engines later fitted with Westinghouse brake received screw couplings in place of the normal three-link type.

Sandboxes of oblong section were provided ahead of the leading splasher and originally similar, but smaller ones, to the rear of the driving wheel splasher. When side tanks were added, the rear sandboxes were removed and the replacements were in some cases of a more modern design and placed under the bunker. (cf. figs. 35 and 36).

The bunkers were originally devoid of coal rails although two or three were added later and plated inside. As on class B.T.P., the outline of the tank inside the bunker could clearly be seen by the curved line of rivet heads on the bunker sides. The well part of the tank located at the rear between the frames brought the water capacity to 650 gallons. The addition of side tanks augmented this and gave a total of 1280 gallons.

The cab was originally without eaves to the door opening, but these were added later. The cab steps were of a characteristic shape being wide and set back just below the footplate. The leading step provided to give easy access to the motion was a single one on a waisted bracket, but this was moved forward when the side tanks were fitted, straight-sided brackets being used in some, if not all, cases.

The boilers fitted when the engines were first built had open domes with two spring-balance safety valves and a small brass valve cover over the firebox with two bell-type whistles mounted between this valve cover and the cab, whilst the smokebox originally had wingplates. All these engines ultimately acquired chimneys of the later N.E.R. pattern, though some had previously had the original replaced by an earlier Worsdell pattern which had a larger base diameter than those later fitted. Rebuilding with standard Worsdell boilers with closed domes and Ramsbottom valves necessitated the whistles being moved to the cab roof, whilst the new smokeboxes lacked any wingplates.

Brakes

Although nominally goods engines, some of this class did work passenger trains and were Westinghouse fitted. Nos. 124/71, 598/9 and 610 had been fitted by 1903 and Nos. 197/8 and 211 were fitted in 1908 with apparatus for the train only. The standard position for the pump was the front face of the left-hand side tank (fig. 36), but on at least No. 124 it was mounted on a separate vertical bracket in front of the right-hand tank (fig. 35). This mounting was reminiscent of the type used on B.T.P. engines. No. 197 also had the pump on the right-hand side, but the actual position is not known. From 1910 several of the engines with continuous brakes (e.g. Nos. 124/71/97, 599) were equipped with steam heating apparatus.

Allocation and Work

In N.E.R. days the allocation of these engines varied very little; for example in 1907 the class was spread amongst the sheds at Stockton, Ferryhill, Darlington, West Auckland, Heaton and Neville Hill. No. 124 was at Ferryhill in the early years of the century and typically worked two passenger trips each weekday over the branch to Coxhoe with as many goods trips as were required and could be fitted in. Over the first thirty years of its life it averaged almost 30,000 miles per year on work of this kind. The only alteration up to 1920 was the addition of one to Tyne Dock and a loss of one at West Auckland.

By June 1922 no fewer than five of the ten had moved to Hull, Nos. 193, 598, 602 and 1059 being at Dairycoates, where they were used in the extensive yards and docks,

whilst No. 171 became pilot at the former H. & B.R. shed at Alexandra Dock.

These transfers to Hull caused the class to disappear from Stockton, Tyne Dock and Darlington, although No. 171 did return to Darlington for the last nine months of its life. At Neville Hill Nos. 197/8 and 211 continued as shunters in Wellington Street goods yard, but in December 1925 No. 211 was despatched to Starbeck where it remained until withdrawn. Apart from a six-month period at Darlington in 1925, No. 124 spent most of its life working at Ferryhill.

In November 1925 the four Dairycoates engines were transferred to the Southern Area. This move resulted from the construction that year of the ten J72's at Doncaster which were sent to the N.E. Area, whereupon a like number of older N.E.R. 0-6-0T's were despatched to the Southern Area. Initial allocation of the four J76's was to New England, though Nos. 193 and 602 later worked at Boston whence both engines were sent back to the N.E. Area in 1928 and were scrapped shortly afterwards. Nos. 598 and 1059 also returned north for withdrawal from N.E. Area stock, the former being sold in November 1926.

Sales

No. 598 was withdrawn in November 1926 and was bought by G. Cohen & Sons, being despatched from Darlington to Milford Haven on 2nd April 1927. It was named *Ajax* by the Milford Dock Co. and scrapped in 1944.

Engine Diagram

Section D, 1924. Shows engines with 4ft. 9in. wheels only.

Summary of J76 Class

1923 No.	*Maker*	*Built*	*Withdrawn*
124	Darlington	8/1881	2/26
602	,,	8/1881	1/29
1059	,,	9/1881	3/27
193	,,	9/1881	10/28
197	,,	12/1881	12/27
198	,,	12/1881	1/28
599	,,	1/1882	6/26
598	,,	2/1882	11/26
171	,,	2/1882	10/27
211	,,	3/1882	7/28

CLASS J77

N.E.R. CLASS 290—FLETCHER/W. WORSDELL
4ft. 1¼in. ENGINES

ENGINES AT GROUPING (Built 1874-84, rebuilt 1899-1921): 15, 37, 43/7, 57, 71, 105/38/45/51/64/6/73/99, 276/90, 305/19/24/ 33/44/54, 597, 604/7/12/4/23, 948/53/4/6/8/ 98/9, 1000/21/33, 1115/6, 1313/40-4/6-9, 1430-3/5/8/9/60/1/2. TOTAL 60.

The J77 class engines were all rebuilds from the former North Eastern Bogie Tank Passenger class. Not all the engines of this 0-4-4 well tank class were rebuilt in this way, some being withdrawn unaltered, a number surviving long enough to become L.N.E.R. class G6 (see Part 7, pp. 99-103), and one was rebuilt as a 2-2-4T to become L.N.E.R. class X2. Details of the engines as built are given under class G6.

The B.T.P.'s were robust engines, but with the introduction of large numbers of class O (L.N.E.R. G5) 0-4-4T's in the period 1894-1901, some became surplus to requirements. The later additions to stock of the much larger engines of class W (see L.N.E.R. A6) and class D (see L.N.E.R. class H1 and A8) in 1907-8, 1913-14 and 1920-22 made further B.T.P. engines available for rebuilding.

The first forty were rebuilt at York Works between 1899 and 1904. After these works

were closed, the task of rebuilding further engines was carried out at Darlington, ten in 1907-8 and ten in 1921.

In addition to replacing the bogie with trailing coupled wheels and making the necessary alterations to the frames, new 17in. cylinders were fitted to any engines still having 16in. cylinders. The earlier rebuilds retained the original cab, but new side tanks were fitted and the bunker was reduced in size. The last ten rebuilds were given new cabs and bunkers in addition to new side tanks and this gave them a much more "Worsdell" appearance. However, all the engines retained the deep vertical valence to the running plate which was a characteristic of the original Fletcher design.

Withdrawal commenced in 1933 when there was insufficient work for them to do, but most survived until after nationalisation and the last one was not withdrawn until 1961. Many of the engines were very long-lived with No. 954 (68392) lasting for nearly eighty-six years, forty-six years as a passenger engine. By contrast No. 354 (68410) which had a life of over eighty-three years was a shunting engine for sixty years.

Date	Works	Engines Rebuilt
1899	York	47, 138, 290, 607/14, 1033 (6)
1900	,,	43,57, 151/73, 305/33/54, 998, 1000, 1460/2 (11)
1901	,,	71, 166, 276, 623, 1115/6, 1313, 1439 (8)
1902	,,	344, 948/99, 1341/6 (5)
1903	,,	958, 1343, 1435 (3)
1904	,,	105/45, 597, 612, 1021, 1430/8 (7)
1907	Darlington	37, 199, 1347/8/9, 1433/61 (7)
1908	,,	319, 953, 1344 (3)
1921	,,	15, 164, 324, 604, 954/6, 1340/2, 1431/2 (10)

N.E.R. and L.N.E.R. Renumbering

Five of the engines had been renumbered before being rebuilt to class "290". Nos. 37, 138/66/73/99 were Nos. 1465/75, 1469, 1467/8 respectively prior to February 1885 and at an even earlier date had in all probability carried other numbers (see Part 7 of this series at p. 100).

When the L.N.E.R. renumbering scheme was drawn up in 1943, Nos. 164/73, 333, 999,

1021, 1343, 1439/60 had already been withdrawn. The remaining fifty-two engines were allotted Nos. 8390-8441 in the order built, except for Nos. 1115 and 354 which were reversed. The numbers 8394, 8403/11/8/39 were not in fact used, the engines concerned being withdrawn before the scheme was put into effect in 1946, whilst No. 8419 only carried its new number for one month.

Standard L.N.E.R. Dimensions at Grouping

Cylinders (2 inside)	17″ × 22″
Motion	Stephenson with slide valves
Boiler:	
Max. diam. outside	4′ 3″
Barrel length ...	10′ 7″
Firebox length outside ...	4′ 6″
Pitch	6′ 9⅜″
Diagram No. ...	68
Heating surface:	
Firebox ...	84 sq. ft.
Tubes (205 × 1¾″)	1025 sq. ft.
Total	1109 sq. ft.
Grate area ...	12.8 sq. ft.
Boiler pressure ...	160 lb./sq. in.
Coupled wheels ...	4′ 1¼″
Tractive effort (85%)	17,560 lb.
Length over buffers	29′ 9¼″
Wheelbase ...	7′ 8″ + 8′ 6″ = 16′ 2″
Weight (full) ...	43т 0c
Max. axle load ...	14т 16c
Water capacity ...	700 gallons
Coal capacity ...	2т 5c

The L.N.E.R. engine diagram related to the 1921 rebuilds. The earlier rebuilds had a shorter rear overhang and were lighter. The details taken from the N.E.R. diagrams for these engines were:

Length over buffers ...	29′ 3¼″
Weight (full)	41т 15c
Max. axle load	14т 1c

The water capacity was 700 gallons, but the amount of coal that could be carried was not given and may have been less than 2 tons 5 cwt.

Rebuilding

Before being rebuilt to class " 290 " many of these engines had already undergone some degree of reconstruction. In July 1882 a new iron boiler was fitted to No. 1349 and a similar one to No. 1343 in May 1886. After this all new replacement boilers fitted were constructed from steel plate and were of standard Worsdell pattern. Almost all the engines had received these new steel boilers before they were rebuilt as shunting engines, but Nos. 138, 290, 1343 had them fitted when rebuilding to " 290 " class took place. The fitting of Worsdell boilers meant that many Fletcher features disappeared as new smokeboxes and boiler mountings were also fitted at the same time. However, the original style cab was retained on those engines rebuilt between 1899 and 1908, but those converted in 1921 received new cabs of Worsdell pattern (cf. figs. 37 and 39).

The earliest engines built were fitted with 16in. cylinders and many of these had already been rebuilt with new 17in. cylinders before rebuilding to 0-6-0T took place and any still retaining 16in. cylinders when reconstructed received new 17in. cylinders at that time.

Individual rebuilding dates from B.T.P. to " 290 " class are given in the Summary, but dates of the fitting of Worsdell boilers and 17in. cylinders will be found in the following table.

No.	Worsdell Boiler	17″ cyls.	No.	Worsdell Boiler	17″ cyls.
15	3/94	11/98	954	8/92	12/87
37	11/91	6/95	956	4/91	4/91
43	10/93	2/00†	958	10/89	10/89
47	9/93	10/99†	998	11/94	3/00†
57	12/93	11/00†	999	5/95	*
71	7/92	8/96	1000	11/97	*
105	3/93	8/04†	1021	8/93	12/04†
138	9/99†	*	1033	3/92	10/99†
145	3/92	10/04†	1115	6/91	12/01†
151	6/93	*	1116	11/95	3/01†
164	1/94	1/94	1313	4/97	*
166	4/97	*	1340	6/91	1/98
173	12/91	7/97	1341	8/92	1/02
199	12/91	*	1342	10/92	10/86
276	8/94	8/94	1343	12/03†	11/94
290	6/99†	*	1344	10/92	10/92
305	12/96	*	1346	9/89	9/89
319	6/91	5/95	1347	11/94	12/97
324	5/92	8/04	1348	5/89	4/94
333	4/92	2/97	1349	4/95	4/89
344	11/88	6/02	1430	3/91	6/87
354	3/92	10/98	1431	6/92	6/92
597	3/95	9/04†	1432	10/90	10/90
604	12/92	*	1433	7/90	7/90
607	8/94	12/99†	1435	5/88	5/97
612	10/93	12/04†	1438	9/92	10/90
614	2/89	9/96	1439	1/90	4/87
623	2/93	*	1460	12/95	5/00†
948	5/91	3/87	1461	12/92	*
953	7/88	8/92	1462	12/95	*

† Worsdell boiler or 17in. cylinders first fitted when rebuilt to " 290 " class.

* These engines had 17in. cylinders when built.

From about 1908 a number of boilers which were still quite young and in good condition, having been built between 1897 and 1904 for long-boilered goods engines of classes " 93 ", " 120 " and " 1001 ", became surplus to requirements and were shortened so as to be suitable for B.T.P. (G6), " 190 " (X3), " 290 " (J77) and " 124 " (J76) class engines. No. 956 received such a boiler while still class B.T.P., but was given a normal boiler when rebuilt to " 290 " class in 1921. In the case of Nos. 37, 166, 276, 354, 607/12/4, 998, 1021, 1313, shortened boilers were fitted but had been replaced by Grouping, whereas Nos. 199 and 1116 carried them after Grouping, receiving standard boilers in December 1924 and July 1930 respectively. These boilers could be readily identified because the shortening had been carried out at the smokebox end and the dome was therefore further forward on the shortened barrel than was normal.

After the rebuilding to class "290" was carried out, no further significant alteration took place. No new boilers were built for some years after Grouping as withdrawal of the B.T.P. engines provided sufficient spares. The boiler design was altered in 1937 to incorporate a single-plate barrel with a plate thickness of $\frac{9}{16}$in. rather than $\frac{1}{2}$in. with the butt-jointed type. Boilers to this pattern, which were easily identified because the dome was 1ft. 9$\frac{1}{4}$in. further back (fig. 42), were built from 1939 (first fitted March 1940) until there was a total of forty by November 1945. Altogether forty-six engines carried the new pattern of boiler at one time or another (see Summary), some reverting to the original type. Of the engines withdrawn with B.R. numbers, 68398, 68417/28/36 ended their days with the old pattern, the remainder having the single-plate type. Unlike most of the other redesigned N.E.R. boilers, the Diagram 68 pattern was not given a separate classification (e.g. 68A).

Details

The detail variations of these engines prior to rebuilding from 0-4-4T to 0-6-0T are referred to in Part 7 under class G6. Some of these variations of detail had already disappeared before their conversion to shunting engines and others went in the process of rebuilding. Nevertheless many remained and more were in fact introduced in the reconstruction.

There were originally two main types of frames used. The majority of the engines as first built had deep frames between the coupled wheels with oval cut-outs at either side of the point where the motion plate was fixed to the frames (in a few cases only the rear slot was cut). A few of the last engines to be built had shallow frames without slots. The rear section of the frames was shallow in all cases. On rebuilding, the front part was retained and a new rear portion of shallow construction was provided to take the rear coupled wheels. The engines rebuilt in 1921, which received the Worsdell pattern cabs and bunkers, had frames six inches longer than those which retained the Fletcher type cab and bunker (fig. 39). Those engines which on rebuilding had the shallow frames throughout (Nos. 138, 290 and 305) also had the springs for the leading wheels below the axle (fig. 38). Because as rebuilt the wheels were smaller in diameter than before, the running plate and footplate were raised relative to the frames and a small arc was cut out of the front of the frame below the bufferbeam. The height of the buffers was also changed from the lowest to the highest possible position on the bufferbeam. The overall effect of these changes and the deep valence to the running plate was to give the "290" class engines a somewhat squat appearance.

The B.T.P. design included wooden bufferbeams at the front and rear, but on rebuilding to shunting engines these were changed to the steel plate type. In many cases the front bufferbeam was later altered by the addition of a wooden sandwich mounted in front of the steel plate (fig. 42), but not all engines received this modification. One which did, No. 68410, ran for some time with the front beam wrong way up so that the buffers were set low.

The buffers of the original design had been of the square-based, hollow-stemmed Fletcher type, but so far as is known all rebuilds had the Worsdell tapered shank type or hollow stemmed type having a circular base. In some cases circular pads were later fitted behind the base plates and some engines received L.N.E.R. Group Standard buffers, but only in B.R. days, No. 68423 being the first recorded, in September 1948. So far as is known, it was only engines with the vacuum brake which received G.S. buffers.

The cab footsteps of the B.T.P. class engines (which were one of the characteristic parts of this design) were replaced by new steps of a standard pattern. There were several variations of the single front steps (figs. 37, 41 and 42), the 1921 rebuilds apparently having new ones designed to conform to the cab steps (fig. 39). The earlier rebuilds had either the original steps, or a cut-down version, mounted in line with the vertical part of the running plate. One engine only, No. 1344, is known to have had the steps set back as on class J76.

The engines rebuilt in 1921 differed from the remainder of the class in that they received new cabs of the Worsdell type whereas all the others retained either the typical Fletcher outline, or in the case of Nos. 290 and 305 (which had been built at York) their special style of cab (fig. 38). The engines rebuilt from the original Neilson series, Nos. 947-58, lost the characteristic shape of the cab, being altered to conform to the more usual Fletcher outline. The cab opening was altered so that it extended neither as far forward nor as far down (compare fig. 40 with fig. 180 in Part 7). One of these engines, No. 958, also had the round spectacle windows of that batch changed to the square Fletcher type, but at the front only. The remaining engines rebuilt between 1899 and 1908 had the cab opening altered to a somewhat lesser degree to maintain the line of the top of the side tanks. Finally, of the engines rebuilt in 1907-8, Nos. 199, 319, 1344/8 received round spectacle windows in place of their original square pattern. (No. 953 also had round spectacles, but this was one of the Neilson batch, which were so constructed).

One further variation to be noted in the cabs of the earlier rebuilds was that at first the gutter over the cab opening curved slightly round at the front and rear of the opening and, except when the engine was at rest, any rain water on the windward quarter probably blew straight back into the cab (fig. 37). In L.N.E.R. days many engines had the gutter extended forward about half way to the front edge of the cab (fig. 41) and the majority of these also had a similar extension to the back edge of the cab (fig. 40). An odd one out was No. 68406 (ex-No. 1433) which had an extended gutter fitted above the older one.

The bunkers were fitted with two rails in the earlier rebuilds and they were plated behind before Grouping, some engines having an additional rail added. The 1921 rebuilds always had three rails with plating behind them. Some of the engines had a single footstep added to the back of the bunker.

A variety of whistle combinations were to be found. The organ, large and small bell types were all used and combinations noted are one organ, one bell, one organ and one bell, one large and one small bell. Some engines which had the organ type changed later to bell whistles.

The three alternative positions of the dome already referred to were sufficiently distinctive to show which J77 class engines had modified " 1001 " class boilers, normal three-plate barrels or the later single-plate barrel.

In North Eastern days all the boilers had Ramsbottom safety valves and these were still carried by most engines during the early L.N.E.R. period. From the mid-1930's pop valves appeared (fig. 42), sometimes with a cover round their base. Because escaping steam impaired visibility, the shapely casing formerly used with the Ramsbottom valves was generally refitted.

Three further small changes of boiler fittings which took place were the positioning of the clack valves, at first on the middle of the front boiler ring, then moved slightly to the rear and then finally disappeared from sight when combination injectors were fitted on the backplate. In many cases the boiler hand-rail was removed at the cab end in later years and some engines had the wheel and handle smokebox door fitting at first, whereas latterly all had the two handle type of fastening.

Unlike some of the rebuilds of Fletcher engines carried out in the Worsdell/Raven period, the " 290 " class had the characteristic Fletcher oblong sandboxes mounted at the side of the smokebox, the only exceptions being Nos. 138, 290 and 305. These three engines, which had shallow frames and underhung springs to the leading wheels, were fitted with integral leading wheel splashers and sandboxes (fig. 38). Even the Neilson series of B.T.P. engines, which originally had combined splashers and sandboxes, lost these on rebuilding to class " 290 " (cf. fig. 40 and fig. 180 in Part 7).

No. 956, based at Shildon, carried shunting poles (see p. 13) until late 1933, when they were removed.

Brakes

Before rebuilding, all the B.T.P. engines had Westinghouse brake, the pump being mounted on a vertical plate on the right-hand side slightly in front of the cab. On rebuilding, the Westinghouse was removed and only steam brake fitted except in the case of Nos. 37 and 1347 rebuilt at Darlington in April and May 1907 respectively. These engines either retained the Westinghouse brake, or had it refitted almost immediately, using the same form of mounting placed in front of the right-hand side tank and not mounted on the leading edge of the tank (fig. 41). These brakes were removed in December 1938 and June 1940 respectively. From 1945 twelve of the engines (see Summary) were fitted with vacuum brake and these could be easily identified by the conspicuous pipe along the right-hand side from cab to smokebox, and below the footplate (fig. 43).

Most of these vacuum-fitted engines also received carriage heating equipment, but No. E8433 did not. In the case of Nos. 8412/20 this was not fitted until some years after the vacuum brake was added, but the remainder either received both together or had the heating equipment added shortly afterwards. The pipework for the steam heating was below the left-hand footplate valance and was noticeably lagged.

British Railways

Forty-six J77's entered B.R. stock on 1st January 1948 and of these, Nos. 8390/6, 8400/4/15/6/33/41 were withdrawn without receiving 60,000 series numbers, although Nos. 8404/33 were given an E prefix to their numbers and carried " BRITISH RAILWAYS " on their side tanks.

Allocation and Work

To enginemen and enthusiasts alike the " 290 " class engines were always firm favourites and embodied in no small measure the Fletcher quality of rugged durability.

At Grouping the sixty engines were scattered throughout the length and breadth of the N.E.R. system, examples being at no less than twenty-one sheds, the largest allocation, seven, being at Dairycoates. As well as acting as general shunters, they marshalled mineral trains in and around the principal coal exporting harbours and also propelled rakes of wagons over dock lines to coal hoists and high level shipping staiths. Thus the sheds at the ports of Middlesbrough, North and South Blyth, Hull, Stockton, the Hartlepools and the Teesside assembly point of Newport accounted for no fewer than thirty-four of them, while the busy centres of Tyne Dock, Percy Main and Sunderland only supported token examples which they were soon to lose and never regain. The J77's were also employed in the main line marshalling yards. In 1923 two were based at the essentially Midland outpost of Normanton, where for many years the N.E.R. kept several engines for working in the Altofts reception sidings sorting wagons destined to travel on to N.E.R. metals via Castleford to York. One of the pair, No. 998, remained there until 1935, when it was replaced by a J71.

Up to the end of 1935 only seven J77's had been withdrawn, and the general pattern of allocation and duties remained much the same as that which obtained some twelve years earlier. The York contingent had, however, risen to nine at the expense of odd representatives at Shildon, Thirsk and Blaydon. At this time No. 604 had found a new home at Northallerton and more surprisingly No. 623 was based at the passenger shed of Botanic Gardens in Hull, this shed being adjacent to several small yards in the Stepney area where No. 623 was daily employed. It eventually departed for Tweedmouth in 1939. Nos. 37 and 1347 at Tweedmouth were fitted with Westinghouse brake so that in emergency they could work the Kelso line passenger train forward from Tweedmouth (where a reversal was necessary) to Berwick. Some of the Kelso trains terminated at Tweedmouth, passengers for Berwick normally proceeding thence by a connecting train on the main line. If this connection was not made, the Tweedmouth pilot would be called upon to work the Kelso branch train over the Royal Border Bridge to Berwick.

As with many other N.E.R. freight classes, several J77's were sent to the Southern Area of the L.N.E.R. The first to go was No. 1313 which was at Ardsley from October 1925 to March 1926. In November 1925 No. 1439 was sent to Doncaster, but moved to Immingham later the same month. Then in January, 1931 three more were moved to the Southern Area, No. 614 to Ardsley and Nos.

948 and 1349 to New England. Allocation of J77's to the latter shed was of short duration and No. 948 soon moved to Grantham and No. 1349 joined No. 614 at Ardsley. The Grantham engine returned to the N.E. Area in December 1932. The pair at Ardsley were found to be suitable for work on the East & West Yorkshire Union lines, although No. 1349 was sent back to the N.E. Area in July 1932. No. 614 continued alone at Ardsley until February 1935 when it too was returned north, its place being taken by No. 1439 (which had been at Immingham for nearly ten years) and this engine stayed at Ardsley until it was withdrawn in June 1939.

Just prior to the 1939 War, all those at Dairycoates were transferred to Alexandra Dock, where they stood out in the open. They did however visit Springhead for servicing. Although the War saw considerable changes in the deployment of whole classes of N.E.R. engines, the J77's were unaffected, and many remained at the same sheds for several decades. Thus one could always expect to find Nos. 43, 344 and 1115 at Middlesbrough, 138, 290, 1000, 1348/9 at York, and 71 and 1462 at Neville Hill.

Despite a big drop in coal shipments, the class worked hard throughout the War and the cessation of hostilities found forty-seven still at work, spread over twelve sheds. This contraction in the number of depots to which they were allocated saw the disappearance of the class from West Hartlepool, whilst the odd examples at Gateshead and Sunderland were transferred to Blaydon, although even the allocation of J77's at that shed soon vanished. The single representative at Darlington gained four companions. The numbers at York and Alexandra Dock remained static at seven each, but in 1946 York surrendered several to Starbeck and one to Heaton, whilst over the next few years three of them went to Selby for use on marshalling of trains in the two yards at Gascoigne Wood. Withdrawals continued to occur, but no fewer than thirty-two were doing yeoman service at the close of 1954, with strong contingents still at Alexandra Dock, Teesside and Blyth.

Coal shipping staiths have long been a familiar feature at many of the North-East coast ports, perhaps the most famous being the North, West and New Staiths at the busy coal exporting harbour of Blyth. The J77's were well nigh inseperable from these staiths, first preparing rakes of laden coal trucks on the level, and then at frequent intervals and with abounding energy and ear-shattering exhaust they would accelerate full out, either singly or in pairs, up the fearsome man-made gradient, propelling as much as 550 tons. Having attained the summit of one of these

Fig. 37   Class J77 No. 276 at Starbeck, July 1932.

Leading springs above footplating, Fletcher cab with square windows and
short rain strip above opening, steel plate front bufferbeam, two
coal rails, oblong front sandboxes, deep front footstep.

Fig. 38   Class J77 No. 305 at Middlesbrough shed.

Leading springs underslung, front sandbox and splasher combined,
York style cab.

Fig. 39   Class J77 No. 1432 in store.

1921 rebuild (with Worsdell type cab, longer bunker and wider front
footstep), three coal rails.

Fig. 40   Class J77 No. 953 at East Hartlepool shed,
April 1939.

Neilson-built engine with circular cab windows, rainstrip on cab
roof extended at both ends.

Fig. 41   Class J77 No. 1347.

Westinghouse brake, waisted front footstep, cab rainstrip extended at
front only.

Fig. 42   Class J77 No. 8417 at Darlington, August 1947.

Boiler with single-plate barrel (dome further back), Ross pop safety
valves, sandwich type front bufferbeam, short front footstep.

Fig. 43   Class J77 No. 8433 at Selby, April 1950.
Vacuum ejector.

Fig. 44   Class J78 N.E.R. No. 590 at Springhead,
July 1924.
50-cwt. capacity crane, additional dumb buffers, front footstep fitted,
Wilson cushion tyres to wheels.

Fig. 45   Class J78 N.E.R. No. 995 at Gateshead,
November 1924.
3-ton capacity crane.

Fig. 46 Class J78 No. 590 at York, about 1928.

With normal wheels.

Fig. 47 Class J79 No. 407 at Middlesbrough shed.

Large tanks, hopper shaped sandboxes.

Fig. 48 Class J79 No. 1787 at Middlesbrough shed.

Small tanks, smaller sandboxes.

Fig. 49   Class J80 H. & B.R. No. 68 (L.N.E.R. 2449).

Domeless boiler with uncased Ramsbottom safety valves, single bell
whistle, buffers with parallel shanks.

Fig. 50   Class J80 No. 2449, about 1924.

N.E.R. "901" class boiler with clack boxes on side of barrel and with
uncased Ramsbottom safety valves, buffers with tapered shanks,
re-railing jack retained.

Fig. 51   Class J80 No. 2448 at Immingham, April 1926.

Diagram 71B domed boiler with Ross pop safety valves, twin whistles.

Fig. 52   Class J81 N.B.R. No. 1216 at Parkhead shed, 1923.
Storm sheet attached to front weatherboard.

Fig. 53   Class J82 N.B.R. No. 1328 at Parkhead shed, 1923.
Dual-fitted, three coal rails.

Fig. 54   Class J82 No. 10330 at Perth shed, about 1924.
Westinghouse brake.

ponderous, lengthy, baulk-timber edifices, they pushed the trucks along the high level decking to the appropriate chutes for the coal to be loaded into the holds of the collier berthed beneath, prior to easing the empties back off the staiths to the assembly sidings at ground level. For several decades the successful operation of these staiths was dependent on the excellent power/weight ratio of the J77's and their ruggedness and capability certainly extended the lives of those based at North and South Blyth, where they continued to perform this slogging repetition until well into 1959, their duties then being taken over by diesels. The handful of survivors then spent their last months at York, Hull and West Hartlepool, except for No. 68408 (old 1438) which was retained as a reserve at South Blyth until February 1961 and was the last J77 to be withdrawn.

Sales

After No. 8396 was withdrawn in April 1950 it was sold to the Ministry of Fuel and Power and used at Crofton Mill Screens until they closed in 1951 when it was transferred to the Swalwell Screens. It was scrapped in 1955.

No. 8416, withdrawn at the same time as No. 8396, also went to the M.O.F.P. and worked at the Broomhill Opencast Screens.

It was sent to Messrs. Bagnalls of Stafford for repairs in November 1951 and afterwards went in May 1952 to Skiers Spring Screens, Wentworth, Yorkshire. In 1954 it went to Watnall Opencast site, Nottingham and then in May 1955 to the Upper Blaenavon Opencast (Deakin's Slope) site, only to move to Gwaun-cae-Gurwen Opencast site in June 1957 before returning later the same year to Upper Blaenavon. Further repairs were carried out by Adams of Newport in May 1958 after which it worked at Tirpentwys Site, Abersychan until at least the middle of 1960. It was scrapped about 1960-61.

Engine Diagrams

Section D, 1924. Shows Darlington 1921 rebuild type only. Trailing overhang given as 6′ 11$\frac{3}{8}$″ corrected in December 1924 to 6′ 11$\frac{5}{8}$″.

Section D, 1939. Darlington 1921 rebuilds, showing the single plate barrel with the dome further to the rear. Details of boilers before and after 1937 given.

N.B. Both drawings were incorrect in that they implied that the motion plate (between the two frame slots) was 6ins. nearer to the middle axle than was the actual case.

Classification: Southern Area load class 3; Route availability 2; B.R. power class 2F.

Summary of J77 Class

B.R. No.	1946 No.	1923 No.	Maker	Works No.	Built	Rebuilt J77	Brake at Gpg.	Later alterations	Boiler with Single Plate Barrel	Withdrawn
(68390)	8390 8/46	948	Neilson & Co.	1830	4/1874	York 10/02	S	—	5/43-Wdl.	9/48
68391 5/48	8391 6/46	953	"	1835	8/1874	Darlington 9/08	"	—	11/44-Wdl.	7/57
68392 5/48	8392 3/46	954	"	1836	8/1874	" 2/21	"	—	3/46-Wdl.	5/60
68393 8/48	8393 6/46	956	"	1838	8/1874	" 3/21	"	+ VE 8/48	1/46-8/48, 10/51-Wdl.	5/55
	(8394)	958	Hawthorn & Co.	1840	8/1874	York 8/03	"	—	—	9/44
68395 10/48	8395 6/46	1340	"	1644	5/1875	Darlington 4/21	"	+ VE 10/48	10/48-Wdl.	6/56
(68396)	8396 4/46	1341	"	1645	5/1875	York 1/02	"	—	6/43-Wdl.	4/50
68397 6/51	8397 6/46	1342	"	1646	5/1875	Darlington 5/21	"	—	2/43-Wdl.	1/58
		1343	"	1647	5/1875	York 12/03	"	—	—	4/34
68398 9/49	8398 7/46	1344	"	1648	6/1875	York 7/08	"	—	9/43-9/49	1/53
68399 9/48	8399 6/46	1346	"	1650	6/1875	York 3/02	"	—	5/43-Wdl.	4/58
68400 (8400)	8400 5/46	1347	"	1651	6/1875	Darlington 5/07	W	S 6/40	11/42-Wdl.	10/48
68401 9/48	8401 6/46	1348	"	1652	6/1875	" 10/07	S	+ VE 9/48	7/43-Wdl.	7/54
68402 12/50	8402 6/46	1349	"	1653	6/1875	" 4/07	"	—	6/43-Wdl.	5/58
	(8403)	1430	"	1677	9/1875	" 3/04	"	—	—	3/44
68404	8404 6/46	1431	"	1678	9/1875	York 6/21	"	—	1/45-Wdl.	4/51
68405 5/52	8405 7/46	1432	"	1679	9/1875	Darlington 2/21	"	+ VE 1/48	2/45-Wdl.	12/58
68406 4/48	8406 7/46	1433	"	1680	9/1875	" 3/07	"	+ VE 1/50	12/44-Wdl.	11/59
68407 1/50	8407 6/46	1435	"	1682	10/1875	York 10/03	"	—	1/44-5/47, 1/50-Wdl.	2/56
68408 9/49	8408 6/46	1438	"	1685	11/1875	" -7/04*	"	—	9/45-Wdl.	2/61
		1439	"	1686	11/1875	" 7/01	"	—	—	4/39
68409 4/49	8409 1/46	1115	Darlington	—	6/1877	" 12/01	"	—	9/46-Wdl.	11/59
68410 12/49	8410 6/46	354	Gateshead	—	5/1877	" 4/00	"	—	12/49-Wdl.	10/60
	(8411)	1033	Darlington	—	6/1877	" 10/99	"	—	—	11/45
68412 1/49	8412 6/46	15	Gateshead	—	7/1877	Darlington 3/21	"	+ VE 11/45	9/43-Wdl., 12/44-11/47, 10/50-Wdl.	2/57
68413 10/50	8413 7/46	614	"	—	7/1877	" 6/99	"	—	12/44-11/47	5/54
68414 3/49	8414 6/46	43	"	—	7/1877	" 2/00	"	—	10/46-Wdl.	12/58
(68415)	8415 6/46	47	"	—	10/1877	" 10/99	"	—	12/46-Wdl.	10/49
(68416)	8416 6/46	71	"	—	11/1877	" 9/01	"	—	6/42-Wdl.	4/50
68417 2/51	8417 6/46	607	"	—	1/1878	Darlington 12/99	"	—	11/43-2/51	9/56
		164	"	—	1/1878	York 6/21	"	—	—	9/33
	(8418)	998	Darlington	—	3/1878	" 3/00	"	—	3/43-Wdl.	6/44
68419 7/46	8419 7/46	145	Gateshead	—	3/1878	Darlington 10/04	"	—	4/40-7/44	8/46
68420 12/49	8420 6/46	324	Darlington	—	4/1878	" 5/21	"	+ VE 11/45	3/47-Wdl.	4/55
		1021	Gateshead	—	4/1878	York 12/04	"	—	—	4/33
		1460	"	—	5/1878	" 5/00	"	—	—	11/33
68421 1/50	8421 3/46	276	"	—	7/1878	" 10/01	"	—	3/46-Wdl.	5/54
		333	"	—	8/1878	" 12/00	"	—	—	4/33
68422 3/49	8422 4/46	105	Darlington	—	8/1878	" 8/04	"	+ VE 7/48	9/46-Wdl.	6/54
68423 7/48	8423 6/46	344	Gateshead	—	10/1878	" 6/02	"	S 12/38	5/43-Wdl.	11/57
68424 9/48	8424 7/46	37	"	—	3/1879	Darlington 4/07	W	—	10/45-Wdl.	6/58

48

Summary of J77 Class (continued)

B.R. No.	1946 No.	1923 No.	Maker	Works No.	Built	Rebuilt J77	Brake at Gpg.	Later alterations	Boiler with Single Plate Barrel	Withdrawn
68425 3/49	8425 6/46	612	Darlington	—	4/1879	York 12/04	S	—	3/49-Wdl.	1/60
68426 11/48	8426 1/46	1116	"	—	6/1879	" 3/01	"	—	11/42-Wdl.	8/57
68427 4/48	8427 4/46	597	"	—	6/1879	" 9/04	"	—	7/42-Wdl.	1/58
		173	Gateshead	—	6/1879	Darlington 9/00	"	—	—	3/35
68428 7/50	8428 7/46	319	"	—	6/1879	" 8/08	"	—	4/44-7/50	2/55
68429 3/50	8429 7/46	199	"	—	7/1879	York 10/07	"	—	7/41-Wdl.	1/56
68430 4/49	8430 8/46	57	"	—	12/1879	" 11/00	"	+ VE 6/47	3/40-Wdl.	6/56
68431 8/50	8431 6/46	151	"	—	12/1879	Darlington 12/00	"	—	10/43-1/47, 8/50-Wdl.	2/60
68432 3/49	8432 6/46	604	"	—	5/1880	York 3/21	"	+ VE 3/49	11/45-Wdl.	5/55
		999	"	—	6/1880	" 9/02	"	—	—	5/33
(68433)	8433 2/46	1000	"	—	7/1880	" 10/00	"	+ VE 1/48	1/45-Wdl.	5/51
68434 7/48	8434 3/46	1313	"	—	8/1880	Darlington 4/01	"	+ VE 7/48	11/45-Wdl.	1/57
68435 9/50	8435 7/46	1461	"	—	10/1880	" 3/07	"	—	11/47-Wdl.	10/58
68436 12/48	8436 6/46	1462	Darlington	—	11/1880	York 7/00	"	—	11/43-12/48	6/56
68437 10/48	8437 7/46	623	Gateshead	—	6/1882	" 6/01	"	—	1/46-Wdl.	1/56
68438 12/51	8438 6/46	166	York	—	7/1882	" 2/01	"	—	4/40-Wdl.	2/58
	(8439)	138	"	—	12/1884	" 9/99	"	—	—	9/44
68440 2/50	8440 6/46	290	"	—	12/1884	" 6/99	"	—	7/41-Wdl.	8/54
(68441)	8441 6/46	305	"	—	12/1884	" 7/00	"	—	—	6/48

* No. 1438 was rebuilt to 0-6-0T during the first six months of 1904.

CLASS J78

N.E.R. CLASS HI—T. W. WORSDELL
3ft. 6¼in. CRANE ENGINES

Engines Transferred from Service Stock to Running Stock, August 1926 (Built 1888): 590, 995. Total 2.

These two crane tanks were built by the N.E.R. in 1888 at Gateshead for use at that Works. From the front buffers to the middle axle, the engine portion was identical with the contemporary class H (L.N.E.R. Y7) 0-4-0T's, but the rear end was altered to take an additional coupled axle to provide a stable base for a 3 ton capacity steam-driven crane with friction drive. The domeless boiler was standard with the 0-4-0T's.

Until August 1926 both engines were regarded as being in Service Stock, but were then transferred and recorded subsequently in Running Stock totals. No. 995 was sold in 1933, whilst No. 590 was withdrawn and cut up in 1937.

Standard L.N.E.R. Dimensions at Grouping

Cylinders (2 inside)	No. 590	13″ × 20″
	No. 995	14″ × 20″
Motion	Joy with slide valves	
Boiler:		
Max. diam.		
outside ...	3′ 8″	
Barrel length...	6′ 8½″	
Firebox length		
outside ...	4′ 4″	
Pitch	6′ 9″	
Diagram No. ...	74	
Heating surface:		
Firebox ...	57 sq. ft.	
Tubes		
(139 × 1¾″)	448 sq. ft.	
Total	505 sq. ft.	
Grate area ...	11.3 sq. ft.	
Boiler pressure ...	140 lb./sq. in.	
Coupled wheels...	3′ 6¼″	
Tractive effort		
(85%) ...	No. 590	9,520 lb.
	No. 995	11,041 lb.
Length over		
buffers ...	23′ 5¼″	
Wheelbase ...	6′ 0″ + 4′ 0″ = 10′ 0″	
Weight (full) ...	26т 11c	
Max. axle load ...	10т 15c	
Water capacity...	500 gallons	
Coal capacity ...	6¼ cwt.	

Details

When built, both engines had 13in. diameter cylinders, but in April 1898 No. 995 was given a set of 14in. cylinders of the type fitted to later engines of the H class 0-4-0T's.

As built, only a low weatherboard was provided, but long before Grouping both engines had been fitted with half-cabs of similar style to the front portions of those on the H class.

The original Gateshead drawing for class H1 showed the length over buffers to be 23ft. 2¼in. A change in thickness of the buffing plates later increased this figure by ½in., whilst longer buffers subsequently brought the overall length up to 23ft. 5¼in.

The cranes on both engines originally had the same radius of 10ft. 6in. and lifting capacity of 3 tons, but before Grouping the jib on No. 590 had been extended to give a working radius of 12ft. and the maximum lift was correspondingly reduced to 50 cwts. (figs. 44 and 45). These weight limits were clearly stated on the arm of each crane. The two cranes also differed in that No. 995 had been changed in 1904 from a chain with a cylindrical weight to a wire rope with spherical bob-weight. No. 590 retained a chain and this was fitted with a pair of cylindrical weights. During the L.N.E.R. period little, if any, use appears to have been made of the cranes.

In N.E.R. days both engines had wheels with nine spokes which included what were known as Wilson cushion tyres. These consisted of hardwood blocks fitted between the wheel centre and a normal tyre, giving the appearance of abnormally thick wheel rims (fig. 44). Conventional wheels, having ten spokes, were fitted to No. 995 before Grouping and to No. 590 in November 1926 (fig. 46).

The original boilers were built by York Works, although the engines were constructed at Gateshead, the boilers being similar to those currently being put into the class H dock shunters. These first boilers lasted until October 1910 on No. 590 and to July 1911 on No. 995. The latter was then fitted with a newly-built Gateshead boiler which it continued to carry until withdrawn from service in June 1933. The replacement boiler on No. 590 had been in stock, unused, for eight years, being one of a batch of spares built at Gateshead in 1902. It served more than twenty years on No. 590 until condemned in January 1932. The replacement on this occasion was a boiler Darlington had built in 1923 and used on Y7 class No. 129, this engine being scrapped in November 1931. No. 590 then carried this boiler until withdrawal in April 1937, and held the unusual record of its boilers having been built, in order of fitting, by York, Gateshead and Darlington. All the five boilers used on class J78 were equipped with Ramsbottom safety valves enclosed in shapely brass covers, and the L.N.E.R. engine diagram was in error in depicting Ross pop valves.

The smokebox door on both engines was originally fastened by twin handles. No. 590, however, later had the wheel and handle arrangement, but from January 1932 lost the handwheel and again had two handles.

Both engines only carried a single whistle, mounted above the cab roof. At first this was of the bell type, but was changed to the organ pipe variety before Grouping.

Throughout their L.N.E.R. days this pair of engines presented other differences of detail apart from their cranes already mentioned. No. 590 carried additional footsteps just ahead of the leading axle, these having only a single step; No. 995 had no steps other than those to the cab. Similarly, No. 590 at its front end carried a pair of substantial dumb buffers between its ordinary buffers and the drawhook (fig. 44), but No. 995 was not so equipped. On the other hand No. 995 carried a tallow cup on each side of its smokebox waist for lubricating valves and cylinders and No. 590 was never so fitted, its cylinder lubrication being from oil boxes mounted on the rear of the smokebox base.

For some time after Grouping the cast-brass N.E.R. number plates were retained. Unlike the J79 and Y7 classes, there was sufficient room for these on the bunker sides.

Until its first repaint after Grouping No. 995 was additionally lettered GATESHEAD WORKS (fig. 45) as well as N.E.R., but by 1923 No. 590 only carried N.E.R. as it was by then no longer employed at Gateshead.

Brakes

Braking was by hand.

Allocation and Work

No. 995 served throughout its life as shunter at Gateshead Works and shed. Locomotive repairs ceased at the Works in August 1932 as an economy measure (they were however re-opened during the 1939-45 War) and No. 995 became redundant. It was sold in June 1933.

No. 590 was similarly employed at first, but by 1907 was at West Hartlepool and had moved to Darlington by 1920. In 1923 it was at Percy Main, the old Blyth & Tyne Railway's shed and repair shops, which were used until Grouping by the N.E.R. as their principal location for the scrapping of locomotives. Late in 1923 No. 590 was sent to Springhead Works at Hull, where it stayed only ten months before being transferred to York North as shed pilot. It finished its days there, but was not used to any great extent and only amassed a mileage of 61,932 between the time of Grouping and its withdrawal in April 1937.

A little-known fact is that both engines were loaned to the Admiralty for about three months late in 1918, when they saw service at Immingham Docks.

Sales

In June 1933 Robert Frazer and Sons, the Newcastle dealers, bought No. 995 and it was used subsequently by Hartley Main Colliery, where it became their No. 26. By June 1943 it was standing derelict at Seaton Delaval and was broken up later in that year.

Engine Diagram

Section D, 1924. This showed the longer jib as fitted to No. 590, but was in error in depicting pop safety valves which the class never carried.

There were two clerical errors, the firebox height being given as 3ft. 9⅜in. which was duly corrected to 3ft. 9 3/16 in. at the end of 1924. The other mistake was apparently due to the misreading of the figure of 10т 15c 2Q on the middle coupled axle as 10т 15c 7Q when a copy of the Gateshead diagram was sent to Doncaster for the L.N.E.R. diagram to be prepared, and the 7Q was apparently never questioned!

Summary of J78 Class

1923 No.	Maker	Built	Transferred from Service to Running Stock	Withdrawn
590	Gateshead	12/1888	8/26	5/37
995	,,	12/1888	8/26	6/33

CLASS J79

N.E.R. CLASS H2—WILSON WORSDELL
3ft. 6¼in. ENGINES

ENGINES AT GROUPING (Built 1897): 407, 1787. TOTAL 2.

ENGINE TRANSFERRED FROM SERVICE STOCK TO RUNNING STOCK, 1925 (Built 1907): 1662. TOTAL 1.

Two small tank engines, numbered 407 and 1787, were built at Gateshead Works in 1897. They formed part of a requisition made in March 1896 for five H class 0-4-0T's, but this was later changed to three 0-4-0T's and two 0-6-0T's. The H2 design was derived from the H class 0-4-0T and H1 class 0-6-0T (L.N.E.R. classes Y7 and J78) and carried the same size domeless boiler as both those classes. The cylinders were 14in. diameter, the same used since 1891 on the H class. The wheelbase was one foot longer (from the middle to the rear axle) than class H1, but the front overhang was one foot less than on both the H and H1 designs. Unlike these latter engines, class H2 had a proper rear bunker, which held 1¼ tons of coal, but rather surprisingly the water capacity was slightly less. Westinghouse brake was provided for engine and train instead of hand only, and this enabled No. 407 to take over the passenger and goods working of the 5 mile long Cawood, Wistow & Selby Light Railway when the N.E.R. acquired that line in 1901. For operating it, No. 407 was fitted with larger side tanks.

In January 1907, Wilson Worsdell had requisitioned a further crane tank of class H1, but was turned down by the Locomotive Committee. A month later, another requisition, this time for a class H2, was successful, hence the building of the third engine, No. 1662. This engine utilised one of a batch of spare boilers built in 1902, which had lain unused during that period. No. 1662 was hand braked only and it served as a Gateshead Works and shed shunter until 1930. Until the end of 1925 this engine was in Service Stock, but was then transferred to Running Stock.

Apart from the larger side tanks fitted to No. 407, the J79 class remained substantially as built. Withdrawal took place between August 1936 and August 1937, but all three were sold and served many more years as industrial locomotives.

Standard L.N.E.R. Dimensions at Grouping

Cylinders (2 inside)		14″ × 20″
Motion		Joy with slide valves
Boiler:		
Max. diam. outside		3′ 8″
Barrel length ...		6′ 8½″
Firebox length outside ...		4′ 4″
Pitch		6′ 9″
Diagram No. ...		74
Heating surface:		
Firebox		57 sq. ft.
Tubes (139 × 1¾″)		448 sq. ft.
Total		505 sq. ft.
Grate area		11.3 sq. ft.
Boiler pressure ...		140 lb./sq. in.
Coupled wheels ...		3′ 6¼″
Tractive effort (85%)		11,041 lb.
Length over buffers ...		22′ 4″
Wheelbase ...	6′ 0″ + 5′ 0″ = 11′ 0″	
Weight (full) ...		27T 0c*
Max. axle load ...		9T 16c*
Water capacity ...		475 gallons*
Coal capacity ...		1T 5c

* The weights shown on the L.N.E.R. engine diagram applied to the heaviest engine of the three (No. 407 with the larger tanks), but the drawing itself showed the small tanks and the water capacity of 475 gallons related to these. The weight of the engines with the small tanks, according to N.E.R. records, was 25 tons 0 cwt. and the maximum axle load was 9 tons 2 cwt.

L.N.E.R. Renumbering

In November 1923 No. 1662 received the short-lived sectional suffix (becoming 1662D) when it was repainted in L.N.E.R. livery. Hitherto it had carried the words GATESHEAD WORKS in similar, but smaller letters than the N.E.R. on its tank sides. The D suffix seems to have been obliterated after only a few months.

Details

The original boilers, all built by Gateshead, remained unchanged until life-expired. They were replaced on No. 407 (June 1916), No. 1662 (November 1923) and on No. 1787 (March 1917) by new, but similar, Darlington-built boilers and these were retained until withdrawal and then sold with the engines.

All these boilers were domeless and fitted with Ramsbottom safety valves enclosed in a polished brass cover. The L.N.E.R. engine diagram was incorrect in showing Ross pop safety valves. In 1923, when Darlington prepared this diagram, boilers as used on the J79 class were being built for five new class Y7 engines Nos. 982-6 and these *were* fitted with Ross pop safety valves. It was thus reasonable to assume then that if any new boiler was put on to a J79 engine, it would have had pop valves, but in the event, the new boiler which Darlington built and put on No. 1662 in November 1923 was equipped with Ramsbottom valves.

The earliest N.E.R. records quoted the wheel diameter as one inch less, at 3ft. 5½in., than later diagrams. The pitch of the boiler was accordingly 6ft. 8½in. instead of 6ft. 9in. The fitting of longer buffers increased the overall length from 22ft. 1½in. to 22ft. 4in., the figure shown on the L.N.E.R. diagram.

Although No. 1787, at least, had twin handles on the smokebox door at first, all three had the wheel and a handle fastening throughout most of their career.

Only a single whistle was fitted, on a pipe protruding through the cab roof. Latterly Nos. 407 and 1787 had the organ-pipe type, whilst that on No. 1662 was the higher-pitched bell shape.

No. 1662 carried a curious fitting on its front bufferbeam, adjacent to the drawhook and on its right-hand side (see Part 1, fig. 35). It resembled the anchoring bracket for a shunting pole, but is unlikely to have served that purpose. Its real use is not known, but it may have been used to couple up with the cab drawbars of dead engines needing to be moved at Gateshead Works. No. 1662 never carried front footsteps, whereas the other two were soon fitted with a single step on each side fitted just behind the centre of the leading axle. No. 1787 differed from the other two, at least in its later days, in having somewhat smaller sandboxes, which were filled from above the footplating instead of below. These sandboxes were shaped to the profile of the wheels instead of being of the hopper pattern on the other two engines (cf. figs. 47 and 48).

The very short coal bunkers were topped by three coal rails, originally open, but all had been plated on the inside before the L.N.E.R. took over. As the bunker side-sheets were no more than 21in. across, they were devoid of the usual type of N.E.R. large cast brass numberplate (which measured 23¾in.), and this was instead fitted on the back of the bunker. Strangely, the standard L.N.E.R. 9in. wide cast numberplate was also fitted to the centre of the back of the bunker and not in the usual position on the

sides, although there would have been room for it.

It has already been mentioned that No. 407 had larger side tanks than the other two, which had their tank tops level with the cab cut-outs. The tanks on No. 407 were longer as well as being much deeper, which brought the tops just about level with the top of the boiler, a very noticeable difference in a side view (fig. 47). The alteration in tank capacity has not been ascertained.

Brakes

Westinghouse equipment was fitted to Nos. 407 and 1787 and this was retained to the end of their L.N.E.R. service. The engines were driven from the right and the pump was mounted in the cab on the left-hand side. Hose connections front and rear were attached to the usual swan-neck pipes.

No. 1662 had hand brake only, but early in 1930 Middlesbrough shed wanted a small, vacuum-fitted engine for working horse boxes in connection with Stockton race traffic and No. 1662 was chosen because, of the three J79's, it had the youngest boiler. It left Darlington Works in April 1930 fitted with vacuum ejector on the right-hand side, with hose connections under the bufferbeams. The engine brake was still hand only.

Allocation and Work

In the year in which they were built, that doyen of North Eastern enthusiasts John S. MacLean, noted No. 407 working at Scarborough (presumably marshalling stock in connection with holiday traffic) whilst No. 1787 was at Gateshead Works. Both were working at York around 1900/1. In 1901 No. 407 began to work the Cawood branch, with No. 1787 acting as reserve for this duty, but without the increased tank capacity. In 1908 the branch passenger trains were turned over to the petrol-electric railcars and by Grouping both Nos. 407 and 1787 were working at Middlesbrough. For a week in July 1925, at the time of the Centenary celebrations, No. 407 was on loan to Darlington to help meet the need for the very inflated demands on the Works shunters there in positioning stock for the Exhibition and Procession. Later that year, in October, it put in one of its spells of passenger working, hauling three flat-roofed four-wheelers (the entire coaching stock of the North Sunderland Railway) between Chathill and Seahouses on the Northumberland coast. This was a duty which the N.E.R. and the L.N.E.R. undertook to help their tiny independent neighbour when the only locomotive it possessed was out of action, and No. 407 was the usual performer. Otherwise it worked out the rest of its existence around Middlesbrough, mainly shunting on the docks.

The third engine, No. 1662, acted as a Works and shed shunter at Gateshead and when, in 1930, it was decided to fit this engine with the vacuum brake, it and No. 1787 exchanged sheds in April of that year. No further moves were made by these two engines. All three were entered on the programme of withdrawals for 1935 and from July of that year Nos. 407 and 1787 were laid aside to be offered for sale, but were not withdrawn from stock until firm disposal had been arranged. No. 1787's going was not for a cash consideration. By some mischance at Jarrow an L.N.E.R. engine ran down and wrecked one of the shunting engines belonging to the Bowes Railway, and, as recompense, No. 1787 was handed over to this company in August 1936. Sale of the other two was effected in June and August 1937.

Sales

As just mentioned, No. 1787 went to the Bowes Railway in 1936 and became No. 5, working from their shed just outside Gateshead. It was scrapped in October 1946 by D. S. Bowran of Gateshead.

No. 407 was sold to the Whitwood Chemical Co. of Castleford who named it *Jean*. In July 1939 this company became part of Briggs Collieries Ltd. After a thorough overhaul, a repair which took from December 1941 to November 1942, *Jean* was sent to Briggs' Savile Colliery and remained there until about October 1947, when it was transferred to N.C.B. Middleton Broom Colliery on the south-east outskirts of Leeds. By June 1949 it was partly dismantled and complete scrapping occurred at the end of 1953 or in early 1954.

The last one, No. 1662 went much further afield, being purchased by the British Sugar Beet Corporation for use at their Cantley factory near Norwich. It was withdrawn in 1955 and scrapped on site by A. King & Co. of Norwich in 1957.

Engine Diagram

Section D, 1924. Whilst the diagram gave the maximum weights (only applicable to No. 407), it showed the smaller tanks as carried by Nos. 1662 and 1787. Ross pop safety valves were incorrectly shown.

Summary of J79 Class

1923 No.	Maker	Built	Brakes At Grouping	Later Alterations	Withdrawn
407	Gateshead	3/1897	W	—	6/37
1787	,,	3/1897	W	—	8/36
1662	,,	10/1907*	Hand	VE (4/30)	8/37

* No. 1662 was in Service Stock until the end of 1925, when it was transferred to Running Stock.

CLASS J80

H. & B.R. CLASS G2—M. STIRLING
5ft. 0in. ENGINES

ENGINES AT GROUPING (Built 1892): 2448/9/50 (H. & B. 67/8/9). TOTAL 3.

These three 0-6-0T's were the first Hull & Barnsley Railway tank engines to be designed by Matthew Stirling. With the domeless boiler, the outline was neat and conformed to the Stirling tradition. They were delivered from R. Stephenson & Co. (Works Nos. 2781/2/3) in 1892.

All three engines received domed boilers soon after Grouping. Withdrawal occurred during 1930-31.

Standard L.N.E.R. Dimensions at Grouping

Cylinders (2 inside)	18″ × 26″
Motion	Stephenson with slide valves
Boiler (domeless):	
Max. diam. outside	4′ 3″
Barrel length ...	10′ 0″
Firebox length outside ...	5′ 6″
Pitch	7′ 2″
Diagram No. ...	71A

Heating surface:		
Firebox	...	100 sq. ft.
Tubes (198 × 1¾″)		950 sq. ft.
Total		1050 sq. ft.
Grate area		16.25 sq. ft.
Boiler pressure ...		150 lb./sq. in.
Coupled wheels ...		5′ 0″
Tractive effort (85%)		17,901 lb.
Length over buffers		31′ 7″
Wheelbase ...	7′ 3″ + 8′ 3″ =	15′ 6″
Weight (full) ...		45T 15C
Max. axle load ...		17T 6C
Water capacity ...		850 gallons
Coal capacity ...		3T 5C

N.E.R. and L.N.E.R. Renumbering

After the H. & B.R. was amalgamated with the N.E.R. on 1st April 1922, 3000 was added to the running numbers of the H. & B. stock. Nos. 3068/9 were so dealt with, but it is uncertain whether No. 67 was actually renumbered, though this is probable. During 1924 the L.N.E.R. renumbered 3067/8/9 to 2448/9/50.

Rebuilding

The official H. & B.R. figures for the heating surface of the boilers of the class in their early years were as follows:—

Firebox	...	...	96 sq. ft.
Tubes	...	...	937 sq. ft.
Total	...	...	1033 sq. ft.
Grate area		...	16 sq. ft.

New fireboxes would have been fitted by 1923 with possibly an altered tube arrangement, which would account for the different figures shown on the L.N.E.R. diagram. Originally the capacity of the coal bunker was given as 86 cu. ft. (say 2 tons) and the L.N.E.R. figure of 3¼ tons seems to be too high.

By Grouping new boilers were required by the class. In May 1923 No. 3068 (as it then became) was equipped at Springhead Works with a second-hand domed boiler from an N.E.R. Fletcher " 901 " class 2-4-0, and retained the same boiler until its withdrawal as No. 2449 in July 1931 (fig. 50). This boiler (L.N.E.R. Diagram 69) was three inches longer in the barrel than the original boiler and gave a reduction in grate area to 15.16 sq. ft. The heating surface was as follows:—

Firebox	...	...	98 sq. ft.
Tubes	(205 × 1¾″)		995 sq. ft.
Total	...	...	1093 sq. ft.

The boiler pressure of 160 lb. per sq. in. resulted in an increase in tractive effort to 19,094 lb. After No. 2449 was withdrawn,

its boiler stood spare for three years and then served another four years on N12 class No. 2487, being condemned along with that engine.

The other two members of the class entered Darlington Works early in 1924 and emerged in May of that year with new domed boilers (fig. 51). These Diagram 71B boilers (used also on classes J75, N12 and N13) had the same overall dimensions as the originals, but there was a reduction in grate area to 15.5 sq. ft. and alteration to the heating surface as follows:—

Firebox	...	...	99 sq. ft.
Tubes	(205 × 1¾″)		972 sq. ft.
Total	...	...	1071 sq. ft.

The 175 lb. per sq. in. boiler pressure increased the tractive effort to 20,877 lb.

The 71B boiler from No. 2448, which was withdrawn in the Southern Area, was retained by that Area for stationary purposes and was so used until April 1947. That from No 2450 later served on two engines of the J75 class.

Details

Despite the reboilering in 1923-24, all three engines kept their H. & B.R. chimneys, but all three had their single bell-shaped whistles replaced by the twin N.E.R. arrangement having one bell-shaped and one organ-pipe type (cf. figs. 49 and 51). The change was made on Nos. 2448/50 in May, 1924 when they received Diagram 71B boilers, but when No. 2449 (as 3069) was fitted with a Diagram 69 boiler in May 1923, it retained the single H. & B.R. type whistle. This was replaced by the N.E.R. double variety in April 1927. Other changes to No. 2449 at this visit to Darlington Works were substitution of " LNER " for " L & N.E.R. " on the side tanks, the replacement of uncased Ramsbottom safety valves by Ramsbottom valves in an N.E.R. shaped brass trumpet casing, and the removal of the re-railing jack, hitherto carried alongside the left-hand leading sandbox. At the same time a more dished and larger diameter N.E.R. type smokebox door replaced the H. & B.R. type with the two dog-clip fasteners on the lower half, with corresponding altera-tion of the front portion of the handrail as on the J75 class. Similar alterations to smokebox doors and handrails were made on the other two in May 1924 when they were fitted with 71B boilers, but in their case Ross pop safety valves were provided (fig. 51). It was at this date that they lost their re-railing jacks.

Prior to being taken over by the N.E.R., plating had been fixed inside the three coal rails on the bunker. The coupling rods on these engines were of plain section, whereas the J75 class had fluted side rods.

No. 2449 had lost its buffers with parallel shanks by 1923 and then carried the smaller diameter tapered type (cf. figs. 49 and 50). It also differed from the other two in having delivery pipes and a clack box on the boiler barrel.

Brakes

Originally fitted with the vacuum brake, all three had been converted to steam brake only before being taken over by the N.E.R.

Allocation and Work

These three engines were generally similar to the more numerous and better known J75 class, and although they worked coal trains on the Monckton and Monk Bretton branches when new, their vacuum brakes

and larger wheels enabled them to participate in passenger duties. Up to 1914 they were in demand for light passenger and excursion trains and were particularly useful on the October Hull Fair Specials.

No. 2448 was transferred to the opposite side of the Humber, to Immingham shed, in November 1925 and remained there until withdrawn in September 1930. Nos. 2449/50 spent their L.N.E.R. days on shunting duties at Hull, working from Springhead shed until condemned in July and August 1931 respectively.

Engine Diagrams

Not issued	Engines with H. & B. domeless boilers.
Not issued	Engine 2449 with Diagram 69 domed boiler.
Section D, 1924.	Engines with Diagram 71B domed boilers.

Summary of J80 Class

							Rebuilt Domed Boiler		
1924 No.	N.E.R. No.	H.&B. No.	Maker		Works No.	Built	Diag. 69	Diag. 71B	Withdrawn
2448	5/24	3067	67	R. Stephenson & Co.	2781	8/1892	—	5/24	9/30
2449	9/24	3068	68	,,	2782	8/1892	5/23	—	7/31
2450	5/24	3069	69	,,	2783	9/1892	—	5/24	8/31

CLASS J81

N.B.R. CLASS E—WHEATLEY
5ft. 0in. ENGINE

ENGINE AT GROUPING (Built 1872): 10216. TOTAL 1.

When Wheatley came to the N.B.R. in 1867 the locomotive stock was quite inadequate for the traffic being worked, and there were deficiencies in all types of engine. As regards passenger tanks, the latest class was Hurst's 0-4-2 well tanks of which fourteen had been built between 1857 and 1864. These were neither powerful nor numerous enough to cope with the thriving local and branch services. However, it was

not until 1870 that Wheatley's first passenger tank engines appeared and only two of these were built (see L.N.E.R. class J86). Between 1871 and 1873 fifteen engines of a slightly modified design were turned out by Cowlairs, the L.N.E.R. class J81 being given to the sole survivor of these at Grouping.

N.B.R. Nos.	No. built	Date
149, 229/30, 39, 51, 221/56, 405/6	9	1871-72
62, 113/36, 222/55/61	6	1873

Rebuilding with new boilers took place between 1895 and 1902 by which time the class had been relegated to shunting duties. Thus when the N.B.R. load classification scheme was introduced in 1913 they were placed in category E, among the goods engines. The entire class was renumbered into the N.B.R. duplicate list in 1913/15.

Withdrawal commenced in 1920 and by the end of 1922 fourteen of the class had been taken out of stock.

N.B.R. No.	Withdrawn
1193 (229)	6/21
1194 (230)	9/21
1204 (39)	10/22
1205 (51)	1/20
1209 (149)	11/21
1210 (221)	4/21
1211 (256)	9/21
1215 (405)	1/22
1231 (62)	12/21
1232 (113)	10/20
1233 (136)	10/22
1234 (222)	4/21
1235 (255)	4/21
1237 (261)	4/21

The only engine to be taken over by the L.N.E.R. was No. 1216 (ex-406), and it was withdrawn early in 1924 (fig. 52).

Standard L.N.E.R. Dimensions at Grouping

Cylinders (2 inside)	17″ × 24″
Motion	Stephenson with slide valves
Boiler:	
Max. diam. outside	4′ 0¾″
Barrel length ...	9′ 7″
Firebox length outside ...	5′ 0″
Pitch	6′ 9⅝″
Heating surface:	
Firebox ...	83.70 sq. ft.
Tubes (171 × 1¾″)	775.66 sq. ft.
Total	859.36 sq. ft.
Grate area ...	16 sq. ft.
Boiler pressure ...	140 lb./sq. in.
Coupled wheels ...	5′ 0″
Tractive effort (85%)	13,756 lb.
Length over buffers	28′ 5″
Wheelbase ...	7′ 0″ + 7′ 3″ = 14′ 3″
Weight (full) ...	35т 14c
Max. axle load ...	12т 13c
Water capacity ...	740 gallons
Coal capacity ...	*

* The coal capacity was not quoted on the L.N.E.R. (or N.B.R.) engine diagram, but by calculation would have been about 1 ton 10 cwt.

N.B.R. Renumbering

Transfer to the N.B.R. duplicate list took place as under:—

Old No.	New No.	Date
229	1193	5/1913
230	1194	5/1913
39	1204	11/1913
51	1205	11/1913
149	1209	9/1913
221	1210	9/1913
256	1211	9/1913
405	1215	12/1913
406	1216	12/1913
62	1231	1/1915
113	1232	1/1915
136	1233	9/1915
222	1234	4/1915
255	1235	4/1915
261	1237	4/1915

The engine which survived Grouping was withdrawn in N.B.R. livery without being renumbered.

Rebuilding

When their original boilers wore out, these engines were rebuilt with new boilers of the same size, but with 171 tubes instead of 163. New saddle tanks were fitted whilst certain other features such as chimney, footsteps and brake rigging were brought into line with current (Holmes) practice. An early rebuilding of No. 229, in 1889, has been reported, but the systematic reconstruction of the engines of this class took place between 1895 and 1902.

N.B.R. No.	Rebuilt	N.B.R. No.	Rebuilt
39	6/1895	229	7/1901
51	1/1902	230	11/1901
62	7/1901	255	12/1901
113	7/1901	256	1/1902
136	10/1901	261	1/1902
149	7/1901	405	3/1902
221	12/1895	406	1/1902
222	1/1902		

Comparative weights before and after rebuilding are shown in the accompanying table.

	As Built	As Rebuilt
Leading axle	11т 0c	12т 13c
Driving axle	13т 8c	12т 4c
Trailing axle	11т 18c	10т 17c
Total	36т 6c	35т 14c

Details

At first the customary Wheatley stovepipe chimney was fitted, but on rebuilding the later standard capped type favoured by Holmes was used. Originally a dished door flush with the smokebox was employed but this was replaced (sometimes before rebuilding) by the usual later bevelled pattern. The Wheatley smokebox had snaphead rivets on the front and sides, but countersunk rivets were a feature of the Holmes smokebox giving it a much smoother and neater appearance.

Large numbers of conspicuous rivet heads were also a characteristic of the original saddle tanks which had a straight bottom on either side of the boiler. The dome on the rebuilt engines was placed further back on the boiler barrel and new tanks were fitted. These had countersunk rivets and they curved inwards at the bottom. The original dome cover was open at the top which had a trumpet-shaped extension concealing the safety valves. On the rebuilt engines two lock-up valves were mounted on top of the dome and were clearly visible above the normal-shaped dome cover. In both forms (unrebuilt and rebuilt) the whistle was immediately behind the dome, but whereas the original arrangement was to take steam from an L-shaped union connected to the dome, the rebuilt engines had a straight connection from the dome. In the original design the tank filler was behind the dome and had a flat lift-off lid, but the Holmes version had the filler (with a bevelled and hinged lid) in front of the dome. In the latter case a small handrail was also provided on the tank top.

Protection of the crew against the elements was very meagre, consisting only of a weatherboard at the front of the " cab " and another behind the bunker. Sometimes in later years makeshift extensions were fitted at the driver's side of the front weatherboard. One engine, No. 1215, was fitted in 1910 with a cab somewhat similar to the type fitted to the 0-4-0 tender engines Nos. 1010/1 (one of which became L.N.E.R. class Y10). This cab had no window in the side-sheets and its roof was not extended backwards over the bunker. No toolbox was visible in the earliest days, but before rebuilding some engines acquired one behind the rear weatherboard. After rebuilding it was standard practice to fit a toolbox in front of the rear weatherboard. No. 1216 as running latterly had a tarpaulin storm sheet.

Before rebuilding the cab footsteps were part of a large solid structure which extended in a curved sweep to the rear bufferbeam, whereas most (but not all) the rebuilt engines had the usual narrow type, augmented in late N.B. days by the familiar long wooden shunting step. The buffers of these and other Wheatley classes were of characteristic pattern with square ends bolted to pads on the bufferbeam and thick faces (turned with a large radius at the edges) with a hole

in the centre. Some engines of the class had cast iron wheels with T-section spokes and sometimes axles (of engines with either cast iron or wrought iron wheels) were strengthened by the addition of shrunk-on hoops outside the wheel centres. The cab side sheet was originally a box splasher, but in the rebuilt state was shorter and curved to join the rear splasher.

At various times the N.B.R. made use of a device described in the Directors' minutes as a "tell-tale ". This was a mileage recorder and in 1909 one of these is reported to have been fitted to No. 261 of this class during an investigation of shunting activity at Shettleston, Camlachie, Burntisland, Niddrie and South Leith yards.

Brakes

As built these engines had hand brakes only, but several of the class were fitted with Westinghouse equipment by the 'nineties. Later on there were some conversions to steam brake both from the " hand only " and Westinghouse varieties. The survivor at Grouping, No. 1216, had steam brake.

Allocation and Work

Originally the 5ft. 0in. Wheatley saddle tanks were stationed mainly in Edinburgh (St. Margaret's and Haymarket) and Glasgow (Cowlairs and Parkhead) and were employed on local passenger trains. A notable exception was No. 113 which worked the Carlisle-Langholm service and had the misfortune to overturn in November 1890 near Willow Holme Junction where a similar fate befell D49 2758 *Northumberland* just over forty years later in January 1931. Typical of the lines worked in the early days were the North Berwick and Macmerry branches (Nos. 39 and 230 of St. Margaret's respectively).

Eventually the whole class was employed on shunting duties, mostly in the vicinity of Glasgow and Edinburgh. In Glasgow these engines were to be found at Cowlairs (from Eastfield), and High Street (from Parkhead). In Edinburgh the St. Margaret's engines shunted at Leith Walk whilst those shedded at Haymarket were utilised as pilots at Haymarket goods yard and Waverley station. It is of interest to note that whereas Haymarket employed the 5ft. 0in. engines of this class for carriage shunting at Waverley West, St. Margaret's used the 4ft. 3in. Wheatley 0-6-0 ST's for similar duties at the East end of the station. However No. 113 (formerly of Carlisle) for a time acted as Waverley Goods Pilot, where in addition to the usual discomforts associated with a roofless cab in bad weather, the enginemen had to contend with stones and other missiles dropped by urchins from the Low Calton-Jeffrey Street overbridge, not to mention other more disagreeable schoolboy habits! The class was little known in the Northern District although by 1912 No. 222 was at Dundee.

The only engine to come into the L.N.E.R., No. 1216, was allocated to Parkhead for shunting duties nearby. After withdrawal this engine was not immediately scrapped but was sent to Craigentinny for temporary use as a stationary boiler at the Company's gas works adjacent to the carriage sidings.

Engine Diagram

Section B, 1924.

Summary of J81 Class

1924 No. (10216)	Second N.B. No. 1216	First N.B. No. 406	Maker Cowlairs	Built 2/1872	Withdrawn 2/24

CLASS J82

N.B.R. CLASS R—DRUMMOND
4ft. 6in. ENGINES

ENGINES AT GROUPING (Built 1875-78): 10289/91/4/9, 10306/28/30-3/5/6/48-59. TOTAL 24.

Wheatley had placed in traffic a number of 0-6-0ST engines for local and branch passenger work (see L.N.E.R. classes J81 and J86), but when Drummond became Locomotive Superintendent of the N.B.R. in 1875, more engines were still required for this type of traffic. A new design was produced (Drummond's first for the N.B.R.) incorporating side tanks and many other details in keeping with the Brighton practice of Drummond's late master, William Stroudley. Indeed the whole design was virtually an enlarged version of the L.B.S.C.R. class A (the " Terriers ").

Three batches were turned out of Cowlairs as under:—

N.B.R. Nos.	No. built	Date
165/6, 241/59/84/97	6	1875-76
123/51/8/61/2, 274/95	7	1877
20/2/9, 49, 96/7, 106/7/8, 240, 313, 485	12	1877-78

Rebuilding with new boilers took place during the years 1908-10, and all except one survived Grouping. The engine which failed to do so was No. 1290 (ex-166), withdrawn in November 1922. Almost a year passed before the next withdrawal, but heavy inroads were made into the class during 1924-25, leaving four in traffic at the beginning of 1926. These had all been condemned before the end of that year, the last to go being No. 1328 (ex-123) in November (fig. 53). Thus although these engines worked for some 46-50 years, they were outlived by many of their Brighton " ancestors ", some of which had a remarkable long career.

Standard L.N.E.R. Dimensions at Grouping

Cylinders (2 inside)	15″ × 22″
Motion	Stephenson with slide valves
Boiler:	
Max. diam. outside	3′ 10″
Barrel length ...	8′ 8½″
Firebox length outside ...	4′ 8¼″
Pitch	6′ 6″
Diagram No. ...	86
Heating surface:	
Firebox ...	79.96 sq. ft.
Tubes (142 × 1¾″)	586.10 sq. ft.
Total	666.06 sq. ft.
Grate area ...	13.75 sq. ft.
Boiler pressure ...	140 lb./sq. in.
Coupled wheels ...	4′ 6″
Tractive effort (85%)	10,908 lb.
Length over buffers	28′ 6½″
Wheelbase ...	6′ 4″ + 6′ 10″ = 13′ 2″
Weight (full) ...	36T 0c
Max. axle load ...	13T 12c
Water capacity ...	600 gallons
Coal capacity ...	1T 10c

N.B.R. and L.N.E.R. Renumbering

The whole class was placed on the N.B.R. Duplicate List between 1916 and 1920, the actual dates being shown in the table below. The engines which were still running in March 1924 were allotted new numbers under a scheme devised at Cowlairs to abolish the former N.B.R. Duplicate List. These numbers are also shown in the accompanying table, but only two engines of the class carried them. These were Nos. 1330/58 which became 10007/23 in June and May 1924 respectively, but in August and September of that year respectively they became 10330/58 (fig. 54). No other J82's received L.N.E.R. numbers, but No. 1336 was repainted in L.N.E.R. lined black livery and carried the " B " suffix.

Old N.B.R. No.	New N.B.R. No.	Date	Cowlairs 1924 No.
165	1289	2/1917	—
166	1290	3/1917	—
259	1291	5/1917	10002
284	1294	4/1916	10003
241	1299	6/1917	10004
297	1306	8/1918	10005
123	1328	6/1918	10006
151	1330	7/1918	10007
158	1331	7/1918	10008
161	1332	7/1918	10009
162	1333	8/1918	10010
274	1335	8/1918	10012
295	1336	8/1918	10013
20	1348	2/1920	10014
22	1349	2/1920	10015
29	1350	2/1920	10016
49	1351	2/1920	10017
96	1352	2/1920	10018
97	1353	2/1920	10019
106	1354	3/1920	10020
107	1355	3/1920	9018
108	1356	3/1920	10021
240	1357	3/1920	10022
313	1358	6/1920	10023
485	1359	12/1919	10024

Rebuilding

No. 259 is said to have been rebuilt in June 1889, but this is not recorded officially and the engine was apparently little altered. Similarly No. 274 is sometimes quoted as having been rebuilt in 1895, but here again Cowlairs records are silent and some authorities merely show a heavy repair against this date.

During the years 1908-10 all the engines were rebuilt with new boilers of similar proportions to the originals but fitted with combination injectors (instead of the old non-lifting pattern) and pitched 3in. higher (6ft. 6in. instead of 6ft. 3in.). Comparative heating surface figures were:—

	*Old Boilers	New Boilers
Firebox	65 sq. ft.	79.96 sq. ft.
Tubes	636 sq. ft.	586.10 sq. ft.
Total	701 sq. ft.	666.06 sq. ft.
No. of tubes, 1¾"	146	142

* These were the figures given during the Holmes period. The original general arrangement drawing shows the same number of tubes but 673 sq. ft. of tube heating surface (making a total of 738 sq. ft.) and a grate area of 13 sq. ft.

The meticulous calculation of heating surface figures in the rebuilt version to a hundredth part of a square foot would be difficult for a practical man to justify. However such a degree of theoretical accuracy was not uncommon on engine diagrams, not only on the N.B.R. but on many other railways. The grate area was shown as 13.75 sq. ft. on the rebuilds, the previously published figure being 14 sq. ft. The total weight (full) went up from 33 tons 9 cwt. to 36 tons 0 cwt. (maximum axle load from 11 tons 19 cwt. to 13 tons 12 cwt.), whilst the length over buffers was shown as increased by 3in. (from 28ft. 3½in. to 28ft. 6½in.).

All the engines were dealt with at Cowlairs, the individual rebuilding dates being as follows:—

N.B.R. No.	Rebuilt	N.B.R. No.	Rebuilt
165	7/1909	20	7/1910
166	4/1908	22	5/1908
259	12/1910	29	4/1910
284	4/1910	49	6/1910
241	3/1910	96	4/1910
297	6/1910	97	4/1909
123	5/1908	106	5/1908
151	4/1910	107	7/1909
158	7/1909	108	7/1910
161	4/1909	240	7/1909
162	4/1910	313	5/1909
274	7/1909	485	6/1910
295	4/1909		

The new boilers were standard with those used on the rebuilt small Drummond 4-4-0T's (L.N.E.R. class D51) and indeed the boiler taken off No. 1356 after its withdrawal was later used on D51 10462, and survived the J82 class by seven years.

Details

Whilst on the capital list, the first eleven engines built (i.e. Nos. 165/6, 259/84/41/97, 123/51/8/61/2) had the Wheatley type number plates with raised numerals, whereas the remainder had the Drummond type with sunken numbers filled with black wax. As duplicate engines the whole class had number plates with raised numerals in accordance with latter-day N.B.R. practice. The first batch of six engines (Nos. 165/6, 259/84/41/97) and four of the second batch (Nos. 123/51/8/61) originally had crosshead-driven feed pumps and condenser water heating arrangements which Drummond copied from Brighton practice. All subsequent engines had non-lifting injectors and the engines with pumps were soon altered to have injectors, at the same time losing their condensers. The injectors on the altered engines differed from the rest, being situated between the front and centre axles instead of between the centre and rear axles, and the steam valve was plainly visible high up on the front ring of the boiler, whereas it could not be seen on the later engines. After rebuilding all the class had combination injectors. Some of the older engines of the class had an early form of lock-up safety valves, but most of the class had Ramsbottom valves until after 1883, when both types were replaced by the standard N.B.R. lock-up pattern (in all cases on the dome). Before rebuilding, the valves were widely spaced, being on the old seatings, but on the Reid boilers they were close together although still situated on the dome.

In the early days of the class the cylinder lubricators were "square" in shape with T-screws above, and they were placed in front of the smokebox. Later however the usual bulbous pattern with wheels above and below the cup were employed, these being on the sides of the smokebox. Sometimes this alteration took place on rebuilding, but there were examples of the later type of lubricator on unrebuilt engines. As on the later small Drummond 4-4-0T's (L.N.E.R. class D51), the footplate was very low, and consequently the buffers protruded partly above it. For shunting at North Leith No. 1357 had a dumb buffer in the rear right-hand position to prevent buffer-locking on sharply curved sidings. When this engine was withdrawn the dumb buffer was inherited by its successor, No. 10358. In the original design the bunker had no coal rails, but these were added in the Holmes period, increasing the coal capacity from 1 ton 4 cwt. to 1 ton 10 cwt. There were three coal rails, originally unplated, but Nos. 1291, 1331/48-51/8 had the usual sheet metal coal guards behind the rails in late N.B.R. days.

When built these engines had boiler handrails which terminated behind the smokebox. The left-hand rail contained the rod for operating the blower, and this rod continued forward from the handrail to the usual union on the side of the smokebox. The only handrail on the smokebox was a short curved one on the front. After rebuild-ing, a continuous handrail ran from the front of the side tank round the front of the smokebox, curving above the door, to the other tank. Instead of a boiler rail back to the cab however, the rebuilds had separate rails on the top of each side tank.

A photograph of No. 295 taken about 1908 shows the engine running with the rear coupling rods removed (i.e. working as an 0-4-2T).

Brakes

Hand brake only was fitted in the first instance, but some of the class had steam brake before the adoption of Westinghouse as standard from about 1881 onwards. There was a further complication in so far as certain engines had steam brake on the engine and air brake for the train, but by the close of the Holmes era they all had Westing-house equipment for engine and train. The earlier engines of the class originally had wooden brake blocks which were retained in some cases for a time even after the adoption of Westinghouse brake. Three engines of the class, Nos. 108/23/66, had become dual-fitted (i.e. vacuum ejectors were added) by 1909 but there were no subsequent brake alterations (fig.54).

Names

Following Stroudley's practice on the L.B. & S.C.R., Drummond gave these engines names of places in the vicinity of which they worked. Unlike Stroudley, however, Drummond renamed N.B.R. engines when they were moved from one part of the system to another. No official record of Drummond's N.B.R. engine names appears to have survived, and there is an element of doubt concerning the accuracy and completeness of the undernoted list of names applied to this class.

It will be noted that the name *North-Berwick* had a hyphen (an early photograph of the engine clearly shows this). The name *Bo'ness* may have had a hyphen instead of the later customary apostrophe as it is known that the engine destination boards were at one time marked BO-NESS.

It will also be seen that the name *Coat-bridge* was used on two engines of this class (at different times), and that several of the names were later used on Drummond's small 4-4-0T engines (L.N.E.R. class D51). *Clyde-bank* and *Yoker* probably carried earlier names, but these are not known. At first, some of the engines had the name in lettering with serifs, but subsequently plain bold capitals were used. After Holmes took charge of the N.B.R. locomotive department in 1882 the names soon disappeared.

First N.B.R. No.	Original Name	Later Name
165	Coatbridge	Bo'ness
166	Bothwell	Newport
259	Bellshill	Queensferry
284	Airdrie	Grahamston
241	Roslin	Bervie
297	Penicuik	Leith
123	Westfield	
151	Dalmuir	Guard Bridge
158	North-Berwick	Meadowbank
161	Partick	Buckhaven
162	Milngavie	Loch Leven
274	Dalkeith	
295	Bellgrove	Carnoustie
20	Haddington	
22	Langholm	
29	Granton	
49	Sunnyside	Gretna
96	Arbroath	
97	Bonnington	
106	Slamannan	Tayport
107	Uddingston	Leuchars
108	Hamilton	St. Andrews
240	Coatbridge	Polton
313	Clydebank	Musselburgh
485	Yoker	Blairadam

Allocation and Work

Initially these engines were employed on suburban and local passenger work around Glasgow and Edinburgh as well as branch line working elsewhere. The Glasgow engines were soon replaced by later Drummond types and moved to other districts whereas the Edinburgh ones continued to work short distance passenger trains, throughout most of their lives. In particular the St. Margaret's engines of the class were associated with the North Leith branch, which had no less than six intermediate stations in a 3¼ mile journey,

and called for very smart work. Many of the class were kept at small sub-sheds, a typical example being No. 22 of Carlisle which was out-stationed at Langholm. When horse traction was discontinued on the Port Carlisle branch in April 1914 it was this engine (by then replaced at Langholm) which inaugurated steam haulage.

Apart from suburban and branch line work a certain amount of cross-country running was done by such engines as No. 162 on the Devon Valley line. As with most N.B.R. classes, individual engines often worked the same duty regularly for a long period of years, a case in point being No. 161 on the Methil branch. By late N.B.R. days, although some of the class, like Nos. 1289/94 of Polmont, were still on passenger work, many of them were on shunting duties and several had taken up their abode in the Glasgow district again. Their distribution latterly was fairly widespread as the accompanying summary of their final allocation shows:— Eastfield (5); St. Margaret's (4); Perth (3); Carlisle, Polmont, Dunfermline, Thornton (2 each); Haymarket, Tweedmouth, Parkhead, Bathgate and Stirling (1 each). The Tweedmouth engine was No. 1333 which the North Eastern Area acquired with the stock of Berwick shed when it closed. No. 1356 was station pilot at Perth, whilst Nos. 1291 and 1350 of St. Margaret's were much in evidence as Waverley Goods Pilot and St. Margaret's No. 1 Pilot respectively. On the other hand No. 10358 of St. Margaret's (which was still on passenger work as late as 1923) finished its days shunting in North Leith goods yard (the " Cundy " Pilot).

Engine Diagram

Section B, 1924.

Summary of J82 Class

Second 1924 No.		First 1924 No.		Second N.B. No.	First N.B.R. No.	Maker	Built	Brake	Withdrawn
(10289)		—		1289	165	Cowlairs	11/1875	W	10/23
(10291)		(10002)		1291	259	,,	11/1875	W	1/25
(10294)		(10003)		1294	284	,,	11/1875	W	12/24
(10299)		(10004)		1299	241	,,	1/1876	W	1/25
(10306)		(10005)		1306	297	,,	1/1876	W	2/25
(10328)		(10006)		1328	123	,,	4/1877	W & VE	11/26
10330	8/24	10007	6/24	1330	151	,,	5/1877	W	1/26
(10331)		(10008)		1331	158	,,	5/1877	W	7/25
(10332)		(10009)		1332	161	,,	4/1877	W	6/25
(10333)		(10010)		1333	162	,,	5/1877	W	2/25
(10335)		(10012)		1335	274	,,	/1877	W	6/25
(10336)		(10013)		1336	295	,,	5/1877	W	12/25

Fig. 55 Class J83 N.B.R. No. 828 at Waverley station, about 1923.
Unrebuilt (lock-up safety valves on dome, small front sandboxes), outside
brake pull rods, dual-fitted (showing vacuum ejector pipe alongside
boiler), shunter's footstep below bunker.

Fig. 56 Class J83 No. 9829 at Eastfield shed, about 1930.
Rebuilt (lower dome, Ross pop safety valves on firebox, larger front
sandboxes), dual-fitted (showing Westinghouse brake pump), slip coupling.

Fig. 57 Class J83 No. 9832 at Queen Street station, June 1938.
No shunter's step, slip coupling and cab blind fitted for incline duties,
backing plates to coal rails.

Fig. 58   Class J83 No. 8445 at Kipps shed,
                            May 1948.

Stovepipe chimney, steam brake (with inside pull rods).

Fig. 59   Class J83 No. 68451 at Thornton shed.

1917 ex-J31 boiler with lock-up safety valves on firebox.

Fig. 60   Class J83 No. 8473 at Eastfield shed, August 1947.

Green livery with Gill sans lettering.   Steam brake and vacuum
ejector (pull rods inside).

Fig. 61   Class J83 No. 68472 at Craigentinny carriage
sidings, 1948.
L.N.E.R. green livery with B.R. lettering.

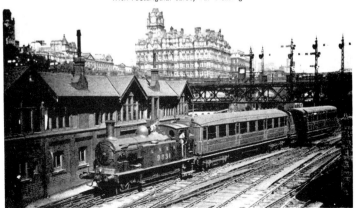

Fig. 62   Class J83 No. 68481 at Waverley station,
August 1958.
B.R. lined black livery, fluted coupling rods, St. Rollox boiler
with rectangular safety valve casing.

Fig. 63   Class J83 No. 9831 at Waverley station,
August 1935.

Fig. 64   N.B.R. No. 439 (later 1266) at Canal shed,
Carlisle, about 1910.

This engine was not one of the three which survived Grouping to
become class J84.

Fig. 65   N.B.R. No. 1238 at Cowlairs Works, September 1920.

No. 1168 of this type survived to become L.N.E.R. class J85 at Grouping.

Fig. 66   Class J86 N.B.R. No. 228 (later 1173) at
Cowlairs shed, August 1902.

With 5ft. 0in. wheels whereas L.N.E.R. engine diagram wrongly showed 4ft. 3in.
wheels.

Fig. 67   Class J84 (E.W.Y.U.R.) No. 3112 at Ardsley shed.
Retaining "E. & W.Y.U.R. No. I" plate on lower part of cab side.

Fig. 68   Class J84 No. 3113 inside Ardsley shed.
Modified frames.

Fig. 69   Class J84 No. 3112.
G.N.R. chimney and smokebox door, separate handrails on sides and
front of smokebox.

Fig. 70   Class J85 (E.W.Y.U.R.) No. 4 at Robin Hood,
September 1923.

As taken over by L.N.E.R.

Fig. 71   Class J85 No. 3114 at Ardsley shed.

With shorter saddle tank and the smokebox off class J84 No. 3113.

Fig. 72   Class J88 No. 843B at Gorgie yard, February 1925.

1905 engine with lock-up valves on dome and non-lifting injectors, two
coal rails, sheet metal buffers with tapered undersides.

Second 1924 No.		First 1924 No.		Second N.B. No.	First N.B. No.	Maker	Built	Brake	Withdrawn
(10348)		(10014)		1348	20	Cowlairs	11/1877	W	1/25
(10349)		(10015)		1349	22	,,	3/1878	W	11/25
(10350)		(10016)		1350	29	,,	3/1878	W	2/25
(10351)		(10017)		1351	49	,,	5/1878	W	8/24
(10352)		(10018)		1352	96	,,	6/1878	W	9/26
(10353)		(10019)		1353	97	,,	7/1878	W	7/24
(10354)		(10020)		1354	106	,,	7/1878	W	10/24
(10355)		(9018)		1355	107	,,	7/1878	W	12/24
(10356)		(10021)		1356	108	,,	6/1878	W & VE	2/25
(10357)		(10022)		1357	240	,,	1/1878	W	12/24
10358	9/24	10023	5/24	1358	313	,,	1/1878	W	8/26
(10359)		(10024)		1359	485	,,	1/1878	W	11/24

CLASS J83

N.B.R. CLASS D—HOLMES
4ft. 6in. ENGINES

ENGINES AT GROUPING (Built 1900-01): 9795-9834. TOTAL 40.

Apart from the very small "pug" saddle-tanks introduced for light shunting (later L.N.E.R. class Y9), Dugald Drummond built no goods tank engines for the N.B.R., and Holmes continued the tradition of using old tender engines for short distance goods trips and heavy shunting. In the 1890's however he rebuilt twenty of Wheatley's 4ft. 3in. 0-6-0 mineral engines as saddle tanks (see L.N.E.R. class J84), and then to help with the traffic boom coincident with the South African War he produced a new side-tank design, of which no less than forty examples were ordered straight away from outside contractors.

These were substantially unaltered at Grouping, but soon afterwards they were all rebuilt with new boilers and other minor alterations were made. Except for No. 8462 (ex-9815), which was withdrawn in September 1947, all the J83's came into British Railways. Ten new boilers for the class entered service in 1951 and it looked as if the engines had a further long lease of life, but within a few years they were being replaced by diesel shunters, some of the latest boilers being cut up after an extremely short life, judged by N.B.R. standards. The class became extinct in 1962.

N.B.R. Nos.	Maker	Works Nos.	No. built	Date
795-814	Neilson, Reid & Co.	5733-52	20	1900-01
815-834	Sharp, Stewart & Co.	4723-42	20	1901

Standard L.N.E.R. Dimensions at Grouping

Cylinders (2 inside)	17″ × 26″
Motion	Stephenson with slide valves
Boiler:	
Max. diam. outside	4′ 5″
Barrel length ...	10′ 1″
Firebox length outside	5′ 5″
Pitch	7′ 2″
Diagram No. ...	84
Heating surface:	
Firebox ...	100 sq. ft.
Tubes (200 × 1¾″)	950 sq. ft.
Total	1050 sq. ft.
Grate area ...	17 sq. ft.
Boiler pressure ...	150 lb./sq. in.
Coupled wheels ...	4′ 6″
Tractive effort (85%)	17,744 lb.
Length over buffers	30′ 2½″
Wheelbase ...	7′ 6″ + 8′ 0″ = 15′ 6″
Weight (full) ...	45T 5C
Max. axle load ...	17T 8C
Water capacity ...	800 gallons
Coal capacity ...	1T 10C

L.N.E.R. Renumbering

Under the Thompson scheme, Nos. 9795-9834 became 8442-81 in numerical order.

Rebuilding

The entire class was rebuilt in 1924-25 (for actual dates see Summary, p. 67) with new boilers of the same size as the originals. Insignificant differences in the published dimensions were as follows:—

	Original Boilers	New Boilers
Heating surface:		
Firebox	100 sq. ft.	99.5 sq. ft.
Total	1050 sq. ft.	1049.5 sq. ft.
Grate area	17 sq. ft.	16.65 sq. ft.

The dome height was reduced from 12ft. 3½in. to 11ft. 6¾in. standard Ross pop safety valves being fitted on the firebox instead of lock-up valves on the dome (figs. 55 and 56).

Other changes made at this time were the enlargement of the leading sandboxes and the provision of helical springs for the trailing axles in place of the laminated type. No revision of the 1924 engine diagram (showing only the unrebuilt form of the class) was issued, and it was not until 1939 that a new engine diagram was published.

In the meantime, to enable the shopping of these engines to be rationalised, a spare Diagram 84 boiler (ex-J31 10166) was made

available. This boiler dated from 1917 and was of the same dimensions as the others, but differed from them in having lock-up valves on the firebox. It was fitted to No. 9801 in April 1933, subsequently passing to No. 9814 in July 1938, No. 9824 in January 1946, and No. 68451 in June 1952 (fig. 59).

No further new (or second-hand) boilers were provided for the class until 1950, when St. Rollox works turned out ten boilers similar to the 1924-25 batch except that the number of tubes was reduced to 197, the total heating surface being given as 1034.5 sq. ft. The tube arrangement in the 1950 boilers was diagonal whereas it was horizontal in the 1924-25 boilers. In B.R. days some of the latter had seven alternate tubes (including the two end ones) removed from the top row, reducing the total to 193, but no revised heating surface figures were issued to correspond. This alteration was not always recorded officially, but it is known that Nos. 68456/8 were affected by the change. No engine diagram revision was issued to cover this variation. The 1950 boilers were recognisable by their rectangular (as distinct from round) safety valve casing, the valves themselves being the standard Ross pops as before (fig. 62). The first engines fitted with these boilers at Cowlairs in 1951 were Nos. 68444/6/7/55/64/6/72/6/80/1 (some of which reverted to the earlier type) and later Nos. 68448/9/71/7 acquired 1950 boilers.

Details

By Grouping all the J83's had tallow-cups at the sides of the smokebox (for the cylinders) and a single-feed lubricator in the cab (for the steam chest). The cab lubricator was of the Wilson & Co. Improved Parel type, later replaced in many cases by one of the Detroit OA pattern, both types of lubricator working on the hydrostatic principle with sight-feed. As running latterly No. 68478 had the tallow-cups on the front of the smokebox instead of at the side. The dual-fitted engines had steam heating apparatus with a hose connection at both ends, and No. 68449 was similarly equipped when supplied with a vacuum ejector in 1952. From about 1907 onwards shunting steps were fitted (to Thornton engines only at first), generally before Grouping, but No. 9832 was not so equipped until very late L.N.E.R. days (figs. 55 and 57). The J83's employed as banking engines on Cowlairs Incline (Nos. 9828/9/32/3/4, not all simultaneously) had slip couplings and cab blinds (fig. 57), whilst a makeshift wooden extension was sometimes attached to the bunker to give increased coal capacity. At Haymarket shed the same purpose was achieved by wedging old engine destination boards into the rear of the bunker. In late N.B.R. or early L.N.E.R. days backing plates were fitted to the coal rails on all engines of the class (fig. 57).

For a few weeks in August 1935 No. 9817, and for a short time in 1946-47 Nos. 8445/8/79, had stovepipe chimneys (fig. 58). Commencing in 1930, fluted coupling rods were fitted to Nos. 9801/5/7/11/2/3/7/20/31/4, in place of the usual plain roads (fig. 62). Drop grates were fitted as follows:—

9800	2/1936	9832	5/1937
9821	1/1936	9833	7/1937
9823	4/1937	9834	11/1936
9829	9/1937		

This resulted in a slight reduction in tank capacity (which was ignored on the engine diagram) because a space had to be cut to accommodate the operating handle and rod.

Brakes

As originally built the whole class had steam brakes, but Nos. 825-34 were soon altered to Westinghouse. These ten engines were additionally supplied with vacuum ejectors by 1916, and in late N.B.R. days Nos. 805/16 also became dual-fitted (figs. 55 and 56).

During and just after the Second World War the foregoing twelve engines had their Westinghouse equipment replaced by a graduable steam brake, working in combination with the vacuum, (for actual dates see Summary). Nos. 9827/31 were altered at Inverurie Works, the remainder being dealt with at Cowlairs (fig. 60).

The vacuum-fitted engines were normally employed on carriage-shunting duties in Edinburgh, Glasgow and Dundee, but in October 1952 No. 68449 was similarly equipped for assembling braked goods trains at South Leith yard. Finally Nos. 68466/70 had steam and vacuum combination brakes fitted in December 1952 and February 1953 to enable them to take over carriage-shunting duties from withdrawn engines of this class.

Before rebuilding the brake pull-rods were outside the wheels on all engines (fig. 55). On rebuilding the steam brake engines had the brake rigging altered to centre-pull (fig. 58), but the dual-fitted engines were not so altered until converted to steam and vacuum brakes (fig. 60). Another alteration which took place on rebuilding was the removal of the steam brake valve from the right-hand to the left-hand side of the cab (where the reversing lever had always been).

Liveries

Until 1928 these engines were painted in the lined black goods livery of the L.N.E.R., but subsequently became unlined. However an exception was made in the case of a few engines employed on shunting duties at Waverley station. Similarly, when the L.N.E.R. re-introduced the green locomotive livery in 1946, some of this class were again selected for early treatment because of their association with Waverley. The engines painted green were Nos. 8472/3/4/7/8/81 (fig. 60), only four of which were actually in use at Waverley at any one time, the other two being available as replacements when the regular engines were in Works or stopped for shed attention.

British Railways

Of the forty engines in this class only one had been withdrawn by the L.N.E.R. All the survivors at nationalisation were subsequently renumbered into the 60,000 series and fitted with smokebox number plates. For a time Nos. 68472/4/81 ran in L.N.E.R. green livery with their B.R. numbers, Nos. 68472/81 being lettered "BRITISH RAILWAYS" (fig. 61) whilst No. 68474 retained its "L N E R" lettering. Subsequently No. 68477 was painted in B.R. lined black livery; at first the "BRITISH RAILWAYS" lettering was retained, but this was replaced by the B.R. emblem. Other engines with B.R. lined black livery and emblem were Nos. 68463/72/4/80/1 (fig. 62). The remainder of the class were unlined and Nos. 68472/7 later became unlined also.

Allocation and Work

In pre-Grouping days all N.B.R. main sheds except Hawick and Stirling had at least one representative of this class. They were employed on transfer goods, mineral trip working, heavy yard shunting and banking duties. At St. Margaret's they worked the transfer traffic between Portobello, Niddrie and other yards around Edinburgh, these trains being known locally as "The Trawlers". For a time, two of the St. Margaret's engines (Nos. 825/6) were utilised on the Musselburgh branch passenger service. In the Glasgow area, the Eastfield engines shunted at Cadder and Maryhill yards and assisted on Cowlairs Incline, whilst those at Parkhead and Kipps were active in High Street yard and the vicinity of Coatbridge respectively. Initially the Fife engines worked coal trains, a typical example being from Auchtertool (on the Kirkcaldy and District Railway cross-country branch) to Burntisland Docks, but they were superseded on this work from 1909 onwards by 0-6-2T's (L.N.E.R. classes N14 and N15). With the construction of large numbers of the latter engines just prior to Grouping most of the J83's were put on shunting duties. Some of the class, already utilised in this way, were also replaced by 0-6-2T's and transferred to other centres (e.g. No. 801 of Berwick and No. 807 of Aberdeen), both of which were moved to St. Margaret's. The advent of the 0-6-2T's enabled two of the St. Margaret's J83's to be assigned to pilot duty at Waverley Station (East End) and some years later Haymarket shed acquired engines of the class for shunting at the West End. These carriage pilots were dual-fitted engines. Dunfermline shed also numbered a dual-fitted J83 amongst its stock, No. 9831, which in addition to the normal shunting and trip duties undertaken by the class at Kelty was also able to work short-distance passenger trains (provided for miners), calling at Cowdenbeath (Old) station long after its closure to normal traffic.

Between December 1925 and February 1926 No. 9806 was employed at Ardsley on trials against engines of the J50, J77 and N5 Classes.

In the 1930's the distribution of the class was as follows:— St. Margaret's 9, Thornton 7, Eastfield 6, Kipps 5, Dundee 5, Haymarket 4, Carlisle 2, Perth and Polmont 1 each. Apart from Waverley and Queen Street, carriage shunting was done by this class at Craigentinny, Cowlairs and Dundee. Some of the Thornton engines were sub-shedded at Methil for work around the docks there and at Kirkland yard, whilst the Polmont engine (No. 9824) was located at Kinneil and shunted at Bo'ness. The Carlisle engines (Nos. 9802/10) were employed at Canal yard, but during the 1939-45 War these two engines were moved to Edinburgh.

In the early 1940's, St. Margaret's employed No. 9830 on the North Leith branch passenger service where it replaced a Sentinel steam railcar. About this time No. 9831, by then shedded at Haymarket, appeared on passenger trains on the Corstorphine branch. The hardest turn of the day on this line was the 8-30 a.m. from Corstorphine, and this train was a sight to behold as it came past Haymarket shed, ten or twelve main line bogie coaches packed with passengers, with a bunker-first J83 sending an enormous column of smoke and steam straight up into the air and emitting a loud continuous roar. Even in British Railways days Haymarket often used a J83 on Corstorphine passenger turns, but not on the 8-30 a.m. which by then was normally Pacific-hauled.

Changes in the allocation of this class were few, but after nationalisation the Perth engine (No. 68469, ex-9822) was moved to Dalry Road, being noted shunting at Morrison Street Coal Depot, and later to St. Margaret's. The introduction of diesel shunters heralded the demise of the class and later transfers were usually to take over duties from withdrawn engines. The J83's were, even by N.B.R. standards, very regular in their habits and individual engines were often employed on the same actual duty for many years. An outstanding example was No. 68464 (originally N.B.R. No. 817) which throughout its lifetime was Leith Walk No. 3 (Trip) pilot. The J83's were most useful engines and invariably kept fully occupied. Only three of the class (all Kipps engines) failed to attain a mileage of one million, and one of the St. Margaret's engines (No. 9830) ran over two million miles. Among L.N.E.R. 0-6-0T classes, their average annual mileage was appreciably higher than their nearest rivals (class J72) and their maintenance costs amongst the lowest.

Engine Diagrams

Section B, 1924. Unrebuilt engines.
Section B, 1938. Rebuilt engines.

Classification: Route availability 4; B.R. power class 2F.

Summary of J83 Class

B.R. No.	1946 No.	1924 No.	Maker	Works No.	Built	Brake at Gpg.	Rebuilt	Vac. Ej. Added	W'house replaced by Steam	Withdrawn
68442 7/50	8442 4/46	9795 6/24	Neilson, Reid & Co.	5733	8/1900	S	6/24			1/62
68443 12/50	8443 4/46	9796 6/24	,,	5734	9/1900	,,	6/24			2/61
68444 5/51	8444 4/46	9797 10/24	,,	5735	9/1900	,,	10/24			1/60
68445 12/49	8445 4/46	9798 10/24	,,	5736	9/1900	,,	10/24			10/62
68446 11/48	8446 4/46	9799 6/24	,,	5737	9/1900	,,	6/24			3/56
68447 8/48	8447 3/46	9800 5/24	,,	5738	9/1900	,,	5/24			2/61
68448 4/50	8448 3/46	9801 11/24	,,	5739	9/1900	,,	11/24			10/62
68449 8/48	8449 3/46	9802 5/24	,,	5740	9/1900	,,	5/24	10/52		9/58
68450 8/50	8450 3/46	9803 2/25	,,	5741	9/1900	,,	2/25			12/57
68451 9/49	8451 3/46	9804 4/24	,,	5742	9/1900	,,	4/24			2/58
68452 3/50	8452 4/46	9805 2/25	,,	5743	3/1901	W & VE	2/25		9/44	6/58
68453 1/50	8453 5/46	9806 12/24	,,	5744	3/1901	S	12/24			10/62
68454 9/50	8454 5/46	9807 11/24	,,	5745	3/1901	,,	11/24			2/62
68455 4/48	8455 3/46	9808 9/24	,,	5746	3/1901	,,	9/24			5/56
68456 4/48	8456 5/46	9809 2/25	,,	5747	3/1901	,,	2/25			1/61
68457 9/48	8457 5/46	9810 9/24	,,	5748	3/1901	,,	9/24			3/60
68458 5/50	8458 5/46	9811 5/24	,,	5749	3/1901	,,	5/24			1/62
68459 8/50	8459 5/46	9812 5/24	,,	5750	3/1901	,,	5/24			5/61
68460 7/50	8460 5/46	9813 12/24	,,	5751	4/1901	,,	12/24			11/58
68461 5/48	8461 4/46	9814 2/25	,,	5752	4/1901	,,	2/25			6/58
—	8462 4/46	9815 12/24	Sharp, Stewart & Co.	4723	4/1901	S	12/24		7/45	9/47
68463 6/50	8463 6/46	9816 1/25	,,	4724	4/1901	,,	1/25			11/58
68464 7/48	8464 5/46	9817 5/24	,,	4725	4/1901	W & VE	5/24			3/58
68465 5/48	8465 5/46	9818 8/24	,,	4726	4/1901	S	8/24			8/57
68466 9/48	8466 4/46	9819 11/24	,,	4727	4/1901	,,	11/24	12/52		12/58
68467 5/48	8467 6/46	9820 11/24	,,	4728	4/1901	,,	11/24			9/59
68468 7/50	8468 5/46	9821 9/24	,,	4729	4/1901	,,	9/24			6/59
68469 12/48	8469 5/46	9822 3/25	,,	4730	4/1901	,,	3/25			10/56
68470 10/49	8470 5/46	9823 1/25	,,	4731	4/1901	,,	1/25	2/53		10/62
68471 10/50	8471 5/46	9824 12/24	,,	4732	4/1901	,,	12/24		8/44	8/61
68472 5/48	8472 6/46	9825 10/24	,,	4733	4/1901	W & VE	10/24		6/45	2/62
68473 4/50	8473 3/46	9826 10/24	,,	4734	4/1901	,,	10/24		12/44	5/56
68474 7/50	8474 1/46	9827 12/24	,,	4735	4/1901	,,	12/24			4/58
68475 7/50	8475 1/46	9828 10/24	,,	4736	5/1901	,,	10/24		4/47	3/58
68476 4/48	8476 1/46	9829 8/24	,,	4737	5/1901	,,	8/24		2/44	3/56
68477 8/49	8477 5/46	9830 4/24	,,	4738	5/1901	,,	4/24		12/44	12/62
68478 10/49	8478 5/46	9831 2/25	,,	4739	5/1901	,,	2/25		3/45	11/58
68479 6/50	8479 3/46	9832 4/24	,,	4740	5/1901	,,	4/24		9/44	10/62
68480 5/51	8480 5/46	9833 1/25	,,	4741	5/1901	,,	1/25		12/44	3/59
68481 5/48	8481 4/46	9834 11/24	,,	4742	5/1901	,,	11/24		1/44	2/62

CLASS J84

N.B.R. CLASS E—WHEATLEY
4ft. 3in. ENGINES

ENGINES AT GROUPING (Built 1873): 10257/9/70. TOTAL 3.

Between 1867 and 1874 Wheatley built thirty-eight 0-6-0 tender engines somewhat similar to his standard 5ft. 0in. class (see L.N.E.R. class J31), but with 4ft. 3in. driving wheels. Most of these engines were displaced from main line duties by the 1880's and many were employed on transfer trips and yard shunting, for which the tenders were not necessary. Twenty engines were therefore rebuilt as saddle tanks between 1889 and 1895, being then rather like a class of 0-6-0ST constructed by Wheatley about twenty years previously (see L.N.E.R. class J85). The engines selected for conversion were the last batch of twenty built at Cowlairs in 1873-74 and numbered 430-49 (fig. 64).

Rebuilding with new boilers (as distinct from conversion to tank engines) took place between 1892 and 1901 and, although the two processes were being carried out concurrently for several years, no engine was rebuilt with new boiler and converted to tank at the same time.

Withdrawal commenced in 1915 with No. 440 which (unlike all the others) never carried its duplicate number, but there were no further withdrawals until 1919, after which scrapping proceeded steadily. By Grouping seventeen of the class had been withdrawn.

N.B.R. No.	Withdrawn
1258 (431)	5/21
1260 (433)	8/21
1261 (434)	12/19
1262 (435)	9/21
1263 (436)	8/22
1264 (437)	4/21
1265 (438)	9/21
1266 (439)	1/19
1267 (440)	4/15
1268 (441)	11/21
1269 (442)	8/21
1271 (444)	9/21
1272 (445)	10/20
1273 (446)	7/19
1274 (447)	1/19
1275 (448)	7/21
1276 (449)	3/19

The three engines which survived the Grouping did not last long under L.N.E.R. ownership and the class was extinct by 1924. The 4ft. 3in. Wheatley 0-6-0's which were not converted into tank engines had all been withdrawn by 1920.

Standard L.N.E.R. Dimensions at Grouping

Cylinders (2 inside)	$16'' \times 24''$
Motion	Stephenson with slide valves
Boiler:	
Max. diam. outside	$4' 0\frac{3}{4}''$
Barrel length ...	$9' 10''$
Firebox length outside ...	$5' 0''$
Pitch	$6' 8\frac{1}{2}''$
Heating surface:	
Firebox ...	83.5 sq. ft.
Tubes ($171 \times 1\frac{3}{4}''$)	795.0 sq. ft.
Total	878.5 sq. ft.
Grate area	16 sq. ft.
Boiler pressure ...	140 lb./sq. in.
Coupled wheels ...	$4' 3''$
Tractive effort (85%)	14,336 lb.
Length over buffers ...	$28' 2\frac{1}{2}''$
Wheelbase ...	$6' 9'' + 7' 9'' = 14' 6''$
Weight (full) ...	36T 11c
Max. axle load ...	13T 13c
Water capacity ...	760 gallons
Coal capacity ...	*

* The coal capacity was not quoted on the L.N.E.R. (or N.B.R.) engine diagram, but by calculation would have been about 1 ton 10 cwt.

N.B.R. and L.N.E.R. Renumbering

During 1915-16 the twenty engines of this class were all transferred to the N.B.R. duplicate list, as follows:—

Old N.B.R. No.	New N.B.R. No.	Date
430	1257	11/1915
431	1258	11/1915
432	1259	11/1915
433	1260	5/1916
434	1261	6/1916
435	1262	6/1916
436	1263	6/1916
437	1264	6/1916
438	1265	12/1915
439	1266	1/1916
440	1267	—
441	1268	1/1916
442	1269	1/1916
443	1270	1/1916
444	1271	3/1916
445	1272	2/1916

Old N.B.R. No.	New N.B.R. N	Date
446	1273	2/1916
447	1274	3/1916
448	1275	4/1916
449	1276	4/1916

No. 440 never actually carried its new number, being withdrawn in 1915.

Of the three which came into L.N.E.R. possession, Nos. 1257/70 were withdrawn before the introduction of the 1924 renumbering. No. 1259 was allotted No. 10001 under the special scheme devised by Cowlairs for duplicate stock, but like Nos. 1257/70 it was withdrawn in N.B.R. numbering and livery.

Rebuilding

Two distinct processes of rebuilding took place in this class, the first being the conversion from the 0-6-0 tender wheel arrangement to the 0-6-0ST type. The standard Holmes pattern of saddle tank with curved base, countersunk rivets and front filler was employed. Individual dates of conversion are given in the table below.

Rebuilding with new boilers took place soon after the alteration from tender to tank, and these boilers were of the same dimensions as those originally fitted. Even the position of the dome was retained so that the recently added saddle tanks would not require alteration or replacement. Thus it will be seen that the dome was further forward than was usual on Holmes boilers. The following table gives both rebuilding dates, but it should be noted that the Cowlairs records available latterly only gave the second (i.e. reboiling) date and made no reference to the conversion from tender engines.

N.B.R. No.	Conv. to ST	New Boiler
430	1892	1/1898
431	1891	1/1895
432	1891	6/1900
433	1894	5/1900
434	1890	7/1900
435	1893	11/1900
436	1891	12/1900
437	1890	1/1901
438	1894	5/1897
439	1893	4/1897
440	1891	12/1892
441	1889	7/1900
442	1890	7/1900
443	1890	1/1901
444	1889	6/1901
445	1889	1/1901
446	1895	6/1897
447	1890	1/1898
448	1890	11/1895
449	1889	6/1900

During the 1914-18 War drawings were prepared for a further rebuilding of this class to incorporate an overall "round" cab reminiscent of G.N.R. practice, but this reconstruction was never carried into effect.

Details

As built these engines had the customary Wheatley stovepipe chimney, replaced when new boilers were fitted by the standard Holmes pattern capped chimney. At the same time new smokeboxes with countersunk (instead of snaphead) rivets were supplied, the door being bevelled with strap hinges instead of the earlier flush-fitting dished type with plate hinge. Holmes fitted the usual tallow-cup cylinder lubricators in the smokebox waist, with a bulb type lubricator in the cab for the steam chest. When running with tenders these engines had a cab with an extremely short (almost non-existent) roof whilst the side sheets had a quite substantial lower portion but very scanty upper section. In their saddle-tank form only front and rear spectacle plates were provided but the lower part of the cab side sheets remained. On top of, and protruding well over, the left-hand side sheet was usually placed the flat wooden driver's seat which was known to the enginemen as the "dickie". This gave the driver a very exposed position and he was often glad to change places with the fireman who at least had a modicum of shelter down "in the well".

In late N.B.R. days the characteristic long wooden step for the shunters was fitted. Before reboilering, the safety valves were totally enclosed in the dome cover (as tender engines) or in an iron casing above the dome (as tanks), but after the second rebuilding the standard lock-up valves were visible above the dome. In the final state the whistle was attached to a flanged distance piece visible behind the dome, whereas previously it was adjacent to the dome, the steam connection not being seen. Cast-iron wheels with T-section spokes were usually employed but in later years several engines of the class had the more usual wrought-iron wheels with normal spokes.

Brakes

Originally these engines had hand brake only, and No. 440 (allotted 1267) was still so equipped when withdrawn. All the rest were fitted with steam brake by about 1916.

Allocation and Work

As tender engines this class had been utilised on main line goods and mineral trains, but by the late 1880's they were widely used on yard shunting and transfer goods work.

After conversion to saddle tanks they were employed as shunting pilots mostly in the Central Lowlands. Two notable exceptions were Nos. 439/44 which were employed at Carlisle and Kelty respectively for many years. At St. Margaret's their duties included carriage shunting at Waverley, as well as the usual goods shunting in the busy marshalling yards at Portobello, Joppa and Niddrie. At South Leith, also served from St. Margaret's, three of the class were assigned to regular pilot duty, the usual trio being Nos. 435/6/7 (later renumbered 1262/3/4). Other sheds

which had engines of this class were Eastfield, Parkhead, Kipps and Polmont, typical duties being Bo'ness Pilot (No. 1272 of Polmont) and Camlachie Pilot (No. 1259 of Parkhead). The latter was one of the L.N.E.R. survivors, the other two being No. 1257 of Kipps and No. 1270 of St. Margaret's. The duties worked by this class were taken over by N15 0-6-2T's, or by J83 0-6-0 side tanks which had themselves been displaced by N15's.

Engine Diagram

Section B, 1924.

Summary of J84 Class

Final 1924 No.	First 1924 No.	Second N.B. No.	First N.B. No.	Maker	Built	Withdrawn
(10257)	—	1257	430	Cowlairs	10/1873	1/24
(10259)	(10001)	1259	432	,,	10/1873	6/24
(10270)	—	1270	443	,,	12/1873	7/23

CLASS J85

N.B.R. CLASS E—WHEATLEY
4ft. 3in. ENGINE

ENGINE AT GROUPING (Built 1870): 10168. TOTAL 1.

This engine was the first of a class of nine engines (three built in 1870 and six in 1873), and the sole survivor of the class at Grouping. Both series were built at Cowlairs, as under:—

Original N.B.R. Nos.	No. built	Date
130/2/52	3	1870
8, 13, 44, 258/60/3	6	1873

They were all rebuilt with new boilers and standard Holmes features between 1894 and 1898, transference to the N.B.R. duplicate list taking place during the years 1912-15 (fig. 65).

Withdrawal commenced in 1919 and by 1921 all except No. 1168 (ex-130) had been taken out of traffic.

N.B.R. No.	Withdrawn
1169 (132)	–/19
1170 (152)	–/20
1212 (258)	4/21
1228 (8)	2/19
1229 (13)	2/20
1230 (44)	11/20
1236 (260)	4/21
1238 (263)	8/20

No. 1168 was not withdrawn until 1924.

Standard L.N.E.R. Dimensions at Grouping

Cylinders (2 inside)	16″ × 24″
Motion	Stephenson with slide valves
Boiler:	
Max. diam. outside	4′ 0¾″
Barrel length ...	9′ 6″
Firebox length outside ...	4′ 4″
Pitch	6′ 7″
Heating surface:	
Firebox	84.81 sq. ft.
Tubes (171 × 1¾″)	755.82 sq. ft.
Total	840.63 sq. ft.
Grate area ...	13.5 sq. ft.
Boiler pressure ...	140 lb./sq. in.
Coupled wheels ...	4′ 3″
Tractive effort (85%)	14,336 lb.
Length over buffers	26′ 11½″
Wheelbase ...	7′ 0″ + 7′ 0″ = 14′ 0″
Weight (full) ...	34T 4c
Max. axle load ...	12T 6c
Water capacity ...	690 gallons
Coal capacity	*

* The coal capacity was not quoted on the L.N.E.R. (or N.B.R.) engine diagram, but by calculation would have been about 1 ton 10 cwt.

N.B.R. and L.N.E.R. Renumbering

The nine engines of Wheatley's " 130 " class were put on the N.B.R. Duplicate List as under:—

Old N.B.R. No.	New N.B.R. No.	Date
130	1168	6/1912
132	1169	7/1912
152	1170	9/1912
258	1212	11/1913
8	1228	12/1914
13	1229	1/1915
44	1230	1/1915
260	1236	4/1915
263	1238	11/1915

No. 1168, which was the only survivor at Grouping, was allotted L.N.E.R. No. 9999 in 1924, but it was withdrawn in N.B.R. livery and numbering.

Rebuilding

In accordance with the usual N.B.R. custom, systematic rebuilding of this class was carried out when the original boilers wore out. The new boilers were constructed in two batches, one in 1893 (two boilers) and the other in 1898 (seven boilers). The actual dates of fitting are given below.

N.B.R. No.	Rebuilt	N.B.R. No.	Rebuilt
8	1/1899	152	7/1898
13	7/1899	258	1/1894
44	9/1898	260	11/1898
130	4/1895	263	11/1898
132	7/1898		

The replacement boilers were of similar dimensions to those originally fitted, but the dome was set further back. New saddle tanks were fitted and other features brought into line with current Holmes practice (see under " Details ").

Details

The original Wheatley stovepipe chimneys were replaced by the standard Holmes capped pattern on rebuilding, and new smokeboxes with countersunk (instead of snaphead) rivets were fitted. The smokebox doors on the re-built engines were of the usual later bevelled pattern with external ring, whereas the original doors were dished and flush-fitting. The sandboxes were usually below the running plate, but one engine (No. 13) is known to have had the leading sandboxes above the running plate. No. 13 also had another unusual feature—two coal rails on the bunker, which was normally quite bare, not even having the rear spectacle plate to be found on other Wheatley 0-6-0ST classes.

The original dome cover was open-topped and bell-mouthed, concealing the safety valves, but on the rebuilds the dome cover was not so tall and had a flat top, above which appeared the customary two lock-up safety valves. On the rebuilt engines the saddle tank had countersunk rivets and a rounded base, whereas the unrebuilt variety had snaphead rivets and a flat base. The tank filler was originally behind the dome and had a detachable lid, but the later version had the filler (with hinged lid) placed in front of the dome. In both cases the whistle was just behind the dome, but the steam pipe from the dome to the whistle was L-shaped in the unrebuilt form and straight on the rebuilt version. An interesting feature of the unrebuilt engines was the " hump " in the whistle operating rod from the cab to enable it to clear the tank filler.

The footplate arrangements were much the same as on other Wheatley saddle tanks, with very little protection for the enginemen. The large structure carrying the cab footsteps was usually replaced by the later standard type of steps, but at least one engine (No. 258) retained the old type after rebuilding. On both types the long wooden shunting step was fitted latterly.

In early records No. 130 is shown as having several non-standard features. The wheel diameter was quoted as 4ft. 2in. as against the usual 4ft. 0in. for Wheatley engines which was given as 4ft. 3in. in later years. The wheelbase of No. 130 was recorded as 7ft. 0in. + 7ft. 0½in. instead of the 7ft. 0in. + 7ft. 0in. shown for the rest of the class, and this engine had an iron firebox instead of the usual copper one. These non-standard features on No. 130 do not appear in later records.

The wheels on this class were of the cast-iron pattern with T-section spokes.

Brakes

Hand brake only was provided on this class when built, and it was not until well into the Reid era that steam brake gear was supplied to all except one of the engines, No. 1169, which retained hand brake only until withdrawal. Originally wooden brake blocks were employed but latterly cast-iron blocks were used. In some cases the iron

blocks were at first fitted on to the original brake gear but entirely new rodding was later provided. The earlier arrangement had the pull rods " dipped " to clear the coupling rod ends, but the new apparatus had straight rods.

Allocation and Work

These engines were usually to be found shunting in various yards around Edinburgh and Glasgow. They were allocated to St. Margaret's, Haymarket, Eastfield, Parkhead and Kipps, with an odd member of the class (No. 13) at Bathgate. The two St. Margaret's engines (Nos. 8 and 44) were employed at Portobello Yard over a long period of years. The sole survivor at Grouping, No. 1168, was an Eastfield engine, its regular duty being Sighthill pilot.

Engine Diagram

Section B, 1924.

Summary of J85 Class

Final 1924 No. (10168)	First 1924 No. (9999)	Second N.B. No. 1168	First N.B. No. 130	Maker	Built	Withdrawn
				Cowlairs	6/1870	9/24

CLASS J86

N.B.R. CLASS E—WHEATLEY
5ft. 0in. ENGINE

ENGINE AT GROUPING (Built 1870): 10173. TOTAL 1.

Wheatley's first two passenger 0-6-0ST engines for the N.B.R. were Nos. 226/8, turned out from Cowlairs Works in 1870 and were slightly different from his later 5ft. 0in. 0-6-0ST's (see L.N.E.R. class J81). Nos. 226/8 had one 4ft. 3in. counterpart (No. 220) and a great deal of confusion has existed in the past because the N.B.R. did not issue a separate engine diagram for Nos. 226/8 (later 1172/3), but erroneously endorsed the 1921 engine diagram for No. 220 (then 1171) as applicable to Nos. 1171/2/3.

Nos. 226/8 were rebuilt with new boilers in 1901, the former was withdrawn as No. 1172 in 1919 leaving No. 228 to come into L.N.E.R. as No. 1173 (fig. 66). The confusion regarding these engines has even resulted in the capital list number of 1173 being quoted

as No. 220, but previous numbers were stamped on the large cast-brass number plates on N.B.R. duplicate engines and No. 1171 (which was withdrawn in November 1922) was actually checked by contemporary observers as ex-220.

No. 1173 was withdrawn in October 1924, having been the last Wheatley 0-6-0ST to remain in traffic.

Standard L.N.E.R. Dimensions at Grouping

Cylinders (2 inside)		16″ × 24″
Motion		Stephenson with slide valves
Boiler:		
Max. diam. outside		4′ 0¾″
Barrel length ...		10′ 2″
Firebox length outside ...		5′ 0″
Pitch		6′ 8¼″

Heating surface:

Firebox ...	...	83.5 sq. ft.
Tubes (171 × 1¾″)		817.0 sq. ft.
Total ...	...	900.5 sq. ft.
Grate area	...	16 sq. ft.
Boiler pressure	...	140 lb./sq. in.
Coupled wheels	...	4′ 3″*
Tractive effort (85%)		14,336 lb.*
Length over buffers		28′ 5¼″
Wheelbase	...	7′ 3″ + 7′ 9″ = 15′ 0″
Weight (full)	...	37T 2c*
Max. axle load	...	13T 9c*
Water capacity	...	759 gallons
Coal capacity	...	†

* These dimensions (and the L.N.E.R. engine diagram) actually applied to one engine (N.B.R. No. 1171) which had been withdrawn before Grouping. Class J86 had 5ft. 0in. coupled wheels and would therefore have a tractive effort of 12,185 lb. Presumably the pitch of the boiler would be slightly higher than the figure given and the weights were doubtless slightly different.

† The coal capacity was not given on the L.N.E.R. diagram but would be approximately 1 ton 10 cwt.

N.B.R. and L.N.E.R. Renumbering

Nos. 226/8 became Nos. 1172/3 on transfer to N.B.R. duplicate list in November 1912. The only survivor at Grouping, No. 1173, never carried an L.N.E.R. number, but under the shortlived Cowlairs renumbering scheme of 1924 it was allotted No. 10000.

Rebuilding

Nos. 226/8 were rebuilt in the usual N.B.R. fashion with new boiler and detail alterations to bring them into line with current practice in 1901 (No. 226 in December; No. 228 in November). These engines had a slightly longer wheelbase than the No. 149 class (see L.N.E.R. class J81) and they retained this difference after rebuilding. Consequently they required a different boiler; this had the same firebox but a longer barrel. The comparative figures were:—

	J81	J86
Wheelbase	7′ 0″ + 7′ 0″	7′ 3″ + 7′ 9″
	= 14′ 0″	= 15′ 0″
Barrel length	9′ 7″	10′ 2″

Weight before rebuilding was given as 36 tons 3 cwt. with a maximum axle load of 13 tons 0 cwt. on the leading axle. The wheel diameter was given in the earliest records as 5ft. 1¾in. Other alterations are dealt with under "Details".

Details

The original stovepipe chimney was replaced on rebuilding by the usual Holmes pattern with cap, but No. 226 had for some years previously a somewhat top-heavy lipped bell-mouth added to its stovepipe. The smokebox and its fittings were altered as on other Wheatley 0-6-0ST classes and likewise the saddle tank was replaced by the more shapely Holmes type. The original boilers had the dome situated on the firebox with open bell-mouthed top to house the safety valves, but the Holmes boilers had the dome further forward with lock-up safety valves protruding above. Unlike the later 5ft. 0in. engines (see class J81), Nos. 226/8 had the leading sandboxes above the running plate, but these were moved (on rebuilding) to the customary position beneath the running plate. The whistle was moved by Holmes from its position immediately in front of the cab to one adjacent to the dome. Both before and after rebuilding the tank filler was fairly well forward, but originally the lid lifted off instead of being hinged (No. 226 is known to have had a hinged lid before rebuilding).

The cab was of the usual scanty proportions associated with Wheatley engines, and in the words of the long-suffering enginemen it had "the sky for a roof". The shape of the side sheets was altered from the box type to the contoured pattern combining with the rear splasher when the engines were rebuilt, but no further protection for the crew was provided beyond the existing two spectacle plates. The substantial rear step was replaced by the later standard N.B.R. pattern on rebuilding. In the early days a primitive form of lubricator was placed behind the chimney, but latterly the familiar tallow-cups were affixed to the smokebox waist.

Brakes

Originally both engines had hand brake only and No. 226 retained this arrangement throughout its life. No. 228 however was equipped with Westinghouse brake during the Holmes period, without subsequent alteration.

Allocation and Work

In their early days Nos. 226/8 were shedded at Cowlairs and worked local passenger trains in the Glasgow area. No. 228 in particular was associated with the Blane Valley line for a long period. In later years they were employed on shunting duties, allocated to Parkhead (No. 1172) and Polmont (No. 1173). Just prior to withdrawal No. 1173 was usually to be found shunting at Grahamston and Springfield Yards, Falkirk.

Engine Diagram

Section B, 1924.

Final 1924 *No.* (10173)	*First* 1924 *No.* (10000)	*Second* *N.B.* *No.* 1173	*First* *N.B.* *No.* 228	*Maker* Cowlairs	*Built* 10/1870	*Withdrawn* 10/24

CLASS J84

E. & W.Y.U.R.
4ft. 0in. ENGINES

ENGINES TAKEN OVER 1ST JULY 1923 (Built 1895-1900): 3112/3 (E. & W.Y.U.R. 1 and 2), E. & W.Y.U.R. 3. TOTAL 3.

The East & West Yorkshire Union Railways Company was taken over by the L.N.E.R. on 1st July 1923. The line was small, with a route mileage of only 9¼, serving collieries south of Leeds. In places, both curvature and gradients were severe. Connections were made with the G.N.R. Doncaster-Leeds line at Lofthouse, near Ardsley, and with the Midland Railway at Stourton.

The locomotive stock of the E. & W.Y.U. Rlys. consisted of four 0-6-0ST's (L.N.E.R. classes J84 and J85) and two 0-6-2ST's (L.N.E.R. class N19), all built by Manning, Wardle & Co.

Two 0-6-0ST's, numbered 1 and 2, were ordered in March 1895 and were delivered in June and July of that year (makers' numbers 1307/8). They had 17in. × 24in. cylinders and 4ft. 0in. coupled wheels. The design had a raised firebox, the top of which was almost level with the top of the saddle tank, the latter being mounted astride the boiler barrel ahead of the firebox. A third engine, No. 3, was ordered in December 1899 and delivered in September 1900 (works number 1489). It differed from the earlier pair only in minor details, such as the special deep tone whistle.

The L.N.E.R. allotted class J84 to these engines and J85 to the other E. & W.Y.U. 0-6-0ST although both classifications were already in use for Wheatley saddle tanks in the Scottish Area. However, the Wheatley engines were scrapped during 1924 and this duplication thereupon ceased.

No. 3 was withdrawn as such immediately after being taken into L.N.E.R. stock, but Nos. 1 and 2 became 3112/3 and were condemned in 1930 and 1928 respectively.

Standard L.N.E.R. Dimensions, 1923

Cylinders (2 inside)	17″ × 24″
Motion	Stephenson with slide valves
Boiler:	
Max. diam. outside	4′ 0″
Barrel length ...	10′ 0″
Firebox length outside ...	5′ 4″
Pitch	6′ 9½″
Heating surface:	
Firebox ...	95 sq. ft.
Tubes (172 × 1⅞″)	868 sq. ft.
Total	963 sq. ft.
Grate area	14.94 sq. ft.
Boiler pressure ...	150 lb./sq. in.
Coupled wheels ...	4′ 0″
Tractive effort (85%)	18,424 lb.
Length over buffers	29′ 3″*
Wheelbase ...	6′ 6″ + 8′ 0″ = 14′ 6″
Weight (full) ...	39T 12c*
Max. axle load ...	13T 19c*
Water capacity ...	850 gallons
Coal capacity ...	1T 10c

* These figures applied to No. 3112 and E. & W.Y.U. No. 3. No. 3113 was both longer and heavier (see " Rebuilding " below).

L.N.E.R. Renumbering

E. & W.Y.U. Nos. 1 and 2 became L.N.E.R. Nos. 3112/3 in July and November 1924 respectively. No. 3 was not allotted an L.N.E.R. number and was in fact withdrawn almost immediately after being taken over. No. 3112 at first retained its old brass numberplates, although these were later removed. The plates, hitherto fitted to the sides of the saddle tank, were now located on the cab sides, underneath the Manning, Wardle maker's plates (fig. 67). No. **3113** received the usual L.N.E.R. small cast number plates, on the cab sides.

Rebuilding

The original boilers lasted a relatively short time, being replaced as follows: No. 1 April 1914, No. 2 March 1916, No. 3 June 1911. These second boilers lasted out the lifetime of the engines.

No. 2 received new frames and cylinders in April 1915. The frames were 6in. longer than the original ones, increasing the front overhang from 7ft. 3in. to 7ft. 9in. They were also more substantial, both thicker and deeper, with no lightening holes between the leading and centre horn gaps. At the ends the lower profile was cut at a straight slant, instead of the usual curve (fig. 68). The total weight of the engine in working order was increased to 42 tons, and the maximum axle load to 14 tons 8 cwt. The factor of adhesion was thus appreciably increased from the already high figure of 4.816. Unfortunately, No. 2 was prone to repeated frame fracturing. This cannot be entirely attributed to a loss of flexibility on the sharp curves as similar trouble was not experienced with No. 4 (class J85).

Details

The handrails on the left-hand side of the saddle tank originally extended back to the cab front but in L.N.E.R. days the rear piece was dispensed with. A vertical handrail was also located on the right-hand side only of the saddle tank. The smokebox handrail crossed in front of the chimney and was joined at the ends to the front plate of the saddle tank. No. 3112 had the later two-handle arrangement to secure the smokebox door, whilst No. 3113 retained its original wheel and handle type of fastening to the end.

In 1928 No. 3112 had its original smokebox handrail removed and replaced by three short rails, one on each side of the smokebox and one on the smokebox door. At the same time the smokebox door straps were shortened and a small door knob fitted, following normal Doncaster practice. The old built-up chimney was replaced by a shorter G.N.R. pattern chimney (fig. 69).

Mechanical lubricators were fitted to all three engines, driven off the coupling rod pin of the leading wheel. The engines had gravity sanders, operating on the leading and trailing pairs of wheels.

When first built, the bunkers held 1 ton of coal. At an early date rails were added to the bunker tops, increasing the capacity by a further 10 cwt.

Brakes

In L.N.E.R. days steam brakes only were fitted, though at one time No. 1 had been fitted with a M.R. pattern Gresham & Craven combined steam brake and vacuum ejector for working passenger trains between Robin Hood and Leeds (see " Allocation and Work " below). The passenger services had been discontinued in 1904, but the vacuum ejector was not removed from No. 1 until about 1914.

Allocation and Work

The double track main line of the E. & W.Y.U. ran from Lofthouse (on the G.N.R.) to Stourton (on the Midland). About half way was Robin Hood, with its sidings, a three-road engine shed (complete with fitting shop), and a turning triangle. From Robin Hood radiated three single line branches. On the main line the 0-6-0 and 0-6-2 saddle tanks could take 20 loaded wagons from Robin Hood to Lofthouse and bring back 80 empty wagons.

For a short period a passenger train service was operated between Robin Hood, Rothwell and Leeds (Wellington), with running powers over the Midland from Stourton. When these services commenced early in 1904 the Midland provided an 0-4-4T to work the trains. Then, in March, 1904 No. 1 was fitted with a vacuum ejector and took over the working. The passenger services ceased to run in the following September, and thereafter the only passenger trains which operated were the occasional excursions at holiday times from Robin Hood and Rothwell to the coast. These were still being run until the early 1960's, usually in charge of J6's, and were subject to a speed restriction of 10 m.p.h. The ruling speed limit on all other traffic was 15 m.p.h., imposed by the severe gradients and sharp curves.

The longest branch was 2¾ miles in length which at its far end served Newmarket Colliery and the coal staiths alongside the River Calder. The branch was worked under staff and ticket regulations as far as Patrick Green, where a compulsory stop was made to pin down the wagon brakes prior to the descent of the " one engine in steam " section to the colliery. An engine could take 22 loaded or 44 empty wagons from Robin Hood to Newmarket, although when shipping traffic was being produced at Rothwell (Rose Pit) a train of 30 wagons of coal could be despatched to the staiths at Newmarket provided a banking engine was supplied as far as Patrick Green.

On the return journey the severe gradient, 1 in 44 in places, restricted the load over the first section to Patrick Green. It was therefore the usual practice to bring a maximum of 12 loaded wagons up to the siding loop at Patrick Green and return to the colliery for a further 12 wagons, which would then be attached to the first lot left in the loop, the whole load then being taken forward to Robin Hood.

The Thorpe branch was about a mile long with rising gradients of 1 in 38, 1 in 30 and finally 1 in 14 at the top end. Half way up the branch was an old tar works where the brake van was always left behind on the running road, attached to any wagons which had to go back to Robin Hood. Up the final stretch the engine would propel a maximum of two loaded or four empty wagons.

In the reverse direction the engine would take up to 13 loaded wagons, with all the brakes pinned down at both sides, as far as the tar works, where the engine would be coupled to the wagons which had been left on the running road. The train would then descend to Robin Hood with the unusual formation of brake van leading and the engine in the middle of the train. Another traffic stop would be made at Robin Hood Coke Works, where probably another half dozen or so wagons would be attached to the rear. These sidings were near to the main Leeds to Wakefield road and traffic was frequently held up for some time at the level crossing by the shunting operations.

The Beeston branch was about ¾ mile long and connected with one end of the turning triangle at Robin Hood. The gradient was not too severe and an engine could propel 24 empty wagons up to Beeston Pit and return with 25 wagons of coal.

The triangle at Robin Hood was also used when necessary for turning wagons of shipping coal to ensure that their end doors were correctly positioned for the staiths at Newmarket.

Such was the peculiar nature of the line that the E.W.Y.U. possessed special purpose engines for working over the sharp curves and steep gradients. All were fitted with raised fireboxes and these were advantageous in that the regulator valves were high up in the firebox near to the faceplate, at the highest point when the engines were climbing the gradients bunker first. The 0-6-2ST's (class N19) were specially suited to the Thorpe branch, with their extremely short rigid wheelbase (9ft. 6in) and radial wheels which had a steadying effect. The 0-6-0ST's had longer coupled wheelbases and were more suited to the Newmarket branch, especially No. 3114, the solitary J85. This engine had the reputation of being the strongest engine on the line and it could bring up to 14 loaded

wagons at a time out of Newmarket Colliery, i.e. two more than the other engines.

The engines were sturdily built and strong, and the L.N.E.R. was hard pressed to find suitable replacements for them when they were withdrawn, particularly for the Thorpe branch.

When the E.W.Y.U. was taken over by the L.N.E.R. in July 1923, one of the 0-6-0ST's, No. 3, was immediately withdrawn. This was no doubt due to extensive boiler repairs being necessary. Most of the repair work was done at Robin Hood and visits to the makers' were infrequent. No. 3's boiler dated from June 1911 and it had last been repaired by Manning, Wardle & Co. in August 1915, when a new set of copper tubes had been fitted. One of the 0-6-2ST's was also withdrawn in July 1923 so that in effect only four E.W.Y.U. engines were taken into L.N.E.R. stock. Of these, No. 2 was in a very bad condition, with fractured frames, and was only steamed when there was a shortage of power.

In February 1924 No. 1 arrived at Doncaster Works for a general repair and was returned to traffic in the July. In the meantime, No. 4 had been laid up at Ardsley for repairs twice (a total of fourteen weeks). The surviving 0-6-2ST had also been stopped for repairs part of this time, leaving the stand-by engine, No. 2, to carry the brunt of the work before it too paid a visit to Doncaster Works in August 1924. No. 2 returned to traffic in November of that year after a general overhaul, renumbered 3113.

No. 3113's next visit to Doncaster Work for a general repair was in January 1928. By the time it was back in traffic three months later, the surviving 0-6-2ST had been withdrawn. Once again No. 3113 bore the brunt of the work, especially in the autumn when No. 3112 was sent to Doncaster for its second general repair there. No. 3112 was returned to traffic on 20th December 1928, and two days later No. 3113 was withdrawn.

No. 3112 was withdrawn in June 1930, rendering class J84 extinct.

Robin Hood shed closed in July 1926 and its engines and men were transferred to Ardsley. The first ex-G.N.R. engine to be tried out on the E.W.Y.U. was a J54, No. 3679. Being domeless, it had an advantage over the J52's which were used later. The steam for the vacuum ejector was obtained from the faceplate and was therefore trouble-free on the gradients. With the J52's, the steam was obtained from the dome, half way along the boiler, and on the gradients the vacuum brakes were occasionally rendered useless by water entering the ejector. However, No. 3679's maximum load over the final section of the Thorpe branch was one loaded wagon, to avoid the risk of stalling.

The next G.N.R. saddle tank to be tried was No. 3686, one of the J57 class. With its smaller diameter wheels it would seem to have been a better choice than the J54, but the wheelbase was still too long for the curves. On a trial trip up the steeply graded Thorpe branch engine first, water entered the vacuum brake, rendering it inoperative. It was consequently regarded as unsuitable for this particular branch. No. 3686 was withdrawn in August 1929.

In September 1930 ex-G.C.R. saddle tank No. 5888 (class J62) arrived at Ardsley and was used on the E.W.Y.U. line until its withdrawal in July 1937. Then in 1931 two ex-N.E.R. J77's, Nos. 614 and 1349, were sent to Ardsley. No. 1349 left in July 1932 and was not replaced. No. 614 was exchanged for No. 1439 in February 1935, and the latter lasted until April 1939. All these engines were used on the Thorpe branch until they were displaced by the more successful J69's.

Between 1935 and 1944, several ex-G.E.R. J69's were shedded at Ardsley, viz. Nos. 7352/67/70/84. No. 7370 in particular was there from May 1935 to September 1944. These engines were found to be well suited to the Thorpe branch, with their 4ft. diameter wheels, 13ft. 10in. wheelbase and steam brakes, although at least one driver used to descend the 1 in 14 gradient by applying the brakes, jumping off and following on foot!

In the meantime ex-G.N.R. J52's had appeared on the E.W.Y.U. line, although not at first on the Thorpe branch. Commencing in mid-1938 a number of these engines returned to Ardsley and eventually they appeared on the Thorpe branch, of necessity, although they were not really suitable and their vacuum brakes were unreliable. By now traffic by rail from the brickworks at Thorpe had fallen off and trips up the branch were infrequent. The J52's stayed on the E.W.Y.U. line until March 1961 when the last survivor at Ardsley was withdrawn. They were replaced by ex-W.D. J94's which remained on the line to the end.

Apart from the above-mentioned 0-6-0T classes, between 1936 and 1938 three ex-H. & B.R. 0-6-2T's were used on the E.W.Y.U. These engines (class N12) worked on the Newmarket branch.

Thus over the last forty years or so the line had seen quite a variety of classes, in an effort to match the capability and sturdiness of the original engines.

Actually, the main line from Lofthouse to Stourton was not as restricted as the branches, and from time to time tender engines were utilised when the coal traffic was particularly heavy.

Engine Diagram

Section N, 1924. Showing unmodified engine 3112.

Not issued. Engine 3113 as modified in 1915.

Summary of J84 Class

1924 No.		E.W.Y.U. No.	Maker	Works No.	Built	Withdrawn
3112	7/24	1	Manning, Wardle & Co.	1307	6/1895	6/30
3113	11/24	2	,,	1308	7/1895	12/28
—		3	,,	1489	9/1900	7/23

CLASS J85

E. & W.Y.U.R.

3ft. 9in. ENGINE

Engine taken over 1st July 1923 (Built 1898): 3114 (E. & W.Y.U.R. 4). Total 1.

Three 0-6-2ST's were delivered by Manning, Wardle & Co. during 1898/9 to the East & West Yorkshire Union Railways Company and were numbered 4, 5 and 6.

They were of similar design to the 0-6-0ST's (L.N.E.R. class J84) supplied to the Company by the same builders, but had 3ft. 9in. instead of 4ft. 0in. coupled wheels.

In August 1919 No. 4 was completely rebuilt as an 0-6-0ST by Manning, Wardle. It became class J85 on the L.N.E.R.

(duplicating temporarily the classification already in use for an ex-N.B.R. saddletank) and lasted until February 1933.

The remaining two 0-6-2ST's were not rebuilt and survived to become class N19 on the L.N.E.R.

Standard L.N.E.R. Dimensions, 1923

Cylinders (2 inside)	17″ × 24″
Motion	Stephenson with slide valve
Boiler:	
Max. diam. outside	3′ 10″
Barrel length ...	10′ 5″
Firebox length outside ...	5′ 9″
Pitch	6′ 8″
Heating surface:	
Firebox	99 sq. ft.
Tubes (150 × 1⅞″)	789 sq. ft.
Total	888 sq. ft.
Grate area ...	16.3 sq. ft.
Boiler pressure ...	140 lb./sq. in.
Coupled wheels ...	3′ 9″
Tractive effort (85%)	18,342 lb.
Length over buffers	31′ 8″
Wheelbase ...	6′ 3″ + 8′ 3″ − 14′ 6″
Weight (full) ...	40T 0c
Max. axle load ...	16T 0c
Water capacity ...	1,000 gallons
Coal capacity ...	2T 0c

L.N.E.R. Renumbering

No. 4 became L.N.E.R. No. 3114, following on after the J84's.

Rebuilding

As 0-6-2ST's, Nos. 4, 5 and 6 found special favour on the sharply curved Thorpe branch of the E.W.Y.U., where the trailing wheels had a steadying effect. This advantage was achieved at the expense of a relatively poor factor of adhesion, when compared with the 0-6-0ST's on the line. Therefore No. 4 was rebuilt as an 0-6-0ST just under four years prior to being taken over by the L.N.E.R. and quickly gained the reputation of being the strongest engine on the E.W.Y.U. line.

In its original form the firebox had been located between the rear coupled wheels and the trailing wheels, enabling a short rigid wheelbase to be provided, i.e. 9ft. 6in. As rebuilt, the firebox had to be located between the middle and rear coupled wheels, and of necessity the coupled wheelbase had to be lengthened. The wheelbase became 14ft. 6in., as in the original 0-6-0ST's, although the centre pair of wheels were actually 3in.

further forward in No. 4 because of the longer firebox.

New 1¼in. thick frames were provided, with a profile resembling the set fitted to No. 2 in 1915. The original saddle tank, with its typical Manning, Wardle appearance, was replaced by a new one which was 2ft. 1in. shorter in length. The top of the new tank was 6in. higher than before to increase the capacity, and almost semi-circular in cross-section to avoid obscuring the driver's vision (fig. 70).

Details

The handrail on the left-hand side of the saddle tank extended back to the cab front, and a vertical handrail completely encircled the tank. The smokebox handrail crossed in front of the chimney and was joined at both ends to the front plate of the saddle tank. The smokebox door differed from those on the J84's in having a flat rim around the edge and short straps which only extended across half the width of the door. The door was secured by the two-handle arrangement. The smokebox diameter was 1in. less than in the J84 class and at the bottom the smokebox sides were vertical.

In July 1929 No. 3114 was modified during a visit to Doncaster Works (fig. 71). Evidently some components were retrieved from class J84, No. 3113, which had been withdrawn at the close of 1928 but not broken up until May 1929. The saddle tank from this engine was put on No. 3114, which reduced the water capacity from 1,000 to 850 gallons. The smokebox door was also utilised, complete with its original wheel and handle door securing arrangement and longer straps. The smokebox and saddle tank handrails were altered: the vertical rail was now located on the right-hand side only, as in No. 3113. The rear piece of the horizontal handrail was dispensed with between the saddle tank and the cab front. The original smokebox handrail was replaced by three separate rails, one on each side of the smokebox and one on the smokebox door.

Brakes

No. 3114 had steam brake.

Allocation and Work

As rebuilt, No. 4 was especially favoured on the Newmarket branch. Notwithstanding its lower nominal tractive effort, it was capable of hauling more wagons than the comparable J84 class engines, which had larger wheels and less adhesion.

Fig. 73   Class J88 No. 9237 at Eastfield shed, June 1929.
1909 engine with lock-up valves on dome and combination injectors, four coal rails.

Fig. 74   Class J88 No. 9152 at Eastfield shed, August 1937.
1912 engine with lock-up valves on firebox, combination injectors, four coal rails (plated in).

Fig. 75   Class J88 No. 9844 at Gorgie yard, about 1925.
1905 engine with 1925 boiler (pop valves on firebox with flared casing).
Showing slotted frames and sheet metal dumb buffers.

Fig. 76   Class J88 No. 68339 at Gorgie yard, April 1952.

Carrying last surviving 1908 boiler with lock-up valves on dome

Fig. 77   Class J88 No. 68345 at Alloa, June 1956.

Stovepipe chimney, rectangular safety valve casing.

Fig. 78   Class J88 No. 68335 at Methil, April 1955.

Vacuum ejector.   Shows solid frames.

Fig. 79   Class J90 No. 6839 at Kittybrewster about 1928.
Ramsbottom safety valves.

Fig. 80   Class J90 No. 6811 at Inverurie, 1934.
Ross pop safety valves.

Fig. 81   Class J91 No. 6841 at Kittybrewster shed, about 1928.
Ramsbottom safety valves.

Fig. 82   Class J91 No. 6838 at St. Combs, October 1926.
Cowcatchers for unfenced branch line.

Fig. 83   Class J93 No. 095 at South Lynn.
10-spoke wheels with built-up balance weights (ex-C.M.R. engine), tall
vacuum standpipe arranged to fold down sideways, Deeley pattern
smokebox door.

Fig. 84   Class J93 No. 099 at Melton Constable, May 1938.
12-spoke wheels with crescent balance weights, hopper bunker.

Fig. 85   Class J93 No. 096 at South Lynn, 1938.
Johnson style smokebox door, short vacuum standpipe.

Fig. 86   Class J93 No. 8484 at Cambridge shed, April 1948.
Tall stovepipe chimney, vacuum standpipe removed.

Fig. 87   Class J93 No. 8485 at Stratford after withdrawal,
March 1948.
Short stovepipe chimney.

Fig. 88   Class J94 Nos. 8048 and 8049 at Darlington,
July 1946.

In W.D. livery and with L.N.E.R. shaded lettering and numerals.

Fig. 89   Class J94 No. 8064 at Gorton, 1946.

Unshaded L.N.E.R. lettering and numerals.

Fig. 90   Class J94 No. 8068 at Grimsby Dock, June 1947.

Small unshaded numerals on bunker.

rformance, it 'e of its class, T's continued after Grouping the E.W.Y.U. the closure of was the last surviving E.W.Y.U. engine when it was withdrawn in February 1933.

See also under class J84 for further details of the operation of the E.W.Y.U. line.

Engine Diagram
Section N, 1924.

Summary of J85 Class

Maker	Works No.	Built	Withdrawn
ining, Wardle & Co.	1398	9/1898	2/33

CLASS J88

N.B.R. CLASS F—REID
3ft. 9in. ENGINES

ENGINES AT GROUPING (Built 1904-19): 9066/87, 9114/6-9/21/30/2/52, 9233-8/71/7/9/ 88/9/90, 9836-47. TOTAL 35.

The standard N.B.R. dock shunting engine from 1882 until 1899 had been the Neilson 0-4-0ST (L.N.E.R. class Y9), but when further locomotives of this category were required in 1904 W. P. Reid produced a new 0-6-0 side tank design. For a post-Drummond Cowlairs drawing office design these engines had three noteworthy peculiarities, viz:— (1) right-hand drive (2) outside cylinders (3) absence of smokebox wingplates. With slight modifications this class remained the N.B.R. standard for light shunting work until Grouping by which time a total of thirty-five had been constructed, all at Cowlairs.

Nos. 9836-47 were rebuilt in 1925 with new boilers having Ross pop safety valves on the firebox (fig. 75). Their original boilers were scrapped and there was no systematic rebuilding thereafter. Three lots of new boilers were subsequently built, thus enabling boilers to be circulated around the class. As a result some of the later engines had from time to time boilers with safety valves on the dome, from the batch built in 1909.

The class was intact at nationalisation, and the first casualty was No. 68341 which was condemned in November 1954 after falling into Kirkcaldy harbour. Regular withdrawal began in November 1955 and the class became extinct in December 1962, having been superseded by diesel shunters.

N.B.R. Nos.	No. built	Date	Safety-valve position	Injectors	Coal rails
836-41	6	1904-05	Dome	Non-lifting	2
842-7	6	1905	Dome	Non-lifting	2 (fig. 72)
233-8	6	1909	Dome	Combination	4 (fig. 73)
66, 114/6/7/8/9/21/30/2/52	10	1912	Firebox	Combination	4 (fig. 74)
277/90/88/9, 87, 271/9	7	1919	Firebox	Combination	4

79

Standard L.N.E.R. Dimensions at Grouping

Cylinders (2 outside)		$15'' \times 22''$
Motion		Stephenson with slide valves

Boiler:

Max. diam. outside		$3'\ 10''$
Barrel length ...		$8'\ 8\frac{1}{2}''$
Firebox length outside ...		$4'\ 8\frac{1}{4}''$
Pitch		$6'\ 6\frac{1}{2}''$
Diagram No. ...		87

Heating surface:

Firebox ...		65.7 sq. ft.
Tubes ($142 \times 1\frac{3}{4}''$)		585.5 sq. ft.
Total		651.2 sq. ft.
Grate area ...		14.5 sq. ft.
Boiler pressure ...		130 lb./sq. in.
Coupled wheels ...		$3'\ 9''$
Tractive effort (85%)		12,155 lb.
Length over buffers		$26'\ 6\frac{3}{4}''$
Wheelbase ...	$5'\ 3'' + 5'\ 9'' = 11'\ 0''$	
Weight (full) ...		38т 14c
Max. axle load ...		15т 12c
Water capacity ...		850 gallons
Coal capacity ...		2т 1c

The above dimensions agreed with those shown on the N.B.R. engine diagram applicable to the 1912 and 1919 engines. Another pre-Grouping diagram existed for the 1904-05 and 1909 batches showing the weight full as 36 tons 5 cwt., the maximum axle load as 13 tons 3 cwt., and the coal capacity (of the 1904-05 series only) as 1 ton 11 cwt. Possibly this diagram was intended to become L.N.E.R. class J87 which in fact always remained blank.

L.N.E.R. Renumbering

Under the 1946 scheme the J88's were renumbered 8320-54 in date order, except that Nos. 9288/9 were slightly out of sequence at the end of the series.

Rebuilding

The first twelve engines were rebuilt with new boilers fitted with combination injectors and Ross pop safety valves on the firebox, the actual dates being as follows:—

No.	Date	No.	Date
9836	5/1925	9842	3/1925
9837	5/1925	9843	6/1925
9838	4/1925	9844	4/1925
9839	5/1925	9845	5/1925
9840	5/1925	9846	4/1925
9841	4/1925	9847	3/1925

This was the last instance of the traditional N.B.R. practice of systematic rebuilding of a class (or part of a class) when boiler renewals became necessary. Instead, the policy was now adopted of putting new boilers into circulation on engines passing through shops, and gradually scrapping the worn-out boilers. In the case of J88, three further lots of boilers were constructed, entering service on the undermentioned engines:—

1929-33 : Nos. 9087, 9121/32, 9233/77/88 (boilers dated 1928).
1950-51 : Nos. 68326/45/6/9/52.
1954-55 : Nos. 68324/33/41/7/50.

The 1928-built boilers, which were made at Cowlairs, were the same as the 1925 batch, but the later examples (constructed at St. Rollox) had 136 tubes (total heating surface 626.7 sq. ft.) and were distinguishable by having a straight-sided rectangular casing for the safety valves instead of the former flared round pattern (cf. figs. 75 and 77). All the boilers used on this class were of the same general dimensions.

As a result of the change in boiler maintenance policy, the following engines ran for a time with 1909 boilers (i.e. with safety valves on the dome):—Nos. 9114/30, 9290, 9842/5/7 and Nos. 8348/54. The last of these boilers to remain in use was condemned (along with engine No. 68339) in October 1958 after almost fifty years of active service (fig. 76).

Details

Apart from the boilers, already referred to, the 1904-05 engines differed from the remainder of the class in four other respects. (1) They had slotted frames, instead of the solid plates used on the later engines (cf. figs. 75 and 78).

(2) They had short dumb buffers, replaced before Grouping by the longer pattern (straight or tapered) as on the rest of the class (see figs. 72 and 75).

Incidentally all the J88's had wooden buffer-beams, and another peculiarity of the class was the absence of drawhooks (these were later fitted in some instances).

(3) They had strap ends on the coupling rods, soon replaced by the solid bush type employed on the 1909-19 engines.

(4) They had two coal rails on the bunker whereas the subsequent batches had four rails. The earlier engines were never altered in this respect, but all the J88's eventually acquired backing plates to the rails.

By Grouping all the engines of the class had been equipped with the long wooden footsteps characteristic of N.B.R. shunting locomotives, and another general fitting was a spark arrester, usually of the horizontal wire screen variety inside the smokebox, but Nos. 8345/7/9 had these on the top of the chimney from about 1943 until withdrawal. The old N.B.R. bulb-type lubricator on the front spectacle plate (inside the cab), which fed the steam chest, and the tallow cups on the running plate which supplied oil to the cylinders, remained in use throughout the lifetime of these engines. An official record that Nos. 9066 and 9116 had Detroit OA sight-feed lubricators in late L.N.E.R. days is quite unsupported by photographic or other evidence.

Engines fitted with drop grates were:—

No.	Date	No.	Date
9130	12/1937	9290	11/1937
9152	8/1938	9842	2/1938
9234	1/1939	9843	12/1939
9237	1/1937	9847	4/1939

In March 1956, whilst on loan to Blairhall Colliery, No. 68345 had its chimney damaged in a mishap and a very austere home-made stovepipe was substituted at Dunfermline shed. This was retained by No. 68345 for the rest of its career (fig. 77).

Brakes

Steam brake was fitted on all the engines of this class and no alterations took place in N.B.R. or L.N.E.R. days. After nationalisation however, Nos. 68332/5 were equipped with steam and vacuum combination brakes for handling fitted goods vehicles at Markinch (fig. 78). The dates of alteration were November 1952 and November 1953 respectively.

British Railways

The whole class came into British Railways, all the engines being repainted in B.R. livery complete with smokebox number plate.

Allocation and Work

The J88's were usually allocated to sheds responsible for dock working both on the East and West coasts of Scotland and for shunting sharply-curved sidings (or sidings with short shunting heads) in the industrial Lowlands. Their distribution did not alter a great deal over the years, the allocation of 1935 being typical:—St. Margaret's 9, Eastfield 8, Thornton 7, Kipps 4, Polmont 3, Stirling and Haymarket 2 each.

The St. Margaret's engines were employed at Leith Docks and Granton Harbour (including the Duke of Buccleuch's extension to the Edinburgh Corporation Gas Works). One of the class shunted at St. Leonard's (terminus of the erstwhile Edinburgh and Dalkeith Railway) where a sub-shed had existed in N.B.R. days, and except for very brief spells when trials of other classes took place, No. 9066 (ultimately B.R. No. 68338) was regularly on this duty throughout its lifetime. Two St. Margaret's J88 pilot duties with trip working were those at Heriothill and Lochend. These and the St. Leonard's pilot were customarily rostered for ex-main line drivers who lavished great affection on their charges, undertaking such maintenance work as adjustment of brakes and gland-packing, and kept their regular engines highly polished. One of the Haymarket engines shunted at Gorgie, the other being kept as a spare, until the installation of a wheel drop at Haymarket shed when the second J88 became " Drop Pit Pilot ".

Until the opening of Thornton new shed in July 1933, Burntisland was a main shed, but it then became a sub-shed of Thornton. Before this date, Kirkcaldy was supplied by Burntisland, but subsequently Thornton was responsible for all J88's working in Fife. Dock working was done at Burntisland, Kirkcaldy, Leven and Methil, the Kirkcaldy harbour being approached by a branch line on a gradient of 1 in 25. Over the years this was the scene of many hair-raising descents and " narrow squeaks ", but on two occasions (separated by an interval of over forty years) disaster ensued. On the second of these (12th November 1954) No. 68341 ran out of control down the branch with nineteen loaded wagons (an excess of seven over the permitted number). After colliding with the stop block on the quayside, the engine toppled into the water and after recovery was withdrawn from service (the first of the class). Apart from dock working, Thornton J88's also shunted the sidings at Kirkcaldy and Markinch. For a time Perth and Dundee had individual engines of the class, but by the mid-1930's the only other Northern District shed besides Thornton with a J88 allocation was Stirling. This was for working Alloa Harbour and when the sub-shed at Alloa was transferred to the jurisdiction of Dunfermline in B.R. days, the two J88's concerned were officially moved to the latter shed. The class was not unknown at Dunfermline, because No. 9289 had been there in early L.N.E.R. days.

One of the Polmont engines was usually out-stationed at Kinneil for use in Bo'ness docks, whilst another found employment on the Rough Castle pilot. The Kipps engines shunted in the industrial sidings of the Coatbridge neighbourhood, such as Whifflet, and one did trip work on the Moffat Mills branch previously done by the Y10 0-4-0 tender engine No. 1011. Incidentally other J88 workings formerly undertaken by 0-4-0 tender engines were those at Lochend, Alloa and Markinch. Eastfield kept an allocation of J88's for shunting at Princes Dock, Queen's Dock and Rothesay Dock (these engines being sub-shedded at Stobcross) and for shunting at Eastfield shed itself.

For many years Y9 " pug " saddle-tanks were available for hire to private owners, usually as a temporary replacement for a locomotive under repair, and in later years J88's were occasionally requisitioned for this type of duty.

As recounted above, No. 68341 was withdrawn in 1954 after a mishap, and the remainder of the class followed it to the scrapheap between 1955 and 1962. The status of the J88's seemed to improve with the passage of time, and many of their trip workings came after Grouping. Even in B.R. days the Heriothill Pilot (No. 68348) was given the additional job of running the empty fish vans in the morning from Waverley to North Leith, the return loads being worked by a V1 in the afternoon. However, the J88's had to make way for diesel shunters, but most of them had by then completed well over forty years of active service. Several of the class spent brief periods at former Caledonian sheds including Balornock, Dawsholm, Grangemouth and Motherwell, where their duties were similar to those undertaken on their native section.

Engine Diagrams

None issued.	Engines with lock-up safety valves on the dome and (a) with two coal rails on the bunker (1904-05 engines) (b) with four coal rails on the bunker (1909 engines)
Section B, 1924.	Showing lock-up safety valves on the firebox (i.e. applicable to the 1912 and 1919 engines)
Section B, 1939.	Same as 1924 but showing pop safety valves and insignificant alterations in firebox height and size of journals.

Classification: Route availability R.A.3; B.R. power class 0F.

Summary of J88 Class

B.R. No.		1946 No.		1924 No.		Maker	Built	Withdrawn
68320	3/50	8320	7/46	9836	12/24	Cowlairs	12/1904	6/60
68321	9/49	8321	7/46	9837	6/24	,,	12/1904	6/58
68322	4/48	8322	7/46	9838	3/25	,,	12/1904	12/58
68323	1/50	8323	7/46	9839	7/24	,,	12/1904	10/56
68324	6/48	8324	3/46	9840	7/24	,,	1/1905	7/58
68325	12/50	8325	1/46	9841	4/25	,,	1/1905	3/61
68326	3/51	8326	3/46	9842	3/25	,,	9/1905	10/59
68327	7/51	8327	7/46	9843	6/25	,,	9/1905	7/58
68328	1/52	8328	7/46	9844	4/25	,,	9/1905	3/58
68329	5/49	8329	7/46	9845	12/24	,,	10/1905	2/59
68330	5/49	8330	7/46	9846	4/25	,,	10/1905	8/58
68331	1/49	8331	7/46	9847	3/25	,,	10/1905	3/59
68332	11/49	8332	4/46	9233	3/27	,,	3/1909*	8/60
68333	5/48	8333	1/46	9234	4/25	,,	3/1909	3/58
68334	4/49	8334	3/46	9235	11/24	,,	3/1909	6/59
68335	6/50	8335	3/46	9236	8/26	,,	3/1909*	10/62
68336	3/49	8336	5/46	9237	3/26	,,	4/1909	5/62
68337	10/51	8337	6/46	9238	2/25	,,	4/1909	11/55
68338	7/49	8338	6/46	9066	10/25	,,	4/1912	9/61
68339	10/51	8339	1/46	9114	5/25	,,	4/1912	10/58
68340	7/49	8340	3/46	9116	4/24	,,	5/1912	2/58
68341	3/51	8341	5/46	9117	2/25	,,	5/1912	11/54
68342	6/50	8342	5/46	9118	6/25	,,	5/1912	2/62
68343	10/49	8343	6/46	9119	3/24	,,	6/1912	10/60
68344	2/50	8344	6/46	9121	5/25	,,	6/1912	1/61
68345	7/51	8345	1/46	9130	9/25	,,	7/1912	12/62
68346	9/48	8346	1/46	9132	8/25	,,	7/1912	10/62
68347	8/50	8347	3/46	9152	2/25	,,	7/1912	8/58

B.R. No.		1946 No.		1924 No.		Maker	Built	Withdrawn
68348	11/49	8348	6/46	9277	3/25	Cowlairs	9/1919	8/58
68349	10/50	8349	5/46	9290	12/24	,,	9/1919	8/60
68353	7/48	8353	6/46	9288	6/25	,,	10/1919	2/62
68354	3/51	8354	1/46	9289	7/25	,,	10/1919	9/60
68350	7/48	8350	7/46	9087	3/25	,,	11/1919	7/62
68351	2/51	8351	5/46	9271	11/25	,,	11/1919	1/57
68352	6/48	8352	6/46	9279	1/25	,,	11/1919	6/60

* Steam brake was standard on the class, but vacuum ejectors were added to Nos. 68332/5 in November 1952 and November 1953 respectively.

CLASS J90

G.N.S.R. CLASS D—MANSON
4ft. 6in. ENGINES

ENGINES AT GROUPING (Built 1884):
6808/11/5/6/39/42. TOTAL 6.

The G.N.S.R. acquired a number of tank engines from subsidiary companies, but these were generally short-lived. On the other hand two 0-4-0 well tanks built for the G.N.S.R. in 1856 had a very long existence. They were sold for industrial use before Grouping, but one of them actually lasted until 1943. Most of the shunting and local work, both passenger and goods, on the G.N.S.R. was therefore done by older tender engines (all of the 2-4-0 or 4-4-0 wheel arrangement) until the introduction of this class of six conventional 0-6-0 side tank engines by Manson in 1884. Numbered 8, 11/5/6, 39 and 42, they were built by Kitson & Co. (Works Nos. 2650-5). Three further 0-6-0T's followed in 1885, but they were slightly different and became L.N.E.R. class J91.

All six engines of this class were rebuilt with new boilers during 1907-11, and all became L.N.E.R. property. Withdrawal commenced in 1932 and the whole class had been eliminated by 1936.

Standard L.N.E.R. Dimensions at Grouping

Cylinders (2 inside)		16″ × 24″
Motion		Stephenson with slide valves

Boiler:
Max. diam. out-side		4′ 0″
Barrel length ...		10′ 6″
Firebox length outside ...		4′ 9″

Pitch		6′ 11″
Diagram No. ...		91
Heating surface:		
Firebox ...		71.8 sq. ft.
Tubes (158 × 1¾″)		774.2 sq. ft.
Total		846.0 sq. ft.
Grate area ...		14.82 sq. ft.
Boiler pressure ...		150 lb./sq. in.
Coupled wheels ...		4′ 6″
Tractive effort (85%)		14,507 lb.
Length over buffers		30′ 0¾″
Wheelbase ...	6′ 10″ + 6′ 10″ = 13′ 8″	
Weight (full) ...		42T 0c
Max. axle load ...		16T 0c
Water capacity ...		900 gallons
Coal capacity ...		1T 10c

Rebuilding

New boilers were provided in 1907-11, the individual dates being as under:—

G.N.S.R. No.	Date Rebuilt	Maker of Boiler
8	5/1908	Vulcan Foundry
11	12/1910	Inverurie
15	10/1911	,,
16	1/1908	Vulcan Foundry
39	11/1907	,, ,,
42	6/1911	Inverurie

The replacement boilers had the same maximum diameter (on the rear ring) as those originally fitted, but ½in. plates were used instead of $\frac{7}{16}$in. and there was a significant increase in weight. Comparative dimensions are shown in the accompanying table.

83

	As built	As rebuilt
Boiler diam. (front and centre rings) (outside)... ...	3′ 10¼″ and 3′ 11⅛″	3′ 10″ and 3′ 11″
Heating surface (sq. ft.):		
Tubes	690	774
Firebox ...	66	72
Total	756	846
No. of tubes (1¾″ diam.)	140	158
Grate area (sq. ft.)	15	14.8
Boiler pressure (lb./sq. in.)... ...	140	150
Weight (full) ...	37T 8c	42T 0c

As rebuilt the engines showed little change in appearance although certain minor alterations were carried out when the new boilers were fitted (see under " Details ").

Details

Originally tall chimneys of typical Manson built-up pattern were fitted, but on rebuilding shorter tapered Johnson-type chimneys were provided. Consequently the height of the chimney above rail level became 12ft. 5¼in. instead of 12ft.9$\frac{15}{16}$in. The smoke-box doors were always of the customary G.N.S.R. dished form, but for a time plate hinges were used until replaced by the standard ⊐-shaped hinge straps favoured by the G.N.S.R. Ramsbottom safety valves were used, originally with casing for the base only, but later with casing for the columns and spring also (fig. 79). In L.N.E.R. days standard Ross pop valves took the place of the Ramsbottoms (retaining the casing around the base) on Nos. 6811/6/42 (fig. 80). Following customary G.N.S.R. practice, two whistles were provided and at first these were on the cab roof. On rebuilding, however, the whistles were moved to the more usual position behind the safety valves. Nos. 6815/42 had the brake whistle removed after Grouping.

The cabs were notable (at the time of the introduction of the class) in having gangway doors, and another feature which mitigated the effects of inclement weather was the sliding shutter on each side enabling the size of the cab aperture to be reduced according to the crew's requirements. Initially the bunker was devoid of coal rails but these were added before rebuilding; after Grouping backing plates were affixed to the rails on Nos. 6815/6/42. Sometimes makeshift arrangements were made to increase the coal capacity further. All engine diagrams for the class (with or without rails) showed a coal capacity of 1 ton 10 cwt.

Sanding was originally by gravity, but on rebuilding steam-operated gear was substituted. The leading sandboxes were joined to the splashers, but unlike most Scottish examples the sandbox was wider than the splasher itself. Roscoe and Furness lubricators on the sides of the smokebox gave way before Grouping to a Detroit sight-feed lubricator situated in the cab. Steam heating equipment (with a pipe to both ends) was fitted as under:—

No.	Date
6808	6/1925
11	3/1922
15	12/1920
16	6/1919
39	12/1920
42	4/1919

The G.N.S.R. normally fitted safety chains at the rear end of tender engines and at both ends of tank engines, including class J90, but these were usually removed by the L.N.E.R. The position of the date plate in G.N.S.R. and early L.N.E.R. days was on the leading sandbox, but later the date plate was moved to the side of the bunker. No. 6842 was unusual in retaining its G.N.S.R. date plate on the sandbox when fitted with its L.N.E.R. combined number and date plates on the bunker. The G.N.S.R. number plate was placed centrally on the side tank, but whereas on class G10 this plate was retained (but moved to the bunker) at the first repainting in L.N.E.R. livery, on class J90 it was removed as soon as L.N.E.R. lettering was applied to the tank side. When working the St. Combs service (known locally as the " Bulger trainies ") No. 8 had cowcatchers at each end.

Brakes

Originally these engines had hand brake only, but by 1890 Nos. 15/6, 39 and 42 had been equipped with Westinghouse brake for working Aberdeen suburban trains. Nos. 8 and 11 were similarly altered soon afterwards. Pipe connections were under the bufferbeams and swan-neck fittings were only used on this class in one instance, namely on No. 6808 probably from June 1925 onwards.

Allocation and Work

Latterly this class was usually associated with local goods working and shunting at Kittybrewster and Waterloo, but in G.N.S.R. days these engines were also to be found on main line pick-up goods trains. The Aberdeen suburban trains (known as " Jubilee Trains " from the date of their introduction, 1887) were regularly worked by this class prior to the appearance of the 0-4-4T's in 1893. All the 0-4-4T's were not employed on these services at first, and for some years the 0-6-0T's shared this work with the 0-4-4T's. Eventually the 0-6-0T's were relegated mostly to goods work, but one of the class (usually No. 8) worked passenger trains, as well as goods and mixed trains, on the Fraserburgh-St. Combs branch.

About the time of Grouping, No. 6842 was regular goods engine on the Alford branch, and at various times Nos. 6815 and 6842 were utilised on shunting duties at Keith.

Engine Diagram

Section S, 1924.

Classification: Northern Scottish Area Second Class.

Summary of J90 Class

1924 No.		Maker	Works No.	Built	Withdrawn
6808	6/25	Kitson & Co.	2650	5/1884	4/32
6811	?	,,	2651	5/1884	6/34
6815	12/25	,,	2652	5/1884	4/35
6816	10/24	,,	2653	5/1884	5/35
6839	7/25	,,	2654	6/1884	5/34
6842	8/24	,,	2655	6/1884	3/36

CLASS J91

G.N.S.R. CLASS E—MANSON
4ft. 6in. ENGINES

ENGINES AT GROUPING (Built 1885): 6837/8/41. TOTAL 3.

These three engines were generally similar to the six Manson 0-6-0T's described under class J90. Their G.N.S.R. numbers were 37/8 and 41, and they came from Messrs. Kitson & Co. in 1885 (Works Nos. 2835/6/7). The boiler was the same size as that employed on the preceding class, but it was set further forward. There was an increase in overall length and also in total weight, but the latter was distributed in such a way as to bring about a reduction in the maximum axle load. The width over the side tanks was 1¼in. greater than in the preceding class.

Rebuilding with new boilers took place concurrently with that of the J90 class during 1908-11, the boilers being interchangeable between the two classes. The other detail differences remained. All three duly became L.N.E.R. stock and were withdrawn between 1931 and 1934.

Standard L.N.E.R. Dimensions at Grouping

Cylinders (2 inside)	16"* × 24"
Motion	Stephenson with slide valves
Boiler:	
Max. diam. outside ...	4' 0"
Barrel length ...	10' 6"
Firebox length outside ...	4' 9"
Pitch	6' 11¾"
Diagram No. ...	91
Heating surface:	
Firebox	71.8 sq. ft.
Tubes (158 × 1¾")	774.2 sq. ft.
Total	846.0 sq. ft.
Grate area	14.82 sq. ft.
Boiler pressure ...	150 lb./sq. in.
Coupled wheels ...	4' 6"
Tractive effort (85%)	14,507 lb.
Length over buffers	30' 4½"
Wheelbase ...	6' 10" + 6' 10" = 13' 8"

Weight (full)	...	43т 5c
Max. axle load	...	15т 15c
Water capacity	...	900 gallons
Coal capacity	...	1т 10c

* Erroneously given as 18in. on the 1924 Engine Diagram; corrected with the December 1924 alterations.

Rebuilding

The boilers used on this class were identical with those fitted to the preceding class and, being of approximately the same age, they became due for replacement during the same period. The new boilers for the two classes were made in two batches, one lot of four coming from Vulcan Foundry and the other five from Inverurie (see also class J90). Actual rebuilding dates were:—

G.N.S.R.	Date	
No.	Rebuilt	Maker of Boiler
37	3/1911	Inverurie
38	11/1911	,,
41	8/1908	Vulcan Foundry

These replacement boilers on classes J90 and J91 were retained by the engines to which they were fitted until withdrawal. The comparative dimensions of the old and new boilers are shown in the table on p. 84. Whereas the weight full was originally 37 tons 12 cwt., after rebuilding it became 43 tons 4 cwt.

Other minor alterations carried out at this time are mentioned under the heading " Details ".

Details

The original Manson chimneys were replaced by the shorter Johnson pattern when the engines were rebuilt, giving a height above rail level of 12ft. 5¼in. instead of 12ft. 9$\frac{15}{16}$in. Other alterations at this time included the removal of the two whistles from the cab roof to the firebox and the substitution of steam-operated for gravity

sanding. Ramsbottom safety valves (originally with seat casing but later with column and spring casing also) were fitted (fig. 81), but latterly No. 6837 had Ross pop valves.

As running in L.N.E.R. days the left leading sandbox on No. 6838 had a right-angle flanged top instead of the usual plain rounded top. By Grouping Nos. 37 and 38 had a sight-feed lubricator in the cab instead of the earlier Roscoe and Furness pattern on the smokebox, but No. 41 still retained the last named. Steam heating equipment was fitted to the class as follows:—

G.N.S.R.	
No.	Date
37	5/1921
38	5/1920
41	4/1919

Brakes

Westinghouse brake was fitted to these engines when built. The hose connections were below the bufferbeam and none appears to have been fitted with swan-neck standpipes.

Allocation and Work

The engines of this class were chiefly employed on yard shunting at Kittybrewster and Waterloo, with trip work and assisting between these two points. Before the advent of the 0-4-4T's (L.N.E.R. class G10) they were also used on the Aberdeen suburban trains. Passenger and mixed trains were handled by the class on the Fraserburgh-St. Combs line, No. 6838 being the regular branch engine in early L.N.E.R. days. When on that duty it was fitted with a cowcatcher at each end (fig. 82).

Engine Diagram

Section S, 1924.

Classification: Northern Scottish Area Second Class.

Summary of J91 Class

1924 No.		Maker	Works No.	Built	Withdrawn
6837	3/25	Kitson & Co.	2835	6/1885	6/31
6838	8/24	,,	2836	6/1885	7/33
6841	10/25	,,	2837	6/1885	6/34

CLASS J93

M. & G.N. "SHUNTING" CLASS—MARRIOTT
3ft. 7in. ENGINES

ENGINES TAKEN OVER 1ST OCTOBER 1936
(Built 1897-1905): 015/6, 093-9. TOTAL 9.

These engines were designed and built by the M. & G.N. at Melton Constable, but the influence of Midland Railway practice was apparent in many features of the design. The boiler drawing was made at Derby in 1896, and many other details were similar to those on contemporary Derby designs, notably the cab, tanks, boiler mountings and smokebox door, but the chimney was similar to the standard Melton Constable "3rd type", tapering in towards the base.

The nine engines were built at Melton Constable between 1897 and 1905, seven being numbered in the duplicate list. In 1907 the engines with "A" numbers were renumbered 93-99 in order of their original numbers.

Engine No. as Built	Renumbered	Date Built
14A	98	1897
1A	93	1898
11A, 3A	96, 95	1899
15	—	1901
17A, 12A	99, 97	1902
2A	94	1904
16	—	1905

When built, most if not all of the engines carried "Rebuilt Melton Constable" plates, and Nos. 93-8 were reputed to have been rebuilt from 0-6-0T's inherited by the Eastern & Midlands Railway (the predecessor of the M. & G.N.) from the Lynn & Fakenham Railway, and which had started life on the Cornwall Minerals Railway. (See pages C.72-74 in R.C.T.S. *Locomotives of the G.W.R.*, Part 3).

Eight of these ex-Cornwall Minerals engines (built by Sharp, Stewart & Co. in 1874) had been acquired by the Lynn & Fakenham in 1880-81, of which four (Nos. 3, 13, 14 and 18) were rebuilt to 2-4-0 tender engines in the early 1890's, whilst the remainder (Nos. 1, 2, 11 and 12) survived as 0-6-0T's until withdrawn. The 1936 M. & G.N. stock register shows the nine J93's as *new* in 1897-1905, and Mr. G. B. Clarke, who was Mr. Marriott's draughtsman at Melton Constable when the 0-6-0T's were built, once stated emphatically that they were new engines.

Nos. 93-8 should correctly be considered as *replacements* of the ex-C.M.R. engines,

whilst No. 99 (old 17A) replaced a Black, Hawthorn 0-6-0ST, and Nos. 15 and 16 took the numbers of the two Fox, Walker 0-6-0ST's built in 1877.

The wheels from the Cornwall Minerals engines are believed to have been used on some of the J93's, and at various times Nos. 16, 95/6/8 were noted with wheels of the same design as those on the ex-C.M.R. engines. These wheels had 10 spokes and built-up balance weights, whereas the new wheels, where fitted, had 12 spokes and cast-in crescent-shaped weights (cf. figs. 83 and 84). No. 98 had received the new pattern wheels by April 1933, and No. 096 was fitted with 12-spoked wheels some time after July 1936, but No. 095 retained the old pattern 10-spoked wheels until withdrawn in 1947 as No. 8485. The fourth engine, No. 016, finished its days in 1949 as No. 8489 with 10-spoked leading and trailing wheels, but the driving axle had a 10-spoked wheel on the left-hand side and a 12-spoked wheel (with the crescent-shaped balance weight) on the right! All photographs so far examined of Nos. 015, 093/4/7/9 show 12-spoked wheels.

It has not been possible to identify any other second-hand material, although the layout of cylinders, slide bars and motion brackets was very similar to that on the earlier engines. The use of much old material was prohibited by the longer wheelbase of the new engines—13ft. 9in. compared with 11ft. 0in.

Although taken over by the L.N.E.R. on 1st October 1936, the M. & G.N. locomotives were not added to L.N.E.R. stock until 1937.

The 0-6-0T's were shown on the original L.N.E.R. diagram as "Class Shunting Tank", but in July 1942 they became class J93. All were withdrawn between 1943 and 1949.

Standard L.N.E.R. Dimensions, 1937

Cylinders (2 outside)	16″ × 20″
Motion	Stephenson with slide valves
Boiler:	
Max. diam. outside	3′ 11″
Barrel length ...	9′ 7″
Firebox length outside ...	4′ 3″
Pitch	6′ 4¼″
Diagram No. ...	46D

Heating surface:

Firebox	67.2 sq. ft.	
Tubes (145 × 1¾″)	662.6 sq. ft.	
Total	729.8 sq. ft.	
Grate area ...	11.3 sq. ft.	
Boiler pressure ...	150 lb./sq. in.	
Coupled wheels ...	3′ 7″	
Tractive effort (85%)	15,181 lb.	
Length over buffers	28′ 2″	
Wheelbase ...	6′ 3″ + 7′ 6″ = 13′ 9″	
Weight (full) ...	37т 14c	
Max. axle load ...	14т 2c	
Water capacity ...	800 gallons	
Coal capacity ...	1т 10c	

L.N.E.R. Renumbering

The final M. & G.N. numbers of these engines were prefixed by cyphers after being taken over by the L.N.E.R. When the general renumbering scheme was drawn up in 1943, No. 097 had already been withdrawn, but the remainder were allotted Nos. 8482-9, in order of construction. Nos. 015, 093/9 were withdrawn before the renumbering was put into effect in 1946.

Details

The boilers, although not standard with any Midland Railway boilers, were typical of S. W. Johnson's Midland designs of the period, made in three rings, with two Salter safety valves in the dome and a lock-up valve on the firebox. Five of the original boilers were built by the Midland Railway at Derby, but the remaining boilers, including replacements, are thought to have been built at Melton Constable.

The original Derby boiler drawing of 1896 showed 190 tubes 1⅝″ diameter, but the grate area and all external dimensions were the same as the standard L.N.E.R. figures quoted above. New boilers were fitted between 1927 and 1930, and in 1936 the M. & G.N. stock register showed all nine engines as having 145 1¾″ diameter tubes with a tube heating surface of 672.62 sq. ft. This figure included the front tubeplate, a practice at one time in vogue on the Midland Railway, which accounts for the variation between the M. & G.N. and L.N.E.R. heating surface figures. The boilers are shown as Class M.R. on an undated L.N.E.R. boiler diagram.

An M. & G.N. document dated 1936 shows No. 93 as running with a 1922 boiler off 4-4-0T No. 9A, but no confirmation has been found of fitting this boiler, which would be 9in. shorter in the barrel than the 0-6-0T boilers.

In the course of repairs at Stratford in 1941 No. 096 received a stovepipe chimney (fig. 86), and similar chimneys were fitted to Nos. 8485/8 by 1946. A much shorter stovepipe had appeared on No. 8485 by the time it arrived at Stratford for scrapping in December 1947 (fig. 87), and No. 8489 had the standard height stovepipe when withdrawn in 1949.

When the 0-6-0T's were built, flush-fitting smokebox doors of Johnson's Midland Railway pattern were fitted, similar to those on the C class (later D52) 4-4-0's, but the Midland Deeley pattern secured with clamps began to be fitted in the late 1920's (fig. 83). No. 096, however, kept its Johnson smokebox door until at least 1938 (fig. 85), but received a Deeley door in later years.

In order to clear the smokebox door, the front vacuum pipe was mounted on a swivel connection, but this arrangement was later replaced on Nos. 015/6, 094/6/7/8 by a fixed pipe mounted lower on the bufferbeam (cf. figs. 83 and 85).

Each pair of wheels was sprung differently, with laminated springs on the leading wheels, twin coil springs on the drivers, and a single inverted laminated spring mounted transversely for the trailing axle. An appearance of antiquity was given to the engines by the coupling rod and connecting rod bearings which were half brasses secured by cotters.

When new, no independent blower was fitted to these engines, and the small ejector had to be used as a blower. This again was a feature of contemporary Midland practice, but all the class had received separate blowers before being taken over by the L.N.E.R. The existence of the blower could be detected by the presence of a small-bore steam pipe running along the side of the boiler above the left-hand side tank.

Between about 1930 and 1934 hoppers were fitted to the bunkers of all nine engines to ease coaling at the new coaling plants at South Lynn and Yarmouth Beach (fig. 84). Most of the engines retained the hoppers until withdrawn, but that on No. 16 was removed some time after 1938.

It is believed that none of the class was repainted with the full lettering " L N E R " after the war, and certainly the three which survived into B.R. stock retained their wartime " N E " lettering until withdrawn.

Brakes

All nine engines had the normal Midland Railway arrangement, with vacuum brake for the train, and steam brake for the engine controlled by the vacuum. Following contemporary Derby practice, the large ejector was mounted on the right-hand side of the boiler immediately behind the smokebox, and operated by rodding along the tank top, whilst the small ejector was on the firebox backplate. The brakes acted on the driving and trailing wheels only, and a distinctive feature was the " ship's wheel " for operating the handbrake.

The vacuum train brake pipes had been removed from Nos. 8485/8 by 1946, and from No. 8484 by 1948 (fig. 86), but in all cases the large ejector remained in place on the side of the boiler, albeit with the connections in varying stages of disintegration. It is not known whether the small ejector (inside the cab) was retained to control the steam brake, or whether a simple steam brake valve was substituted for the Midland-pattern driver's brake valve on the three engines. No. 8489 retained its vacuum brake gear apparently intact until withdrawal in 1949. It is not known if any others of the class lost their brake pipes in their later years.

British Railways

Three engines, Nos. 8484/8/9, survived long enough to enter B.R. stock on 1st January 1948, but No. 8488 was withdrawn during that month and Nos. 8484/9 were also condemned without having been renumbered into the 60,000 series.

Allocation and Work

The J93's were employed principally on shunting and station pilot work at South Lynn, Melton Constable, Norwich City and Yarmouth Beach. The South Lynn engines were also used on trip workings between the South Lynn yards and King's Lynn station and harbour. At one time they also worked some of the passenger trains between South Lynn and King's Lynn.

In January 1926 the allocation of the class was:—South Lynn 95/7, Melton Constable 93/6/9, Norwich City 15/6, Yarmouth Beach 94/8. In January 1937 the allocation was:—South Lynn 94/5/6/8, Melton Constable (including sub-shed at Norwich) 93/7/9, Yarmouth Beach 15/6.

Subsequently there were several changes in allocation between these three sheds, but the only engine which strayed off the M. & G.N. was No. 098 which from September 1939 to June 1940 was stationed as far afield as King's Lynn! Nos. 094/5/6, however, remained at South Lynn continuously from 1937 until they were withdrawn, and the last survivor, No. 016 (later 8489), spent its last six years at Melton Constable.

Engine Diagram

Section M. & G.N., 1937.

Classification: Route availability 2; B.R. power class 1F.

Summary of J93 Class

B.R. No.	1946 No.		1937 No.		1907 No.	Orig. No.	Maker		Built	With-drawn
—	8482	8/46	098	8/37	98	14A	Melton Constable		10/1897	1/47
—	(8483)		093	12/37	93	1A	,,	,,	8/1898	6/44
(68484)	8484	8/46	096	3/37	96	11A	,,	,,	4/1899	5/48
—	8485	8/46	095	5/37	95	3A	,,	,,	12/1899	12/47
—	(8486)		015	11/37	15	15	,,	,,	1/1901	12/45
—	(8487)		099	3/37	99	17A	,,	,,	3/1902	7/45
—	—		097	2/38	97	12A	,,	,,	12/1902	3/43
(68488)	8488	8/46	094	12/37	94	2A	,,	,,	1/1904	1/48
(68489)	8489	12/46	016	5/38	16	16	,,	,,	5/1905	8/49

CLASS J94

W.D. AUSTERITY CLASS—RIDDLES
4ft. 3in. ENGINES

ENGINES PURCHASED FROM MINISTRY OF SUPPLY (Added to stock 1946-47): 8006-80. TOTAL 75.

On 1st January 1943 the prototype "Austerity" 0-6-0 saddle tank, W.D. No. 5000, was steamed. Over the ensuing four years, 377 (with a further five ordered, but cancelled) were mass-produced for the Government and many saw active service in France after the Normandy landing in 1944.

With the cessation of hostilities in Europe in 1945 their war-role ceased. British manufacturers continued to turn out further engines, although the production rate was slowed down and, in fact, engines delivered after June 1945 were simply put into store at Longmoor. For a full account of these locomotives as supplied to the Ministry of Supply for the War Department see *Railway Observer* Vol. 29 (1959) pp. 78 et seq. and pp. 120 et seq. In addition, many more were built later for private use, the last being as late as 1962.

In 1944 a number were loaned to the Ministry of Fuel and Power for work at opencast coal sites, and in October 1944 the various railway companies agreed to undertake the six-monthly boiler inspections of such locomotives, as well as effecting repairs in special cases. By January 1945, the L.N.E.R. had become responsible for the maintenance of some twenty-five of these engines and so it is perhaps not surprising that before long one of this type should be loaned to the L.N.E.R.

In November 1945 No. 71486 was allocated to Doncaster for trials. The ruggedness and simplicity of the design resulted in the purchase of seventy-five of these engines, including No. 71486, on 22nd May 1946. With the immediate post-war shortage of raw materials, it was clearly preferable to purchase surplus Government locomotives: to have built an equal number of J50's in the Company's own workshops might have taken three or four years.

Of the seventy-five engines purchased, twenty-nine were already in service at various military establishments in Britain, forty were recorded as being new (including No. 71486), and the remainder were still under construction by Andrew Barclay & Co.

The second-hand engines were examined by the L.N.E.R.'s representative and nearly all were found to be in urgent need of repairs. The forty "new" engines, which were in store at Longmoor, were little better: the main trouble being signs of over-heating of bearings.

Most of the engines were handed over to the L.N.E.R. in June and July 1946, and were usually worked light to the nearest L.N.E.R. transfer point. They were recorded as being added to stock as from the date of their arrival on the L.N.E.R. system, although many were in no fit condition to enter traffic straight-away. Several received at Neasden from Longmoor were despatched to Stratford Works for attention to their axleboxes, but the classic example was that of No. 71535 (later 8074) which broke down at Immingham on 9th July 1946. No. 8074 was subsequently despatched to its makers, Andrew Barclay, for what was officially described as a "light repair", and was not returned until 30th January 1948. The last of the six engines still under construction at the time purchase arrangements were completed was not delivered until January 1947.

Withdrawals from the class started in 1960 and were completed in 1967 when the last two members were withdrawn.

Standard L.N.E.R. Dimensions, 1946

Cylinders (2 inside)	18″ × 26″
Motion	Stephenson with slide valves
Boiler:	
Max. diam. outside	4′ 3″
Barrel length ...	10′ 2″
Firebox length outside ...	5′ 8″
Pitch	7′ 5½″
Diagram No. ...	120
Heating surface:	
Firebox	87.5 sq. ft.
Tubes (181 × 1¾″)	872.5 sq. ft.
Total	960.0 sq. ft.
Grate area ...	16.82 sq. ft.
Boiler pressure ...	170 lb./sq. in.
Coupled wheels ...	4′ 3″
Tractive effort (85%)	23,870 lb.
Length over buffers	30′ 4″

Wheelbase	...	$5' 9'' + 5' 3'' = 11' 0''$
Weight (full)	...	48т 4c/49т 2c*
Max. axle load	...	16т 6¼c
Water capacity	...	1,200 gallons
Coal capacity	...	2т 5c/ 3т 0c*

* The engine diagram was re-issued in 1952 showing additional details of the engines fitted with 3 ton capacity coal bunkers. A note on the diagram recorded that the empty weight was increased from 37 tons 12 cwt. to 37 tons 15 cwt. and the weight on the trailing coupled axle, in working order, was increased from 15 tons 17 cwt. to 16 tons 5 cwt.—leaving 10 cwt. unaccounted for.

W.D. and L.N.E.R. Numbering

The first of these 0-6-0T's were numbered in a series starting at 5,000. Subsequently, 70,000 was added to the number of the W.D. stock to avoid confusion with U.S.A. Transportation Corps engines and others. A second series was started at 71437, the complete class being numbered 71437-56/62-99, 71500-36, 75000-199, 75250-331.

The engines purchased by the L.N.E.R. were allocated their Nos. 8006-80 more or less in order of date of construction. This involved a reshuffle within classes Y5 and Y6 which were originally allocated Nos. 8080/1/2 under the 1946 renumbering scheme.

Nos. 8006-34 were allocated to the engines which were already in use by the War Department. Nos. 8035-74 were given to the forty new engines in store at Longmoor, excepting No. 8070 which had been on loan to the L.N.E.R. (as No. 71486) since November 1945. Nos. 8075-80 were allocated to the six engines still under construction at Andrew Barclay.

In most cases the engines were renumbered at the shed to which they were allocated, and this was normally carried out soon after their arrival (fig. 88). A hitch occurred over the renumbering of No. 71463 to 8077, as at the time that the J94 was delivered from the makers, the number 8077 was still carried by a class F3 2-4-2T. This was the result of a mishap involving a J70 tram engine, No. 7125, which for legal reasons could not be renumbered 8224 until after the inquiry had been held, thus preventing the F3 from taking the number 7125. By the time that the number 8077 had become available for a J94, Nos. 71463/4/5 had been renumbered 8078/9/80, so the final engine, No. 71466, became No. 8077 in February after delivery at the end of January 1947.

Development

In July 1942 preparations were being made for the invasion of the Continent and it was realised that large numbers of main line and shunting locomotives would have to be built capable of operating over European as well as British lines. Mr. R. A. Riddles, then Deputy Director of R. E. Equipment, was put in charge of the design work. As far as the shunting design was concerned, to save time the standard Hunslet 18in. inside-cylinder industrial 0-6-0ST was adopted, with slight modification. The wartime version was not intended to last and various economies in construction were introduced to facilitate quick production and reduce in particular the use of steel castings. For instance, the wheel centres were made of cast-iron and the main frame structure was largely fabricated from welded steel plate. Cast-iron slide valves were used, the valve chests being placed between the cylinders. A large saddle tank was provided, extending forward from the cab to the front of the smokebox. The tank, cab and bunker were all of welded construction. The boiler barrel was made in two rings and a round-topped firebox (with a copper inner shell) was fitted, on which were mounted two Ross pop safety valves. Reversing was by means of a lever on the right-hand side of the engine, but the regulator and brake valves could be operated from either side. Steam sanding was fitted, sand being applied to the front of the leading wheels and rear of the trailing wheels.

Details

Among features which required immediate modification to make the engines suitable for duties on the L.N.E.R., the more important included the fitting of new cab seats, cab side doors and L.N.E.R. standard lamp irons. These alterations were carried out at the sheds in most cases. The major modification proposed in November 1946 was an increase in capacity of the coal bunker, provision of a ladder and steps at the back end and the fitting of new rear cab windows. This was to be carried out at the works responsible for the maintenance of the engines concerned, and the first to be dealt with was No. 8006 in August 1947 at Gorton (fig. 91). This was in fact the first of only two engines to be so dealt with by the L.N.E.R., No. 8012 being the second, in November. Others were altered by B.R. between 1948 and 1951. Gorton Works invariably altered the J94's as they were shopped there, but those shopped at Gateshead or Darlington were not always altered. The shape of the bunker extension was similar to that introduced by Thompson on his L1 class 2-6-4T's, the extension only occupying the centre portion of the bunker. The rear cab spectacles were changed from the original circular shape to a narrow vertical rectangle.

The final L.N.E.R. modifications authorised in February 1947 included the fitting of an additional handrail on the tank side to facilitate access to the tank filling hole. This handrail was fitted at an angle. An additional footstep was secured to the underside of the tank, immediately below the new handrail and the handrail on the running plate immediately above the leading step was positioned further forward (fig. 92). These changes were carried out in due course on all the others.

A B.R. modification was the fitting of an additional footstep half way along the running plate (fig. 93), but not all the engines were so fitted. Those known are:— 68006/9/12/3/4/7/9/20/2/3/4/5/9/30/5/6/8/9/40/7/9/50/1/3/4/8/62/71/3/5/80. From about October 1948 onwards the cast-iron slide valves were gradually replaced by new ones made of phosphor bronze.

When No. 68030 of Rowsley shed was received at Gorton Works for repairs in August 1957 it was found that the high bunker had been removed. This was put back and the engine was returned to traffic in September. Two months later No. 68006 was received for repairs and it was noticed that it, too, had had its high bunker burned off. Upon enquiries being made it was established that the high bunkers had been deliberately removed at Rowsley to facilitate coaling at the Middleton Top stage. The engines concerned were Nos. 68006/13/30/4 and later Nos. 68012/79 were similarly altered. One or two of these, e.g. Nos. 68012/3, also had their additional ladders and steps removed from the back of the bunker at the same time as the bunkers were cut down. Nos. 68006/30/79, at least, are known to have retained the ladder and steps.

Another feature, peculiar to the J94's working on the High Peak line, was the fitting of oval shaped buffers, a precaution against the possibility of buffer-locking on sharp curves.

Not all the J94's in the North Eastern Region received high bunkers, but very late in life at least one engine, No. 68019, had a makeshift high bunker fitted at the shed. A ladder was also provided. No. 68019 also had another experimental fitting in the early 1960's, but which was removed later—shields were fitted on either side of the safety valves to prevent steam from blowing down and obscuring the driver's view. These additions seem to have been unofficial.

Brakes

All the L.N.E.R. engines of this type had steam brake only, although some of the others had Westinghouse pumps.

Livery

The J94's were painted khaki when they were received from the Ministry of Supply, with the W.D. number carried on the sides of the saddle tank and on the front buffer-beam, and the letters " W.D. " on the cab side. The engines which were renumbered by the L.N.E.R. at the sheds retained their khaki livery for the time being, although there was a difference in practice between the sheds. Those dealt with in the North Eastern Area received shaded numerals and letters on the side of the saddle tanks (fig. 88). The Gorton engines received plain unshaded numerals and letters, again on the side of the saddle tanks (fig. 89), whilst those at Immingham simply received their L.N.E.R. numbers, usually on the bunker sides (fig. 90), without reference to ownership, although for good measure 8028 was numbered on both bunker and tank. Certain engines were renumbered at Stratford Works, e.g. Nos. 8020/2/54/5, and they were painted black at the same time.

At their first shopping, the J94's were painted unlined black. In many cases this was not until after nationalisation. None was ever lined out.

British Railways

All seventy-five engines received numbers in the 60,000 series and were fitted with smokebox numberplates.

Allocation and Work

No. 71486 was loaned to the L.N.E.R. on 1st November 1945 and allocated to Doncaster, where it remained until July 1946, apart from a short spell at Immingham between 25th November and 2nd December 1945.

Seventy-five engines were delivered to the L.N.E.R. between May 1946 and January 1947, including No. 71486, and these were divided between the Southern Area (30) and the North Eastern Area (45). The initial shed allocations were as follows:—Immingham (25); Gorton (5); Blaydon (11); Darlington (12); Newport (3); Selby (3); West Hartlepool (5); York (11).

There were several transfers prior to nationalisation, with examples appearing at Scarborough and Sunderland. After 1948, their field of activity was extended, and they appeared at numerous other sheds, including Ardsley, Bidston, Birkenhead, Borough Gardens, Boston, Colwick, Consett, Dairycoates, Gateshead, Goole, Heaton, Hexham, Hornsey, King's Cross, Langwith, Mexborough, Retford, Stockton, Thornaby,

Trafford Park, Tyne Dock, Westhouses and Wrexham.

They were ideal on short distance trip workings as well as shunting in small yards, and took over the working of several branch lines which had given difficulty to the operating department in the past, e.g. the Brymbo branch in North Wales and the East & West Yorkshire Union section (see p. 77). But their most noteworthy workings concerned the Cromford and High Peak line on the L.M. Region. By 1956 the four old North London tanks were past their prime, and on 10th April 1956 No. 68030 was tried out on the upper section of the line, between Middleton Top and Parsley Hay. By the following August Nos. 68006/13/30 were working regularly on the line, with one engine based at Cromford and the other two usually to be found at Middleton Top. At the lower end the engine made transfer trips between the bottom of the incline and High Peak Junction. At the top end, the engines worked to Friden and Parsley Hay. The J94's were regarded as superior to the N.L.R. 0-6-0T's and in August 1957 No. 68034 was also transferred to this section, as were Nos. 68012/68/79 in 1959-62.

Until May 1964, both Cromford and Middleton Top were regarded as sub-sheds to Rowsley. Cromford then became the responsibility of Derby and Nos. 68006/12/3/68/79 were transferred there from Rowsley, which also became a sub-shed under Derby at that time. One month later, the responsibility for Middleton Top was transferred to Buxton shed, and Nos. 68012/79 were accordingly transferred there from Derby. (Nos. 68030/4 had already been withdrawn, in 1962, and 68013 in 1964).

In April 1965 the line was severed at the southern end and the surviving J94's (68006/12/68) were concentrated at Buxton (68068 being withdrawn from Buxton immediately after transfer there). Complete closure of the line between Friden and Middleton Top occurred in April 1967 and the two surviving J94's were made redundant. No. 68006 was withdrawn in May but No. 68012 was despatched to Westhouses and for several months worked at Williamthorpe Colliery. With its withdrawal in October 1967, the class became extinct.

Sales

After withdrawal certain of the class were sold to other users:—

68020	N.C.B. Askern, their No. 50.	June 1963
68050	N.C.B. Ashington.	March 1965*
68067	N.C.B. Manvers Main, No. 63.	February 1963
68070	Sir Lindsay Parkinson & Co. Ltd., Glyn Neath Opencast Site, South Wales.	March 1963
68077	N.C.B. Orgreave Colliery, No. 14.	December 1962
68078	Derek Crouch (Contractors) Ltd., Widdrington Opencast Site, Northumberland.	March 1963

* For spares. Scrapped early in 1966.

In addition, No. 68034 was offered to the N.C.B. for sale, but was scrapped at Darlington in April 1963. No. 68057 was to be offered for sale, but was withdrawn by the C.M.E., and Nos. 68065/6/74/5 were also possible candidates for sale but were found to be unsuitable and all the above were subsequently broken up.

Engine Diagram

1946. Amended 1952 to show bunker with increased coal capacity.

Classification: Southern Area load class 3; Route availability 5; B.R. power class 4F.

Summary of J94 Class

B.R. No.		To L.N.E.R. No.	L.N.E.R. Stock	W.D. No.	Maker	Works No.	Built	Fitted With Extended Bunker	Withdrawn
68006	6/49	8006	9/46 8/46	75094	Hudswell, Clarke & Co.	1755	1/1944	8/47(a)	5/67
68007	11/49	8007	7/46 7/46	75097	,,	1760	2/1944	11/49	10/62
68008	9/49	8008	7/46 7/46	75101	Hunslet Engine Co.	3151	2/1944	9/49	12/63
68009	6/48	8009	9/46 8/46	75108	,,	3158	3/1944	6/48	7/62
68010	1/49	8010	8/46 7/46	75117	,,	3167	5/1944	1/49	5/65
68011	10/49	8011	7/46 6/46	75119	,,	3169	5/1944	10/49	5/65
68012	5/51	8012	7/46 7/46	75124	,,	3174	6/1944	11/47(a)	10/67
68013	11/50	8013	7/46 6/46	75125	,,	3175	6/1944	3/48(a)	8/64
68014	10/48	8014	7/46 7/46	75134	,,	3184	9/1944	10/48	10/64
68015	11/48	8015	8/46 7/46	75139	,,	3190	10/1944	11/48	8/63
68016	12/49	8016	7/46 7/46	75148	,,	3198	12/1944	12/48	5/64
68017	7/49	8017	7/46 7/46	75149	,,	3199	12/1944	—	11/62
68018	11/48	8018	7/46 7/46	75150	W. G. Bagnall & Co.	2738	5/1944	11/48	8/62
68019	9/49	8019	8/46 8/46	75153	,,	2741	6/1944	(b)	10/64
68020	10/48	8020	9/46 6/46	75164	,,	2752	9/1944	10/48	6/63

B.R. No.		To L.N.E.R. No.	L.N.E.R. Stock	W.D. No.	Maker	Works No.	Built	Fitted With Extended Bunker	Withdrawn
68021	10/49	8021	7/46 7/46	75183	R. Stephenson & Hawthorns	7133	4/1944	—	10/63
68022	10/48	8022	9/46 6/46	75184	,,	7134	4/1944	10/48	9/60
68023	7/49	8023	7/46 6/46	75190	,,	7140	6/1944	7/49	5/65
68024	11/49	8024	9/46 9/46	71509	,,	7163	9/1944	—	1/64
68025	11/49	8025	6/46 6/46	71498	Hudswell, Clarke & Co.	1775	11/1944	11/49	10/63
68026	9/48	8026	7/46 7/46	71506	,,	1783	4/1945	9/48	3/61
68027	4/49	8027	6/46 6/46	71440	Hunslet Engine Co.	3204	2/1945	4/49	12/60
68028	1/49	8028	7/46 7/46	71447	,,	3211	4/1945	1/49	9/60
68029	11/49	8029	7/46 7/46	71451	,,	3215	5/1945	—	9/63
68030	11/48	8030	7/46 6/46	71452	,,	3216	5/1945	11/48(a)	4/62
68031	1/50	8031	7/46 7/46	75272	R. Stephenson & Hawthorns	7202	2/1945	—	2/63
68032	11/49	8032	8/46 7/46	75281	,,	7211	4/1945	—	5/64
68033	9/48	8033	7/46 7/46	75287	Vulcan Foundry	5277	6/1945	9/48	10/60
68034	6/48	8034	7/46 7/46	75297	,,	5287	6/1945	6/48(a)	10/62
68035	3/49	8035	7/46 6/46	75320	,,	5310	7/1945	3/49?	10/63
68036	6/49	8036	7/46 6/46	75321	,,	5311	7/1945	—	5/64
68037	1/49	8037	7/46 6/46	75322	,,	5312	7/1945	1/49	5/65
68038	5/49	8038	7/46 6/46	75323	,,	5313	7/1945	—	11/63
68039	2/49	8039	7/46 7/46	75324	,,	5314	7/1945	2/49	10/63
68040	1/50	8040	7/46 6/46	75325	,,	5315	7/1945	—	10/63
68041	2/50	8041	7/46 6/46	75326	,,	5316	7/1945	—	10/63
68042	9/49	8042	7/46 6/46	75327	,,	5317	7/1945	10/49?	12/63
68043	5/49	8043	7/46 6/46	75328	,,	5318	7/1945	—	5/65
68044	9/49	8044	7/46 6/46	75329	,,	5319	8/1945	—	10/62
68045	10/49	8045	7/46 6/46	75330	,,	5320	8/1945	10/49	9/63
68046	12/49	8046	7/46 6/46	75331	,,	5321	8/1945	—	6/64
68047	9/49	8047	7/46 6/46	75258	W. G. Bagnall & Co.	2781	7/1945	9/49	5/65
68048	12/49	8048	7/46 6/16	75259	,,	2782	7/1945	12/49	10/62
68049	3/50	8049	7/46 6/46	75260	,,	2783	8/1945	3/50	9/63
68050	9/49	8050	7/46 6/46	75261	,,	2784	8/1945	9/49	12/64
68051	9/48	8051	7/46 6/46	75262	,,	2785	9/1945	9/48	6/64
68052	10/49	8052	7/46 6/46	75263	,,	2786	9/1945	10/49	6/62
68053	12/49	8053	7/46 7/46	75265	,,	2788	10/1945	12/49	5/65
68054	3/50	8054	9/46 7/46	75266	,,	2789	11/1945	3/50	6/64
68055	5/50	8055	9/46 7/46	75267	,,	2790	12/1945	5/50	7/62
68056	1/50	8056	10/46 7/46	75268	,,	2791	12/1945	1/50	10/62
68057	12/49	8057	8/46 7/46	75269	,,	2792	12/1945	12/49	6/62
68058	4/49	8058	8/46 6/46	75270	,,	2793	2/1946	—	10/62
68059	10/49	8059	10/46 6/46	75271	,,	2794	2/1946	—	12/63
68060	12/49	8060	7/46 6/46	71467	Hudswell, Clarke & Co.	1785	9/1945	12/49	5/65
68061	6/49	8061	7/46 6/46	71468	,,	1786	10/1945	—	12/63
68062	9/49	8062	7/46 6/46	71469	,,	1787	10/1945	9/49	5/65
68063	6/49	8063	7/46 6/46	71470	,,	1788	10/1945	4/50	1/62
68064	7/48	8064	7/46 6/46	71471	,,	1789	11/1945	12/50?	2/62
68065	6/49	8065	6/46 6/46	71472	,,	1790	12/1945	1/50	12/62
68066	2/50	8066	6/46 6/46	71473	,,	1791	12/1945	2/50	12/62
68067	1/49	8067	6/46 6/46	71474	,,	1792	1/1946	8/51?	2/63
68068	3/48	8068	7/46 6/46	71475	,,	1793	2/1946	3/48	5/65
68069	12/49	8069	7/46 6/46	71476	,,	1794	2/1946	12/48	9/62
68070	5/48	8070	6/46 5/46	71486	R. Stephenson & Hawthorns	7295	9/1945	5/48	3/63
68071	2/49	8071	7/46 6/46	71532	Andrew Barclay & Co.	2186	6/1945	2/49	8/63
68072	3/49	8072	7/46 6/46	71533	,,	2187	7/1945	3/49	9/60
68073	7/48	8073	7/46 6/46	71534	,,	2188	10/1945	7/48	8/61
68074	2/50	8074	7/46 6/46	71535	,,	2189	12/1945	7/50	10/62
68075	8/48	8075	6/46 6/46	71536	,,	2190	3/1946	8/48	10/62
68076	1/49	8076	6/46 6/46	71462	,,	2211	4/1946	1/49	9/60
68077	8/49	8077	2/47 1/47	71466	,,	2215	1/1947	8/49	12/62
68078	8/49	8078	7/46 7/46	71463	,,	2212	7/1946	8/49	3/63
68079	10/50	8079	9/46 9/46	71464	,,	2213	9/1946	10/50(a)	10/66
68080	3/49	8080	11/46 11/46	71465	,,	2214	11/1946	4/49	4/61

(a) Extension removed at Rowsley shed to facilitate coaling at Middleton Top stage.
(b) Makeshift extended bunker fitted at Darlington shed late in the locomotive's life.

Fig. 91   Class J94 No. 8006 at Immingham, September 1947.

Modified bunker, with ladder and altered rear windows to cab.

Fig. 92   Class J94 No. 8050 at Darlington shed, June 1948.

Additional handrail and footstep on saddle tank.

Fig. 93   Class J94 No. 68080 at Immingham shed, October 1954.

Extra footsteps midway along running plate.

ACKNOWLEDGMENTS

This Part is mainly the work of Messrs. D. W. Allen, M. G. Boddy, W. A. Brown, E. V. Fry, W. Hennigan, F. Manners, E. Neve, P. Proud, T. E. Rounthwaite, D. F. Tee and W. B. Yeadon. The authors gratefully acknowledge additional assistance from Dr. I. C. Allen and Messrs. A. G. Dunbar, A. Handforth, K. Hoole, R. W. Miller, E. N. T. Platt, K. Plant and the Hunslet Engine Co., H. S. Steel, P. D. Rowbotham of the Industrial Locomotive Society and W. K. Williams of the Industrial Railway Society.

Acknowledgment of Illustrations:—

G. R. Grigs (Fig. 1), R. H. Inness (Figs. 2, 7, 14, 36/8, 47/8), R. D. Stephen (Figs. 3, 79, 81), T. G. Hepburn (Figs. 4, 46, 55, 75), C. L. Turner (Fig. 5), T. E. Rounthwaite (Fig. 6), W. Rogerson (Figs. 8, 19), N. Fields (Figs. 9, 26), J. Robertson (Figs. 10, 21, 61), H. C. Casserley (Figs. 11, 22), Dr. I. C. Allen (Figs. 12, 85), E. V. Fry (Figs. 15, 87, 92), W. H. Whitworth (Figs. 16, 28, 31/5/7, 44/5, 50/2/3, 67/8, 71, 89), P. J. Hughes (Fig. 17), J. W. Armstrong (Fig. 18), C. Lawson Kerr (Figs. 20, 57, 77), G. M. Staddon (Figs. 23, 76,) R. Copeman (Fig. 24), W. A. Camwell (Fig. 25), L. W. Perkins (Fig. 27), W. Beckerlegge (Fig. 30), A. G. Forsyth (Figs. 34, 42), R. J. Buckley (Fig. 40), J. F. Henton (Fig. 43), H. G. Tidey (Fig. 54), B. V. Franey (Figs. 60, 91), W. S. Sellar (Fig. 62), L. Hanson (Figs. 63, 74), H. L. Hopwood (Fig. 66), T. M. S. Findlater (Fig. 72), J. C. Cunningham (Fig. 73), J. L. Stevenson (Fig. 78), J. P. Wilson (Figs. 84, 90), L. R. Peters (Fig. 86), D. A. Dant (Fig. 88), Figs. 13/6, 28, 31/2/5/7, 44/5, 50-4, 67-71, 80/2/9 are by courtesy of Real Photographs Ltd., Figs. 1, 5, 8, 19, 87, 92 of Photomatic Ltd., Figs. 29, 49, 56, 64 of Ian Allan Ltd., Figs. 65/6 of the Locomotive Club of Great Britain, and Fig. 83 of Locomotive & General Railway Photographs.